# Mr Home pronounced Hume

AN AUTOBIOGRAPHY

# Mr Home
# pronounced Hume

AN AUTOBIOGRAPHY

*William Douglas Home*

COLLINS
St James's Place, London
1979

William Collins Sons & Co Ltd
London · Glasgow · Sydney · Auckland
Toronto · Johannesburg

First published 1979
© William Douglas Home 1979
ISBN 0 00 216076 5
Set in 11pt Monotype Fontana
Made and Printed in Great Britain by
William Collins Sons & Co Ltd Glasgow

# Contents

# *Illustrations*

# Acknowledgements

My thanks are due to my secretary, Sue Mumford Smith, for typing and re-typing this manuscript and to Philip Ziegler, of Collins, for encouraging me to try my hand at an unfamiliar medium and, to both of them, for retaining their equanimity throughout the whole operation even though my hand-writing, according to the latter (with, no doubt, the former's silent acquiescence) is the worst he ever grappled with, not excluding Lord Melbourne's.

To Rachel, much loved wife
and most perceptive and constructive
of drama critics

# Chapter 1
# Origins

When I was a little boy, there used to be an outsize picture, hanging in a passage, now demolished, off the entrance hall at Hirsel. Sometimes I would pause and look up at it of an evening, on my way to stalk a rabbit in the garden with my father who was holding up proceedings while his butler, Mr Collingwood, replenished his tobacco pouch.

My brother Alec has now moved the picture to an even less frequented passage in the old part of the house, erected before Flodden, where I renewed my acquaintanceship with it the other day. It still makes me smile, representing as it does a vast tree, of the 'family' variety, on whose extensive branches, stretching out on either side of its enormous trunk in most unnatural profusion, are recorded the descendants of a man who stands beside its roots, clad only in a loin-cloth of fur and carrying a club. This terrifying creature whose appearance indicates, to this irreverent descendant at least, that he would have been much better placed swinging among the branches, would appear to be my first progenitor. His mate is not included in the picture, no doubt lurking in some near-by cave, engaged in giving birth to a man-child who, one would like to think, turned out to be a shade less unattractive than his sire. One also hopes that that trend has continued down the centuries, although at least one portrait of an earlier Lord Home which hangs in Alec's house would seem to indicate that progress was extremely slow.

The Homes were border fighters sandwiched between Edinburgh and England and it was not always easy for them to determine, in those fluid days, whether the English or the Kings of Scotland were their greatest enemies. On some occasions, as at Chevy Chase, they fought against their ancient enemy, the Percys, and again at Flodden they did battle with the English, although some say that the then Lord Home retired a trifle prematurely from the battle, stayed the night at Hirsel, and returned next morning to plunder the dead. At other times they fell foul of their own King – that same Lord Home, for example, being executed some years after Flodden by his fellow countrymen.

The Douglases, an even rougher and more powerful family, who occupied a larger part of southern Scotland further to the west, faced the same problem as the Homes – 'Who is our friend and who our foe?' they used to ask themselves, no doubt, at breakfast every morning as they ate their porridge with their backs to the wall. 'Is the greater danger from the south or from the north? Is our King to be trusted or would it be better to keep in with England until the chance comes to double-cross them both?'

Sometimes this tight-rope walking act worked well, at other times they lost their balance, as when two young Douglases lunched at Edinburgh Castle with their King, one fateful day, and lost their heads as well at the conclusion of the meal.

The union of these two families, the Douglases and Homes, took place in the mid-eighteenth century when a young Douglas heiress married a Lord Home. Her father was Lord Montague, her mother was the daughter of that Archie Douglas whose claim to the Douglas lands had been disputed in the Scottish courts for seven years and had been finally rejected by the Court of Session.

Outlined briefly, this dispute and almost endless litigation came about because Lady Jane Douglas, Archie's mother and the sister of the first and only Duke of Douglas, saw fit to get married at the age of fifty to a retired mercenary soldier ten years older than herself called Colonel Stewart. This ill-assorted couple went to Paris and, in due course, Lady Jane returned to England with a pair of twin sons, Archibald and Sholto, and laid claim to the inheritance on Archibald's behalf. The Duke of Hamilton, the heir to Lady Jane's unmarried brother, incensed by the birth of babies to the fifty-year-old bride, sent lawyers off to Paris, who discovered that two children had been bought from a glass-blower's family at just the time that Lady Jane claimed her twins had been born.

Hence the case (in which a Mr Boswell acted for the plaintiff) and which, after many thousands of pounds had been spent by both sides, went in favour of the Duke of Hamilton. The Douglas family, it seemed, had reached rock-bottom both in reputation and fortune. The House of Lords, however, saw fit to reverse the judgement of the Court of Session. Consequently, Archie Douglas kept his heritage and his grand-daughter, a great heiress, married Lord Home.

At Hirsel, hangs a Raeburn portrait of the controversial Archie, painted in his old age, wearing a black beret, looking, as I am compelled in honesty to point out, every inch a Frenchman. Still, the fact remains that Archie Douglas, never mind the beret or the bags beneath his eyes in Raeburn's picture, whether he were out of Lady Jane by Colonel Stewart or the son of a French glass-blower and his wife, held the Douglas lands and passed them, through his grand-daughter, into the House of Home. It would be churlish to cast doubts upon a judgement which turned out so satisfactorily, especially for this particular descendant who, as a young schoolboy, spent idyllic summer holidays on Douglas land as a direct result of a decision of the House of Lords two centuries before.

Although I loved my holidays at Hirsel too, I found the time I spent at Douglas more romantic. Like Hirsel it was steeped in history, but much more so. It had been burnt down by the English once, then by a Douglas himself with the English garrison therein. Finally, my father had it pulled down just before the Second World War to allow two coal-mines to join up beneath its towering turrets. Now there's nothing left on the site save a tower from the last castle but one, which Sir Walter Scott called Castle Dangerous.

In Douglas Village stands St Bride's Church in which lies the heart of the Good Sir James Douglas, killed in Spain while trying to convey the heart of Robert the Bruce to the Holy Land. Also in the village street there stands a monument to mark the spot where a young Covenanting tailor had his ears cut off with his own scissors by the troops of 'Butcher' Cumberland.

At the west end of the street is an inn called The Douglas Arms and, when I pass it in my car or go in for a drink with brother Henry, I find myself wondering if once there was a landlord of this same hotel called Simpson. Reading up the case of Lady Jane some years ago to make a play on her extraordinary history, called *The Douglas Cause*, I came on an intriguing passage which concerned the father of that Duke of Douglas whom I have already mentioned.

'He,' I read, 'would often go down from the Castle to the village of an evening and indulge in unspeakable obscenities in the inn of one, Simpson.' Ah well, judging from my sessions in the Douglas Arms with Henry, times have changed.

A mile or two along the valley of the Douglas Water up the Ayr Road is a wood called Windrow in which lies the grave of a poor female traveller who died of cholera while journeying to Douglas and was buried near the spot for fear of spreading the infection. When I was a small boy this historic landmark used to send a shiver down my spine as I lay near it waiting for a roebuck to come out and feed at dusk. I looked for the grave last year but I could not find it in the nettles. None the less my youngest daughter who was with me on the search felt the same shiver down her spine.

These memories of times past made my holidays at Douglas unlike any others. When, each summer, the time came to go by car from Coldstream up the Tweed to Biggar, then past Tinto Hill to Douglas, I was in the seventh heaven, grudging every minute that my mother spent in an hotel in Peebles resting after lunch to break the journey. She was not an ardent motorist, inserting notepaper into her corsage to prevent car-sickness and exhorting all her children to do likewise. Once she went to Hamilton and Inches, jewellers of George Street, in Edinburgh, to make a purchase. Having done so, she began to give her name and address when the salesman interrupted. 'That's all right, my lady, I'll copy it off there,' he said, having observed the Hirsel, Coldstream, Berwickshire, embossed on the notepaper which had worked its way above her corsage.

In the afternoon, we would arrive at Douglas, passing, in a low gear, through the herds of Highland cattle roaming in the park, and draw up at the front door in the shadow of the Castle Dangerous tower. Then, down to the gun-room with my father after tea, to learn about the prospects for the grouse from Mr Telfer, the head keeper, and to find out in which wood there dwelt the largest roebuck and which bog held the most snipe. Then to my father's dressing-room to make plans for the future, while he dressed for dinner. One night, I recall, he finished dressing and went downstairs, while I followed later. On the stairs stood Mr Collingwood, a pair of pants in his hand. 'Well, I never, Mr William,' he remarked. 'I saw his Lordship put these on when he was dressing.' 'So did I,' I said. 'Well, then,' said he, 'Houdini isn't in it. Not unless he put both legs through one hole.'

Thus, each year, there began six weeks of happiness marred only by the annual occurrence of a stomach upset which swept through the inmates of the Castle like a plague at the beginning of September caused by the first frost affecting the state of the cows' milk. At any rate, that was the theory. My mother disbelieved it; blaming strawberries and cream and an excess of peaches, until, one summer, retribution fell upon her. Going up the spiral staircase with her sister Violet on the way to bed, both bearing candles, since electric light was not installed at Douglas except downstairs, she was commenting on the lack of restraint displayed by husband, family and friends.

'And Charlie, too,' she said, 'and all those grown-up men and women. One expects it of the children. But they should know better at their age – gorging themselves on strawberries and . . . Violet!'

'What's the matter, Lilian?'

'Bring me that vase from the table on the landing – Quick!'

My mother was a splendid woman, dark, slim and good looking, née Lilian Lambton, hailing from Northumberland beyond the Tweed. According to my Uncle Claud, her brother – who died recently at a great age – my presence on this earth, since he arranged the marriage, was entirely due to him. One winter evening, he was sitting with his sister in the sitting-room at Fenton, near-by Wooler, when they heard the clip-clop of a horse's hooves outside the window in the drive. My mother pulled aside the curtains, peeped into the blizzard raging outside and remarked, 'It's Charlie Dunglass, Claud.'

'Good God,' said Uncle Claud, 'not in this weather!'

'I'm not marrying that red-haired little man,' my mother said.

With that she ran out through the garden door towards the summer house, and disappeared into the blizzard.

In my father came:

'Where's Lilian, Claud?' he asked.

'Don't ask me, Charlie. Have a drink.'

'I need one. I got frozen on that ride.'

'I'll bet you did,' said Uncle Claud, thinking of his poor little sister getting ever colder in the summer house.

'It's sixteen miles,' my father said.

'I wouldn't be surprised,' said Claud, and handed him a drink, assuming rightly that his sister would show up at any moment, if she did not wish to freeze to death.

As he anticipated, she returned with chattering teeth. Tactfully, he left the room and, happy to relate, the red-haired little man and Lilian got engaged. As a result, my brothers and my sisters and, in due course, myself, came into this world. The confirmation of this story can be found in an old game book at the Hirsel. 'Shot at Bonkyl all day (sixteen miles north). Rode after tea to Fenton (sixteen miles south).' Thank you, Charlie. Thank you, Lilian. Thank you, Uncle Claud.

They made a strange pair, did my parents, wholly lovable but still strange. Charlie – small, red-headed and loud-voiced, Lil – dark and frail, but with a character of steel. He praying aloud in the drawing-room before breakfast (so much so that the impeccably polite Bob Laycock once said to my mother in the dining-room, 'I like your parrot, Lady Home, it gives a splendid imitation of your husband.'); she, much quieter and less extrovert, no doubt confining her prayers to her bedroom, since she would have rather been found dead than showing her emotions.

'Get along, you silly little man,' she used to say, trying to scotch, entirely unsuccessfully, a habit that my father had of offering up a prayer every time he left the room, presumably in favour of the group he left behind him playing bridge, or otherwise engaged with crossword puzzles or L'Attaque. I can still see him now, his back foot tapping on the mat, maintaining contact with the room, so to speak, one hand on the handle of the door, the other raised in a kind of forehead-tapping gesture; a salute, presumably, to the Almighty whom he was addressing, pipe in mouth, as always.

None the less, eccentric as he may have been, it cannot be denied that the incessant blessings he called down upon his household created lasting happiness in his home, right through his life, till he walked to look out of the window on a summer evening before dinner, to consult with the barometer about the next day's weather, and fell down dead.

I received the news at dinner with a friend in London. 'You're wanted on the telephone,' my hostess said. 'Take it in our bedroom.'

Up I went, to hear my brother Alec speaking from Westminster. 'William? Alec. Home's dead,' he said. 'Bridget just rang up from Hirsel to say he died in the drawing-room before dinner. Never knew a thing about it.'

'Right,' I said. 'Thanks.'

Later it transpired that Alec, who had been at dinner with Jo Grimond when the telephone call came through for him, went back to the House of Commons to collect his hat and briefcase, but they wouldn't let him in, since he had ceased to be a commoner. A kindly policeman went and fetched them for him.

Next morning I and my fiancée, Rachel Brand, drove up the Great North Road to Hirsel, on our way to stay with Alec at his home, Springhill, a few miles up the River Tweed.

We called on my mother, and she took me in to see my father. There he lay, the same small figure I had waved goodbye to on the doorstep a few weeks before, at peace with God now (he had always been that), and I like to think in closer contact with Him, thus precluding the necessity for any further use of the loud-hailer he had hitherto relied on to establish contact.

There we stood, my mother and I, looking down on him, and then she said, 'Will he be cold? Should I give him a shawl?' 'Why not?' I said. Why not, indeed, if that would give her comfort for the loss of her red-headed little man with whom she had shared so much of her life, both sad and happy, so much love.

The bridge across the River Leet just west of Coldstream was under repair that year, and so the funeral procession went right round the outside of the Hirsel Park and entered Coldstream from the north. On that route it went past a wood called Bob and Peter, in which I had spent so much time in the shooting season when I was a small boy, walking with my father while he posted the guns, shouting 'woodcock over' with him and, more often, at him, since he seemed to have a close affinity with woodcock, even to the point of missing them on purpose.

Many times had Alec and my second brother Henry and myself pushed our way through the bracken and the rhododendrons, flushed a woodcock and directed it towards him, watched its progress, seen it flinch and turn aside, but heard no gun shot, only seen our distant forebear raise his cap in salute.

H.P.H.–B

'Really, Dadda,' we would say to him in unison, as we approached him, soaking wet and sweating. 'Why didn't you fire?'

'Because it's done no harm to me,' he would reply.

'Then why arrange for us to drive it over you?'

'Why not?' he would ask, with match to pipe. 'They're lovely little birds; I like to see them.'

So, past Bob and Peter, past the back lodge leading into Kinsham wood, in which I wrote *The Chiltern Hundreds*, basing the part of the Earl of Lister, played with such panache by A. E. Matthews, on the little red-haired man now leading the procession *en route* for his final resting place in Lennel Churchyard. There they laid him, three feet into Scottish ground, to paraphrase the French Queen's exhortation to King James the Fourth of Scotland, which led to the decimation of the Scottish troops on Flodden Field – where 'shivered was fair Scotland's spear and broken was her shield'.

The then Lord Home, as I have hinted earlier, was sent to guard the crossing of the Tweed and, thinking that it didn't need protection, billeted himself at home for the night. On returning to the scene next morning, he found that Lord Howard, Surrey's son, had executed a successful flanking movement and cut off the Scottish army from the north. Thereafter, the unfortunate Lord Home was thought by his contemporaries, as well as by historians, to have been less than loyal to his King. Maybe he was, maybe he wasn't. Neither possibility disturbed my father overmuch.

I well recall him saying to a keen American, who was determined to discover why the body of the King was never found on Flodden Field, but only those of a few soldiers, dressed like him to draw the fire:

'I daresay my old ancestor got hold of him, brought him back here and dumped him in the lake.'

The visitor looked out towards the lake in dumb amazement. Then my father told him that the lake had not been there in those days, leaving him to wonder if a grave had been dug or not.

So to Coldstream, to the church (Episcopal) in which my father always worshipped. As the slow procession reached it, I recalled the winter when I drove him in his old age, with my mother, to the second service. There was snow on the ground and the first service was still in progress. Through the thin walls, we could hear, from the parked car, the parson in full voice, delivering his sermon.

'Aren't you getting frozen stiff, Lil?' asked my father.

'I'm all right,' my mother answered, her teeth chattering, as they had done at Fenton almost fifty years before.

'He's going on far too long,' said my father. 'I'll go and take a look.'

Then he got out, opened the church door, thus releasing to us the full force of Mr Swinton's sermon, now approaching its conclusion.

'No use going in yet, Lil,' my father shouted from the open door, 'the little devil's still drivelling on.'

Then to the graveyard, where the 'little devil' laid him to his rest.

They called him the 'Wee Lordie' in the town of Coldstream and they loved him dearly. He was 'hail fellow well met' with every citizen, old or young, law-abiding or the reverse – all of them were his adored God's creatures, prone to sin, like all of us and, for that very reason, worthy of redemption and affection, and, above all, tolerance.

His tolerance extended even to his enemies. Once while I was on leave during the war, I saw him pick up the *Sunday Graphic* and glance at it. His eye lit on a photograph of Hitler walking between two high-ranking German Army officers. 'Poor little devil,' said my father, 'nobody dares tell him that his Sam Browne's over the wrong shoulder!'

Once a long-faced housekeeper came to my mother with the information that a young domestic had slipped up.

'In what way?' asked my mother.

'Well, my lady,' Mrs Turnbull said, 'I went into her room last night to give her some instructions for this morning and I saw a pair of army boots' – she paused in some embarrassment – 'well, they were sticking out, my lady, from under the bed.'

'Attached to anything?' my mother asked.

'I wouldn't be surprised.'

'I see. Thank you, Mrs Turnbull.'

Still long-faced, the messenger of doom departed.

'Charlie,' said my mother, later on at dinner, 'Mrs Turnbull says she saw a pair of army boots sticking out from under one of the girls' beds last night.'

'British or Italian?' my father enquired.

'Does it matter?' said my mother irritably.

'Yes, of course it does. I'll bet you it's that splendid little fellow who sings opera across the river every evening on his way back to the prisoner-of-war camp.'

'Then we'd better tell the Camp Commander.'

'No, no. If we do, he'll confine them all to barracks and we'll miss our evening opera. Besides, there's no proof.'

No one should assume from this that my father condoned immorality. That story merely illustrates his penchant for the under-dog. In fact, he was a stickler for etiquette. So much so, that, on one occasion, when my brother Alec asked him if he might ask Betty Sitwell, a twice-married neighbour, up to dinner for a game of bridge, my father jibbed at the idea.

'But why not?' Alec asked. 'She's very nice.'

'I know she is,' my father agreed.

'Well, then,' Alec said, in some annoyance, 'why can't I ask her to dinner?'

'Dear old Campbell might turn up,' was my father's reply.

Old Campbell was the husband who had been divorced from Betty Sitwell twenty years before. His home was in Argyllshire and he never, under any circumstances, came to Berwickshire. And yet my father, tolerant to a fault, tried to put his foot down, not through disapproval of divorce but merely to save dear old Campbell from a million-to-one chance of suffering embarrassment.

'Old Campbell might look in,' he said, again, attempting to convince himself of his own argument. 'And then it might be awkward.'

On that final phrase, the tension broke, to be replaced by laughter in which, finally, my father joined. Betty Sitwell came to dinner, played her game of bridge and went her way, and, strange to say, old Campbell never turned up from Argyllshire.

That is no bad illustration of my father's outlook on life, rigid in his view of what was right and wrong, yet tolerant above all men of those who failed to measure up to his own standard and determined to protect them from themselves beyond the call of duty.

Take drink, for example. Though he liked his whisky and his port on some occasions, he was never what is called 'drink taken', except possibly towards the end of January – the 25th, to be precise. In that month once, in early youth, I heard strange noises on the stairs at midnight. Cross-examining my mother the next morning on the subject, she explained that my father had been returning from the Burns Supper in Coldstream, and had been let down by the failure of a light bulb on the landing.

I can sympathize now. So can brother Henry. Once, in Greenlaw, Henry spoke at a Burns Supper in my presence, sat down to prolonged applause and missed his chair. Edwin O. Hector, chairman of the Burns Club, nature columnist in the *Berwickshire News*, rose to his feet and pronounced: 'I've heard of speakers who couldna' stand up before now, but this is the first speaker I've seen who couldna' sit doon!'

It was not only the victims of Burns Suppers that my father tolerated; he liked drunks as such; not because they drank, but because he knew why they drank, to counteract an overdose of sensitivity. He therefore thought they ought to be admitted to the company of God's more special creatures, since he heartily endorsed the statement that the weak are blessed. Not that he encouraged them, he merely tolerated them in tune with his philosophy of life. Anyone who got drunk in his presence – and this very seldom happened – felt no shame the morning after, only admiration for his understanding which, one likes to think, gave easement to the hangover.

I once wrote a play called *Now Barabbas*, and one of the two ladies in it (not Jill Bennett) lost her part down at the Boltons Theatre before we came to the West End. Arriving at the Vaudeville from Scotland, some weeks later, my father sat down and started studying his programme. Soon he noticed from the cast list that this lady had been replaced. 'Wilkes' (his pet name for me), he called down the row of stalls, 'what's happened to that dear tight little lady I saw at the Boltons?' 'Sacked,' I told him. No doubt, after the house lights had dimmed, he offered up an understanding prayer on her behalf.

I took him round to see the Prison Governor in the play, played by Tristan Rawston. 'Splendid fellow,' said my father, as I opened the dressing-room door. 'What does he do in the daytime?'

My marriage took place later in the month in which my father died. He would have been there, in St Peter's, Eaton Square, in the front pew and singing lustily and, later, have welcomed all and sundry in his bell-like voice at the reception in the Hyde Park Hotel – drunk a toast, no doubt, with A. E. Matthews, his stage counterpart, and got into his sleeper on the night train out of King's Cross, humming happily, lobbing a passing prayer at all those left behind him on the platform and, indeed, in the whole strange, alien city. And he would have smiled himself to sleep in memory of what my best man, Michael Astor, said, as we stood waiting for the bride to turn up fifteen minutes late. 'Don't worry, William, it's like flighting pigeons. They invariably turn up in the end!'

But that was not to be. Instead, my father lay in Lennel Churchyard with the grilse, the sea trout and the incidental salmon boring upstream through the Lennel Water to the Bell, the Otter Rock, the Nether Stream, the Wiel Stream and the Cradle and the Birgham Dub. In all those pools he had fought their forefathers with a Jock Scott as his weapon, or a White Wing in the gloaming and, on one occasion, at least, when the fisherman's too frequent change of fly annoyed him, a successful length of boot-lace trailing from a bare hook.

Also absent from the wedding was my mother, bravely coming to terms with the loss of her red-headed little man – no longer sent to bed at ten each evening. 'Go on, Lil, it's ten o'clock,' he used to say. 'Remember that you've got a dicky heart' – an unsubstantiated diagnosis based on the fact that, when her eldest son was born, her heartbeat had deviated from the norm for a short period.

Now, on my father's death, she terminated at a stroke this prolonged period of convalescence, staying up to watch her television every evening till she died, aged eighty-three. Admittedly, she gave herself a stiff neck doing so, but that was her own fault and not the television's. 'William,' she said one day in her old age, 'why can't they make television sets that don't give you a stiff neck?' 'Turn your chair round a bit, Mamma,' I suggested. 'Thank you,' she said, and then, having done so, 'that's much better.'

After the shock of my father's sudden death, my mother found the void left by his absence slowly filled by the rest of the family – that family which she had supervised so unobtrusively and with such fairness for so long. We became aware that, although outwardly our father had been dominant in the relationship, this was because our mother had effaced herself deliberately and let him rule the roost, dispensing love in dessert-spoonfuls, and holding the centre of the stage in conversation, planning and administration. On his departure, she assumed quite effortlessly the role he had played for so long. She not only watched her television, she observed her ever-growing family over her hazardously balanced spectacles with an impartial interest, gave advice when it was sought, and sometimes when it wasn't, with a turn of phrase both picturesque and individual, even on subjects that one would have thought outside her field of interest.

I remember coming in from fishing for my tea one afternoon, to find my mother sitting with my sister, Bridget, her untiring adjutant, and two of her grandchildren, Rosemary and Frances Scott, dressed fetchingly in trousers. They poured out their tea, and came back to the table, while my mother sat and watched their progress. 'With all you girls wearing trousers,' said she, 'it's no wonder that so many people are going over to men these days.'

'Grannie!' said Rosemary, putting down her slopping-over tea cup. 'Do you know what you've said?'

'Never you mind,' said my mother, 'and get on with your scone.'

She lived for fifteen years after my father died, and never missed a trick. She looked over her spectacles at her sons' wives, assessing their ability to make her menfolk happy, their capacity for tolerance and understanding, and their dedication to a life devoted to the care and maintenance of sons whose failings were an open book to her.

She marked the progress of each grandchild, and rebuked them when they went astray, in the same words and with the same good judgement as she had dealt out to their parents in the past.

She also kept a close eye on the progress of those parents. With impartiality and devastating candour, she would comment on our goings-out and comings-in. Success meant nothing to her – manners everything, and good taste.

If I wrote a hit play, it was not the hit that mattered to her, or my bank balance – only the play. 'I hope it wasn't vulgar,' she would say, if she had missed it. Or, 'I wish it hadn't been so vulgar,' after she had seen it. 'You'll get nowhere with vulgarity. It's just kow-towing to the modern fashion.'

'But it wasn't vulgar, Mamma,' I would argue.

'Well, it would have been,' she used to counter, 'if the actors hadn't been so good.'

I like to think she didn't always mean this, but was looking to the future with a view to scotching any lapse of taste in the next manuscript.

When brother Alec became the Conservative Prime Minister, she took a call from the *Daily Express*.

'You must be a proud mother, Lady Home,' said the reporter.

'I think it should have been Mr Butler,' replied my mother.

Once again the telephone rang down in England. It was sister Bridget saying that my mother had come to her bedroom door that morning and complained of feeling unwell; then, a few minutes later, died. Poor, saintly, Bridget, fated to be present at the ends of both her parents – faithful unto death.

The new bridge into Coldstream was in service by now, so we didn't go by Bob and Peter this time. We went straight down river from Springhill, the Dower House to the Hirsel, where my mother started marriage and came back to in her widowhood – through Birgham and then Coldstream to the little church just short of Lennel, from the steps of which my father had imparted so much stop press news about the progress of the sermon, to his Lil, still waiting in the car. By now, the 'little devil' who had buried him was dead too, and another clergyman performed the ceremony, both in church and in Lennel Churchyard, where the wife my father had loved with so much intensity, was laid to rest beside him.

Uncle Claud was present and Aunt Violet (who lived on to ninety-six), the last survivors of my mother's family. They left the grave-yard arm in arm, the wind blowing Uncle Claud's tails behind him. Was he thinking of that evening, perhaps, back at the beginning of the century when his young sister Lilian pulled aside the curtain and saw Charlie Dunglass riding through the blizzard, up to the front door, to ask for her hand?

Now they were together again, through all kinds of weather, in the keeping of the God they both believed in with such faith and certainty. A faith which made it certain that the inner happiness derived from their intense, though never sanctimonious belief, imparted happiness to those who came in contact with them.

'Honour your father and your mother' so the good Book tells us. Certainly, I did that. But I also loved them dearly since they spread around so much love themselves. When I sing at weddings or at funerals, 'I will look up and laugh and love and live,' I think of them. I know no better, more fitting, memorial.

## Chapter 2

# Brothers and Sisters

'Never sanctimonious,' I wrote in the last chapter, and that was the truth. My father never treated God as anybody very special, merely as a good friend who, although He never came to stay in person for the shooting or the fishing, was a sportsman none the less. He therefore found it natural to treat Him naturally; coming, for example, after reading the First Lesson, down the aisle to Mr Russell, his devoted factor, and discussing in a loud voice, how the tenants had done on the Birgham Dub that week, what flies they had used and how many kelts had been put back, and then, at the conclusion of the psalm sung by a disapproving Mr Swinton, going back to read the Second Lesson, in impeccable style.

Once, however, he caught his eldest son and heir grinning at the faces that I made at him when he came down the aisle from the Communion rail, and dismissed us both from church – one chastened Minister of State, and one embarrassed playwright. Evidently, in our father's estimation, we were not yet close enough to God to warrant such familiar behaviour, so we paid the penalty. Needless to say, our mother heartily supported the unusual use of the whip by her lord and master; with all the more enthusiasm since, at home, it was her normal lot to pass the sentence and to carry out the punishments.

But there were no hard feelings, and at lunch time back at Hirsel, we were talking about salmon, just as though nothing had happened, and we knew that God was looking down on us with a forgiving smile. Thus did the tenor of our lives proceed, though disciplined, in happiness – a happiness transmitted to us from the deep well of our parents' faith in a benign, though sometimes stern, Creator.

To describe the administration by my parents of their seven children as a kind of coalition between an enlightened pacifist and a broad-minded policeman, although fanciful, is not far wide of the mark – father, except on such rare occasions as in Coldstream Church, directing everything towards negotiation, mother knowing, with maternal instinct, that the adolescent mind required, not just example, but a touch of discipline as well. Thus, the descendant of the old-time Border raiders played the peace-maker among us, while the lady he had lifted from across the Border read the Riot Act.

In consequence, although we loved her dearly, in youth at any rate we stood in awe of her, aware that our every fault was known to her and that it was her avowed intention to eliminate them all. In this endeavour, she was aided by her perspicacity, her wit and her devotion to the truth. Nor did she mince her words. Like every Lambton I have ever met, she was outspoken, to the point of rudeness, had her strictures on family and friends and on the world in general not been delivered with charm and a twinkle in the eye.

Where Lambtons came from in the first place is obscure. Some say, most notably Lord Scarborough, that there is a list of silver kept at Lumley Castle, just across the road from Lambton Castle, signed by William Lambton, butler to the Earl of Scarborough. If so the Lambtons made marked progress. My maternal grandfather was Liberal MP for Berwick-on-Tweed. He it was who stood up in the House of Commons, while still in his twenties, and remarked to Mr Gladstone that, if he persisted in his efforts to prevent a certain measure being passed, the Liberals would have to get a new Prime Minister. His twin brother, Lord Durham, was a steward at the famous Epsom meeting when the Derby winner lost the race, not on the course, but in the stewards' room, because he was a four-year-old.

My mother's nephew, Tony, my first cousin, represented Berwick-on-Tweed, like his grandfather but as a Tory, until indiscretion in his private life forced his retirement. None the less, although he lost his seat, he retains his Lambton wit and humour. What my mother would have thought of the affair which ended his political career I cannot tell, since she had died before the scandal broke. To judge from the reaction of her sister Violet, aunt to Tony and myself, and over ninety at the time, it seems likely that she would have taken it in her stride. Aunt Violet saw fit to ignore the whole affair and only when her errant nephew gave a party for Andy Warhol some years later at his house in Hamilton Terrace did she write him a vintage letter. She had evidently come across an article by William Hickey on the subject. 'My dear Tony,' so the letter ran, 'by letting Champagne run in Hamilton Terrace, as William Hickey says, you've dragged the name of Lambton through the mud.' Strong words to use at ninety-five but who shall say she was not right in her priorities?

A student of the stud book, therefore, like another uncle of my mother's – George, who trained Hyperion to win the Derby (when, I'm happy to record, he was a three-year-old) – might be forgiven for assuming that the future form of any colt or filly bred out of a Lambton mare and by a sire of sunny disposition and marked eccentricity, could well be unpredictable.

However, undisturbed by such disquieting prospects even if they were aware of them, my parents bravely buckled to, and brought into the world five children (three M and two F) before the First World War, adding two more (both M) after the armistice.

Of this brood the eldest was my brother Alec. He was something of an athlete, both at school and Oxford, and he took to politics quite early, standing first in a safe Labour seat in Glasgow then, after defeat, receiving well-deserved promotion to South Lanark which he managed to win. When my father mentioned this, with pride, to Mr Telfer, his head keeper, he was met with the response, 'I always tell my boys to leave politics severely alone.' As a result of his early success in politics, I saw less of Alec than I did of the rest of the family. He was, however, popular with all of us. His father called him 'Ikes' for short. We called him 'Dungfly' since his name was Dunglass, and his mother did her best to cure his hypochondria.

'It's funny, Alec,' she would say, 'how every Sunday you've got flu or something worse, yet, every Monday morning, you're in the shooting-brake by half-past nine.'

'Good timing, Mamma,' he would answer, grinning at her with that crooked grin so reminiscent – not that I have ever seen one – of a clown, called from his dressing-room, perhaps, down to the stage-door telephone, while only halfway through his make-up.

It is difficult to paint his character because, unlike his father, he is reticent and discreet. Nor is he flamboyant, like his brother Henry, nor yet vulgar and facetious like the next one down the list. If he resembles any of us, he is more like Edward, the first post-World

War One child, quiet and unobtrusive but at the same time aware of everything that's going on around him and prepared to comment succinctly upon it. Were he not so vague and of a different sex, he would be very like his mother.

'Peking, Alec, Peking, Peking,' his devoted wife, Elizabeth, would constantly repeat to him while walking behind him down the steps of an aeroplane, when he was Foreign Secretary. 'Peking, Peking, Peking,' in order to prevent him saying to his hosts, as he stood up before the microphone, 'I'm very happy to be back in Montreal' (or Rome, or Washington, or Moscow).

Those who criticized him for his casual approach to life, for his lack of emotion and, as many argued, appeal as a politician, missed something worth much more, his integrity, that quality so unmistakable where it exists, and which I sensed in Alec from the start, though I was too young to recognize it then for what it was. If I had to define it, I would say one sensed in him a kind of calmness such as one feels in the atmosphere around a mountain loch – a shade forbidding, perhaps, to a stranger; somewhat chilly, possibly, to any passing hiker who might seek to put his feet in it, but, to all its familiars a well-loved landmark, comforting, impressive and serene, even beautiful, so unobtrusively and neatly does it fit into the rugged landscape.

Once his self-protective glacier was crossed (he never let me touch him, for example, when I was a small boy, thus ensuring constant attempts on my part to do just that, met always with the standard response: 'Take away that slimy toadlike hand') and superficial reservations were disposed of, there was no one kinder than he to his overcrowded family. He wrote long verses to us – mislaid now, alas – when we had croup or flu; he put us in good places in the line of battle when we were teenagers, for which action we rewarded him by missing everything except, with luck, a passing mountain hare, thus earning a rebuke but seldom relegation to the flank.

He still favours this self-effacing policy. The acres that he owns in Scotland are the hunting grounds of brothers, nephews, grandsons and their poaching friends. With his benign approval, these insatiable hangers-on quarter the ground like harriers. Invariably, when he feels the urge to wait for pigeons, drives his car into some promising plantation, parks and switches off the engine, he will hear, as he descends and reaches for his gun, a shot from the exact location at which he had hoped to pass a pleasant afternoon. And what does he do? Stride along the ride in anger and expel the errant brother (nephew? grandson?)? Not at all. He smiles his crooked smile, replaces the gun in the car, starts up the engine quietly, and proceeds towards another favourite wood in which he probably undergoes the same experience.

This may explain why, in his park at Hirsel, daffodils grow in profusion over many acres. Thwarted in his sporting life, he tends to return home, put on a pair of shorts, pick up two buckets filled with bulbs, put one on either side of him as he sits down on some drive-side or in some field, dig one hole with his trowel on his right, another on his left, insert a bulb in each, replace the divots, then move one pace forward on his hands, like some benign ape, and repeat the process. Meanwhile the sound of gun-fire, reaching a crescendo towards twilight, echoes and re-echoes in his ears.

He spent a large proportion of the war encased in plaster, after being operated on for TB of the spine. His only son was born during this period. This fact, the contemplation of which much amuses Brian Johnston, an irreverent family friend, illustrates both Alec's strength of character and his resilience. The rest of his career is common knowledge.

The next child was Bridget who, when she was young, had red hair, quite a lot of which she still retains. She took after her father in this way (with the red hair not the retaining of it) but not only in this. She inherited, as well, his character, his kindness, his affection for his relatives, his inability to do other than love his fellow men and women, good or bad, his universal popularity.

She never married, but, despite that fact, she has a family of loved ones far more numerous than any family she would have had, if she had done so.

Every afternoon, outside her home, the drive is crowded with parked vehicles of every shape and size, reminding one of a commuters' car park at some Surrey railway station, from which pour her brothers, sisters-in-law, nephews, nieces, not to mention great-nephews and nieces, to take tea with her.

Over this motley, chattering assembly, 'Aunt Bridget' holds

court, in her sitting-room first, and, then, moving dining-room-wards, borne on a relentless tide which renders her supporting sticks redundant, where she sits dispensing tea or milk (according to what age group she is serving at the moment), scones and biscuits and, on special anniversaries like birthdays, short cakes made by her devoted adjutant, friend and retainer, Margaret Russell, now retired.

Not only does she entertain these gangs of foraging relations, but she writes to them on every birthday, every wedding anniversary or other notable occasion, such as First Nights, travels-overseas, release from jail, return to school or temporary occupation of Ten Downing Street. In every letter can be found detailed reports of the activities of all her other relatives, transmitted with such vividness and clarity as to prompt Charlie, a discerning nephew and now Foreign Editor of *The Times*, to confide in me once that, in his opinion, his Aunt Bridget would have been unequalled as a journalist.

Though crippled with arthritis, in spite of two operations, Bridget still continues to relay the latest state of play to her adoring family.

'Old so-and-so died last week, poor old thing. She had been off her head for ages. Rory caught a trout below the Bower Bridge. Alec made him put it back, because it wasn't big enough. Henry found a pied flycatcher's nest up by the Obelisk. Rachel rang up last night, and went on for hours – she's quite mad, but I must admit, she's funny. Edward shot three rabbits for me in my garden. Very nice of him but, as I told him, there are hundreds more. They've put an extra seat top on the downstairs loo, so that I can sit down more comfortably. It looks just like a throne, if you see what I mean.

'Elizabeth and Alec went to London last night on the night train. Wish I could have seen your play before it came off! Will it come up here? I hope so.

'Heard a lot of geese fly over when I woke this morning. Read your letter in *The Times* just now. I thought it rather vulgar.'

Dear old Bridget, every word she writes conveys a memory to the recipient – a happy memory, moreover, of a youth spent in the Border land among the geese (who were much rarer then), the Leet trout (many of them put back, too, like Rory's, though not the two-pounder, less one quarter ounce, I caught above the Ladies Bridge), the rabbits in the Springhill garden and the dining-room in which my mother used to sit, her spectacles precariously balanced on her nose, making remarks of keen perception, with a quiet voice and a twinkle. 'Lady Home,' said Jakie Astor to her in old age, 'do stop twinkling those wicked little eyes at me.'

My brother Henry came next. Looking rather like a dissipated version of the Duke of Windsor, he had ridden hard and drunk hard since his Oxford days. His greatest triumph as an undergraduate was to dead-heat with Peter Cazalet on his own horse, the Mole, in one of the grind races (point-to-point, in normal language). After Oxford, he became a house agent in London (an unlikely nesting site for him) then married Margaret Spencer, who bore him three children: Robin, Fiona and Charlie. He spent much of the War as an Army officer in Edinburgh because he was unfit for active service, having smashed himself up in a riding accident, lost touch with Margaret, finally divorcing her (or vice-versa). When peace came, he married a Norwegian lady, whom he met in Oslo after being drafted there at the conclusion of hostilities. This marriage broke up in due course as well, leaving behind it a son called George. Then the indefatigable fellow married for the third time, Felicity Wills who, in her turn, has produced a son called Peregrine (he wished to call him Merlin, but we talked him out of that).

Thus this old sultan has married three wives, sired five children, drunk more bottles of the 'hard stuff' than his other three surviving brothers put together, yet remained throughout his varying domestic problems (now most happily resolved) a dedicated ornithologist and a delightful, charming fellow, driven to rage sometimes by the failings of his fellow men, but always ready to provide them with a drink.

'Your glass is empty, my dear fellow,' he will say to male and female alike. 'Fill it up! Go on, don't be a damned fool – the night is still young.'

The night is usually, in fact, much older than it looks, thus differing in that respect from Henry, who looks older than he is, reminding one of an ancient oak tree, crippled, but withstanding the gales still. I sometimes wonder, looking at him, how many pairs of woodpeckers have studied him in springtime from some near-by vantage point, and contemplated boring into his anatomy in order to provide themselves with an attractive nesting site.

Some other types of bird, less shy than they, like swallows, take advantage of his hospitality, building their nests above his porch (not outside, but inside the house). These visitors, though picturesque, provide a hazard for his guests, and Admiral Sir Peter Reid, who married cousin Jean Dundas, once came into the drawing-room, dinner jacket and bald head be-spattered with the defecations of his fellow guests above the front door. Other swallows, nesting in Henry's bedroom on the picture rail above his own and his wife's pillows, may well be responsible for the fact that he is now wedded to his third.

Henry paints birds as well, and is a good but intermittent artist in that line. My wife and I, whose silver wedding is now over, are still waiting for our wedding present. Readers of his book, *The Birdman*, will, however, note that he has painted quite a few for himself. 'I'll never finish yours,' he tells me – 'too late now. I get cramp in my arse if I pick up a paint brush.'

Another major interest in his life is Flodden Field. Here on 9 September he may be seen, sitting beneath a hedge and listening for sounds of battle at dusk. The most noticeable sound in my experience of these occasions is that of corkscrews opening port bottles. None the less, he manages to keep the battle going with his conversation.

'That damned fellow, Howard, you know, the bloody Admiral, the son of poor old Surrey, who was in a bath chair, riddled with gout, ancestor of Bernard Norfolk, my dear fellow. He stayed in that house just beyond Wooler – look at it tomorrow on your way south – not the new bit, the bit that looks like a pigsty. Anyway, where were we? Ah yes, that damned fellow Howard. Your glass is empty, my dear fellow, where's the bloody corkscrew? Listen! What was that? A clash of armour? – Damn, it's just that bloody tractor in the farm-yard packing up for the night. Fill up, my dear fellow – go on – the night's still young. Pass me back the bottle. Well, as I was saying, that damned fellow Howard ran out of beer and so he rang up our beloved King and said, "Is that you, James the Fourth? Ah, good. Look here – I'm marching off to Berwick to fill up with beer, because we've run short and my father says he knows you'll give me a safe conduct." Bloody lie, of course, but that was what he said and it worked wonders. Our beloved King – the bloody fool – fell

H.P.H.–C

for it – chivalry and all that. He said, "Certainly, Howard, my dear fellow. If your father has such faith in my integrity, of course I'll give you a safe conduct." So he did, and rang off. And Howard, bloody twister that he was, marched off, but didn't go to Berwick. Instead he came over Twizel Bridge and cut off our beloved King from Scotland in a flanking movement. That's when Scotland went down, my dear fellow. As that damned old bore Sir Walter Scott said, "shivered was fair Scotland's shield, and broken was her whatnot".

'And when Bernard used to ask me down to Arundel for cricket, my dear fellow, I invariably told him that he ought to be ashamed of being a descendant of that bounder!'

Thus the evening would wear on, the while the sound of battle ebbed and flowed according to the tempo of the throbbing in ones ears, and soon the empty bottles would be packed away in the boot and the Sixth Lord Home's descendant would begin to weave his way back down the road towards his native land.

> 'And on that dangerous ford and deep,
> Where to the Tweed Leet's eddies creep,
> They ventured desperately.'

So wrote Sir Walter Scott, again, of the rout of the Scottish troops at Flodden on that dark September night, while Henry, nearly five centuries later, went by Coldstream bridge, though no less desperately.

Rachel, the fourth child out of the seven, had strong views in youth, and used to quarrel with her brothers, not excluding this one. Once she threw a glass of water across the table during dinner into Alec's face, drenching his white tie and tails, donned for the Berwickshire Hunt Ball, in retribution for some slight that she imagined he had just inflicted on his father in the course of conversation. Mr Collingwood went to the door and opened it for Alec, on his way to change his tie and collar and shirt, while the dinner party carried on as though nothing had happened. Nor was he whom she had championed on that occasion, always exempt from her wrath. Once, I remember, after an engagement on some long-forgotten subject, she broke off relations, left and went down to the chapel from which emanated, between tea and dinner, sounds of organ music played with the stops full out. Eight o'clock came, Mr Collingwood came in to announce dinner, while the rafters rang still to the thunder of the organ music in the chapel down below.

'Tell Lady Rachel dinner's ready,' said my father. 'Very good, my lord,' said Mr Collingwood, and hurried on his mission of goodwill. 'Come on, Lil, let's go in,' my father said.

We walked along the passage to the dining-room. The organ music, louder in that area, gave place to silence for a moment, then resumed, much louder than before.

We sat down, reaching for our soup spoons, just as Mr Collingwood returned.

'I've told her dinner's ready, my lord,' said he.

'Well, then, why isn't she coming?'

Mr Collingwood blushed.

'What did she say,' my father persisted, 'when you told her?'

Mr Collingwood stayed silent.

'What did she say, Collingwood?' my mother asked, with quiet authority.

'She said his lordship was a bottle-nosed old shark, my lady.'

'Thank you, Collingwood,' my mother said. 'You'd better put her soup back on the hot plate.'

'Yes, milady,' said he – and then someone laughed.

It could have been my father or my mother or myself, or even Mr Collingwood. No matter which it was, the fact is that the laughter echoed and re-echoed round the dining-room until the organ music could be heard no longer, and the organist, become aware of so much merriment, rejoined her family in time to get her soup.

No word was said about the episode again, not in my hearing anyway, although no doubt my father, in his prayers that night, added a codicil to the effect that he was grateful to have been allowed to sire so spirited a daughter.

Ever an eccentric, she once asked me on returning from a Hunt Ball in the Corn Exchange in Kelso (how we lived it up in those days!) to divert the soda syphon from my glass of whisky and direct it, instead, down the cleavage of her evening gown, as she was feeling hot. I did so and she stood there, dark and dripping, while the soda-water ran first, down her body, then her legs and on to the stone floor.

She married Billy Scott. He had a voice and way of using it not easy to describe unless one makes comparison with Woodrow Wyatt's voice, that is to say, loud, drawn-out and definite. He was Conservative MP for Roxburgh and no heckler had any chance against him, not that he was impolite, far from it, but because the weight of any utterance he made exceeded, by a multitude of decibels, the vocal strength of any interrupter from the body of the hall. He also knew his facts and had a telling way of putting them across. I well remember the conclusion of his speeches in one General Election where he was at pains to thwart the challenge from the Liberals.

'The Liberals, ladies and gentlemen,' so ran his peroration, 'are a strong force in this area. You may be tempted to vote for them. Well and good, please do so if you wish to. But, remember, though they talk a great deal about profit-sharing' – then a trenchant pause – 'you never heard them mention loss-sharing, now, did you?' Then he sat down, and, of course, they never had – nor have done, to this day.

The marriage was a very happy one, brought to a close by his untimely death.

The last pre-1914 child bestowed by an impartial providence upon my parents, was myself. But more of him in the next chapter.

Then at the conclusion of hostilities or shortly after, came my younger brother, Edward.

I can still see Dr Fisher, sitting in a deck-chair outside the front door at Hirsel, with my father in another deck-chair and myself, in shorts (as well as great discomfort, due to my small stature) in a third.

'We'd better tell him that he's got another brother, Fisher, hadn't we?' my father said.

'Why not,' said Dr Fisher, 'as he's going to meet him shortly.'

Upstairs I went, in bewilderment and some resentment. 'What was Dr Fisher doing there?' I asked myself. 'What function could he possibly perform from the depths of a deck-chair? Or had he performed it earlier? And, if so, what right had he to perform it – a strange man from Edinburgh, who seemed to know a great deal more about my family than I did myself?'

In the bedroom in the old part of the house, looking out towards the Cheviot Hills, my mother lay, a baby in her arms. I noticed that it had a hare-lip. Worried by this, but endeavouring to hide my reaction, I stretched out a hand and touched the little fellow's cheek (a thing I've never done since, now I come to think of it) and went downstairs again to rejoin Dr Fisher and my father, where they still sat, looking out towards the lake, smoking their pipes, no doubt congratulating themselves on a job well done in their respective spheres.

'So that's what you've been up to, is it, Fisher?' I sat thinking to myself, in some confusion. 'Anybody would imagine that you were my father, from the way you've been behaving, sticking babies in my mother's bed without so much as by your leave.'

My father raised the question of the hare-lip at once, noting my embarrassment, at which the doctor told me Edward would be just like anybody else when his lip had been operated on, which prophecy turned out to be correct. It made him shy, perhaps, in youth and in his early school days, but no shyer than this elder brother who, although his upper lip was in one piece at birth, began life with a patently receding chin.

In due course, Edward went to Ludgrove, then to Eton, in the footsteps of his elder brothers, finally to Balliol, which college he left on the outbreak of war. He went missing in Malaya and a lot of people – I was no exception – thought that he was dead. Then, in September 1945, he came back pale, thin and riddled with malaria, contracted on the Burma Railway while a prisoner of war.

He went and shot a pair of mallard on the River Leet below the drawing-room window, just as he had done before he left in 1940, both these feathered sacrifices serving as an antidote to the embarrassment he suffered at the parting, on the first occasion, and on his return, at the reunion.

The morning after he came back, he went down to the Tweed to fish the Lower Water opposite to Carham House, in which, at that time, lived a family called Straker Smith. The daughter of the house was that day fishing from the Carham boat into the Scottish side, as is the custom on the Tweed. Edward was doing the reverse, casting his fly towards the English girl with sure effect.

Next day, he went down to the river with a picnic lunch for two. With my dramatic antennae unfurled and quivering, I bore my mother the news, tell-tale that I was.

'Edward's gone fishing with two lots of sandwiches,' I told her.

'Oh, dear,' she said. 'I do hope it's not that Straker Smith girl.'

'Why not Mamma? She's a very nice girl.'

'That is not the point. The point is that he won't know how to make up his mind.'

'Why not?'

'Well, he's seen nothing but Japanese women for the last four years!'

'What – on the Burma railway, Mamma? Take it easy,' I said, smiling.

'Never mind that,' she said, 'I hope Edward will!'

But Edward didn't. To everyone's delight, including his Mamma's, he got engaged that week-end and lived happily thereafter, to the great regret of every mallard in the Border country, not to mention all the pheasants and the salmon who are lined up, annually, to pay the price of his renewed good health.

A tall, phlegmatic fellow Edward is, unlike his other brothers in that he is totally without ambition. Life flows on for him in quiet serenity, leaving his humour unimpaired, his cartridge bill colossal and his heart and soul at peace in his beloved Border land.

They found him in Malaya with a bullet through his heart and propped him up against a gum tree, with a water bottle by his side. When they came back to bury him, he was still sitting there. The Army doctor diagnosed that the position of his heart was evidently not that favoured by most other human hearts, when situated in the standard human chassis. This is to speak physically, of course. From every other point of view, it is just where it should be.

The last child, George, arrived at Hirsel two years later, introduced once more by Dr Fisher. In due course, he travelled down to England for his education, but he never went to Oxford as his brothers had, because, at the conclusion of his time at Eton, he went straight into the Air Force, only to be lost in 1942 while training off the coast of Canada. Because he was the youngest, and, without much doubt, the most attractive of the brood, his disappearance struck my parents very hard. Yet he was hardly ever mentioned in the family thereafter. This may sound strange, I concede, but is not so in my family. The fact that we did not discuss his death did not mean that we had forgotten him. Quite the reverse. Somehow, by some strange process, we succeeded, through our reticence, in keeping him alive.

I saw him last in Torquay, I dressed as a private soldier, he in Air Force uniform, before he went to do his training in Vancouver Island. From my billet down in Kingsbridge, I reported to my parents on his cheerfulness and general well-being, and suggested to them that, in Coastal Command, for which he was training, he might have a chance of coming through the War in one piece.

Three months later, word came through that he was missing. Evidently, fog or some Pacific storm had swallowed up all the planes in his training flight, and they had not returned to base. I do not think of him in that predicament, however. I remember him as I last saw him, smiling goodbye in a Torquay street, his forage cap set at a jaunty angle.

No doubt, my father would remember him as he saw him on his final leave, walking down towards the lake with Mr Collingwood, the butler, talking sixteen to the dozen, disappearing into a hide with his camera, and then dispatching his companion back towards the house again, coat-tails flapping in the wind, still talking, so that the Great Crested Grebe would think that George was with him still, because birds cannot count.

I used this portrait of him in my play *The Dame of Sark* when Colonel Count von Schmettau, German Commandant on Guernsey, told his prisoner of his last meeting with his youngest son, killed on the Russian Front, and proudly showed the Dame a photograph of a Great Crested Grebe.

When I think of George's death, I think, too, of a line of Siegfried Sassoon's brought to my attention, once, by Jakie Astor, in another context:

> 'Remember this one afternoon in Spring
> When your own child looks down and makes
> your sad heart sing.'

## Chapter 3

# Myself, Pre-war

My parents' fifth child came into the world in 1912 in Randolph Crescent, Edinburgh, at which address my own son, Jamie, put in his appearance forty years on.

With my mother, I came back to Springhill where my parents lived at that time, since my grandparents still occupied the Hirsel. Two years later, war broke out. Between the age of two and seven I saw little of my father due to his departure in the Army for the Near East, treading in the footsteps of his ancestor, the Good Sir James but, unlike him, arriving safely at his destination and returning in one piece.

He took part in the Dardanelles campaign. In later life, he always had a good word for the Turks, for one specific reason which appeared to him to be decisive. When the wild-geese flighted high over the Allied lines at dusk towards their feeding areas in Turkish territory, a few ambitious wild-fowlers in khaki loosed off their rifles at them and sometimes – although very rarely – contacted some luckless bird, which fell behind the enemy lines. When this happened – so my father always swore – a Turkish officer would walk out into No-Man's-Land under a flag of truce and hand the victim over with a friendly smile and a salute. This sportsmanship, so similar to that displayed by neighbours of his in the Border land, convinced one British officer, at least, that 'Johnny Turk' was nothing like so bad a character as he was painted by the propagandists.

Letters that my father sent his children from this war-zone and from Egypt later, of which I got my full share although I was too young to read them, always contained pictures of the local fauna. In 1918 he went off to Ireland as the Colonel of a bicycle battalion, combining business with pleasure, as this letter illustrates:

Sept. 22 1918                                                    Strabane

My dear William,

I got four little salmon yesterday 10, 5, 5, and 3 lbs.

It rained hard all day. I went there in what they call a light railway. Small engine and small carriages and narrow rails. There are several railways like that in Ireland.

The train at the station near here only stops if someone wants to go by it and then the station master signals to engine-driver.

They only go slowly, on light railways. Hope you are well and like being back at Springhill.

Your loving

Dadda

Letters such as these were my sole contact with the theatre of operations although tanks rolled into Coldstream sometimes and on one occasion stopped in Birgham, while on a recruiting drive. Their crews invited children like myself on board for an inspection. Also on our walks on foot or by pram in the afternoon, we used to come on gangs of German prisoners, laying pipes by the roadside and, occasionally, a group of wounded British soldiers came to take tea in the garden and admire the view across the Tweed.

Because my nurse had told me so, I knew that the pipe-laying Germans, working on the Kelso road, were enemies, while those in khaki, sitting in the garden drinking tea and eating biscuits, were on the same side as I was. Yet I found it hard to differentiate between the two groups since they all appeared to be quite harmless, friend and enemy alike – the latter often smiling at my sister Rachel and myself, thinking, no doubt, of children of their own back in the fatherland. It could be that from that date, and as a result of those experiences, I began, although perhaps subconsciously, to think of war as being an activity as foolish as it was illogical.

If wounded British soldiers could sit on my mother's lawn and drink tea while a lot of German prisoners laid pipes along the roadside just beyond the garden, without flying at each other's throats, why could this peaceful tableau not be permanent? Why did the barrage have to keep on dropping on the trenches in Flanders, filled with men, on either side of No-Man's-Land, of just such peaceful disposition as all those of my acquaintance? Was humanity for ever to be caught up in a situation not of its own choosing and demonstrably against its nature?

I just wrote that phrase 'although perhaps subconsciously' but – now I come to think of it – I can remember thinking all these things as I stood on the lawn at Springhill in my cotton dress, beside my sister Rachel, similarly clad, looking at maimed men of all ages, dressed in khaki, smiling at me from their wheeled-chairs with precisely the same look in their eyes, the same friendliness, even the same bewilderment, as we marked in the eyes of those, their mortal enemies, outside the gate. Thus, possibly, shades of the prison house began to close around the growing boy.

My father hurried back from Ireland on his bicycle at the conclusion of hostilities to carry on where he had left off. But, before the birth of Edward, we transferred from Springhill to the Hirsel, on the death of both my grandparents.

This move we children found exciting since the house was large, mysterious and even, some said, haunted by an ancestor who had been caught cheating at cards and then thrown downstairs to his death by his disgusted guests. This staircase lay below the nursery quarters in the old part of the house and often Rachel and I, lying rigid in adjoining bedrooms, would hear noises which convinced us that the centuries-old drama was being re-enacted for our benefit.

Also, at the entrance to the nursery passage was a little room, called Zisternelli's cupboard, which intrigued us. We were told its occupant had been a foreign music master, who had been attached to the strength by some female ancestor – the innuendo being that this gentleman had played so pretty a tune as to ensure that he did not have to spend too much time in his cupboard.

Just across the passage from this box-room, lay our schoolroom. Instruction from Miss Pattenden, our governess, filled every morning during term time and some of each afternoon. During the holidays we roamed the park and learned in springtime, how to fish for trout in the Leet, which ran just below the house and, when we graduated, how to fish for salmon in the Tweed. We also learned bird lore from Henry, watching him set up his nesting boxes for pied flycatchers (the swifts came later), being taught to find a willow-warbler's nest in the long grass and then to mark it with a bamboo as a warning to the mowing-machine, learning in what sandy bank beside the Leet the kingfisher preferred to nest or from which fir-branch in the rhododendron wood the golden-crested wrens would hang their nest or in which blackthorn we would be most likely to come on the spherical creation of the long-tailed tit.

In winter we would go to Bonkyl, when the woodcock were in, from whence came my father on that fateful day at the beginning of the century, or wait for pigeons in Spylaw, the wood beside which bonfires had been lit to warn of the approaching English cattle-thieves, or stand beside our elders watching them shoot pheasants over the Leet valley.

Then to Douglas in the summer where the woods were a delight to be in, whether one came on a roebuck or not – birches, spruces, soft moss under foot, great beech trees, on whose roots one could sit down and meditate on life in general, while rabbits chased each other round the beds of rushes and wood-pigeons soared and clapped their wings above the silent conifers.

It was my father who had introduced me to the roedeer at an early age, and taken me out looking for them of an evening, while my elder brothers entertained their friends at tennis on a court on which it would not have surprised one to put up a snipe. We used to hear their shouts across the valley as we wandered silently along the rides, myself behind my self-appointed stalker carrying the .22 rifle, moving like a spectre through the clouds of his tobacco smoke. Sometimes, he left me underneath a birch tree while he walked a mile or so across the heather to the far end of the wood to move the deer. More often, he would walk away from me because he had a theory, quite often proven by experience, that roedeer tend to double back.

My mother used to worry about whether I might shoot him by mistake, if some fine roebuck pausing at a clearing edge, should draw my fire, be missed in the excitement and the bullet should continue on its flight. This never happened, although, once, back in the panel-led hall at Hirsel after shooting rabbits, while obeying his instruc-tions to unload, I pulled the trigger by mistake and missed him by a bee's wing. When my mother came down to inspect the bullet hole, she disliked what she saw intensely, but my father took the whole thing philosophically: 'Poor little devil, Lil,' I heard him saying later to her in his loud voice from his dressing-room, 'bad luck there was a bullet in it, that's all. You can't blame him.'

'Yes, I can,' my mother answered, 'he should have unloaded outside.'

'But he didn't know there was a bullet in it,' argued my father.

'Well, he should have done, the silly little boy! He might easily have killed you.'

Then my father started singing, 'Fill the sails and homeward' and went off to have his bath, leaving my mother combing out her long and beautiful black hair, and thinking of her silly little third son with profound distaste.

Thereafter, we reverted to orthodox roedeer stalking, with my father carrying the rifle and his small potential assassinator bringing up the rear. I would look up at the tweed-clad back and large cap, with the fringe of red hair round it, moving down the ride in front of me, and ponder on how strange and unpredictable life was. The entire Turkish Army had failed to achieve, in two years, what one small and careless boy had nearly brought off on his own, in the oak-panelled hall at Hirsel. No doubt God received repeated votes of thanks for His successful intervention, too, if one may judge from the innumerable pauses that my father made in his perambulations for some time thereafter, followed by the lifting of the large cap, its replacement, then continued progress of the stalk with a more jaunty tread.

God also had His part to play in the chase, notably at cross rides where, before my father made his last step forward, with a view to looking right and left, he would pause, hand on peak of cap, to offer up a short request that some large roebuck might be feeding round the corner. History must record, however, that God, in His wisdom, seldom saw His way to intervening in this manner, preferring us to sweat it out, sometimes for weeks, as when a mighty roebuck, spotted by a shepherd's wife one Sunday morning on her way home from the Kirk, held us at bay throughout one long and happy month. At last, one memorable morning, he came through the birches with the sunlight glinting on his antlers, which, when measured, matched the record head my father had secured in the last century

The intervals between these holidays I spent in England at school, Ludgrove first, which was then situated at Cockfosters and later moved to Wokingham. Although my memory informs me that my first imprisonment in England compared unfavourably with my second, written evidence from Ludgrove would appear to contradict this.

'Dear Lady Home' – so wrote the joint-Headmaster's wife, the day after I first arrived there – 'He seems very well this morning and I watched him talking hard to the boy next to him at breakfast (Martin Gilliat, perhaps, a fellow new boy). He was very cheerful last night and so good when Lord Home went away. We went for a walk round the gardens and met Mr Stanborough who took William off to look for birds' nests.'

From the copy of my first report from Ludgrove – the original, according to my father's notes having been burnt as a precaution against scarlet fever – I learn that I came top in everything but History. Progress, later on, was less spectacular. However, in due course, I moved to Eton, taking Upper Fourth, which would have been the more distinguished Remove, according to the other joint-Headmaster, under 'normal circumstances' – i.e. lack of illness. 'We shall miss him very much' – with these words did this kindly fellow, W. J. Oakley, who had played rugger for England – end his last report on a shy, unathletic little boy.

Five years at Eton followed Ludgrove. I spent one year in the house of C. M. Wells with brother Henry; then they both left and the house was taken on by Mr Howson, one of the four Eton masters to die in the Alps, all roped together, some years later. Howson's watch, according to the Press, had stopped exactly at the moment when death came to them; I remembered that same watch in Pupil Room as it ticked on inexorably on his wrist, the while he sat correcting Latin verses, while I stood behind his chair. He was a nice man and a good man; those in his house were happy and the sorrow that we felt when he fell to his death was genuine.

Most Eton masters in my time (and, no doubt, still) had character. Presiding over them was Doctor Alington, white haired, white surpliced, and outstandingly distinguished in appearance, whose daughter, Elizabeth, was to become my sister-in-law. Mrs Alington, her mother, who reminded me of the Duchess in *Alice*, was a lady with a heart as big as herself and a warmth of personality which instantly set even a small, nervous boy like myself at ease at her breakfast table. Once when Mr Gandhi came to stay with Miss Slade, his long-time disciple, Mrs Alington came on her lying on the mat outside her master's bedroom. 'Go to your room, Miss Slade,' said her hostess sternly. 'But I always sleep outside the dear Mahatma's door,' said Miss Slade. 'Not while I'm President of the Mother's Union, you don't,' said Mrs Alington. Nor did she, that night. Alec's wife inherited a happy mixture of her mother's down-to-earthness and her father's wit.

A warning signal, indicating lack of academic scholarship, was hoisted during my last year at Eton when I wrote a one-act play performed in School Hall.

'What with plays and periodicals (a reference to magazines produced by boys to which I had contributed) History has had to occupy a back-seat in Douglas Home's imagination' – wrote Colonel Hills, my History tutor. Then, forgivingly, he added, 'I thought very highly of his play.' So did Howson. 'I agree with Hills,' he wrote in his last letter to my father, 'William's play seemed to me very good.' He also wrote, ironically in view of what was to come later: 'It is largely due to him that discipline has been good.' I was Captain of the House, which job I handed on to a large, cheerful and untidy boy, Jo Grimond.

The only time I let my tutor down – apart from over minor troubles in the adolescent field – was when that same Hills who had liked my play, suggested that I left the Corps, which he commanded, pointing out that I was not of the stuff that made a good soldier. This thought had occurred to me at frequent intervals on College Field, while undergoing weapon-training from a sergeant in the Guards. On these occasions, I had the same feeling as I had experienced at Spring-hill, in my early youth, among the wounded soldiers on my mother's lawn, the same conviction that the role expected of me was not in my nature, the same longing to shout out loud: 'What's all this about? What are you doing, sergeant, wasting your time teaching me to fire machine-guns at my fellow creatures, none of whom have harmed me? Go home, sergeant, go home, Captain Grenville Grey (our Adjutant), in your Guards uniforms, and make love to your wives and pat your children's heads and try to think of ways to turn your unattractive weapons into plough-shares.'

So I left the Corps, most thankfully, without a backward glance. Then I left Eton and proceeded, after failing to get in the first time, to pass into New College, that home of erudition chosen for me by a hitherto frustrated father. This frustration was induced by the fact that his elder sons had scarcely overworked themselves at Christ Church. I, his third one, underwent a change of college in the hope of better things. Scholastically the hopes entertained by my father were to remain unfulfilled, although I made good friends at New College – with Brian Johnston, who had come from Eton with me; Al Hayes, an American, who, as a Wall Street banker later saved the pound on at least two occasions; and Jim Harmsworth, now the Bow Street Magistrate.

During my final year at Oxford, when I moved from College into lodgings, I took up with my old Eton cronies – Hopetown, Hope, Wood, Mercer Nairne – in Mrs Hutton's digs in Merton Street. I little knew that thirty-eight years later Wood would win the Derby in the year in which my own horse, Goblin, ran tenth. As that fact implies, the atmosphere in Merton Street was sporting, yet, in that unlikely milieu, I sat down and wrote my first full-length play.

Arthur Deakin, who had been at Eton, with me had seen fit to join the Oxford Group. The story went that he stopped the Captain of the Oxford Boat Club in the High Street and enquired of him if he was ever troubled with impure thoughts. 'Not at all,' the open-hearted fellow told him, 'as a matter of fact, I enjoy them.' To our house in Merton Street came this out-spoken fellow to convert the Philistines to Buchmanism: Hopetown, Wood and Mercer Nairne in riding breeches, Hope in running shorts just back from the sports field, myself returned, perhaps, from a game of real tennis with Professor A. L. Goodhart. I still see the tableau now; Arthur Deakin, holding a half-furled umbrella, with a cup of tea and a large slice of cherry-cake, haranguing whisky-drinking infidels with great good humour. Nothing came of his attempts to bring about a mass conversion. All of us remained aloof from his appeals. But one of us saw suddenly the plot for a play in this bizarre environment. It came on at the Q Theatre the year that I went down from Oxford, followed by a transfer to the Duke of York's for a short season –

not designedly short, but because the public did not see their way to patronizing it.

'Charles' – James Agate wrote in his review in the *Sunday Times* – 'died out hunting at the end of Act Two. Henry, his great friend, remarked, "He would have liked to go like that." And with good reason,' Agate frostily concluded, 'for in Heaven there would have been no Third Act!'

Certain other critics did record that I showed promise as a playwright but, as Colonel Hills had pointed out at Eton, such activities did no good to my History. After being sent down twice for climbing in and climbing out of Merton Street, and then returning for my Schools, I took a Fourth degree, denoting, as Tom Boase (a History tutor, later to be President of Magdelen) told me, that I had provided interesting answers to a lot of questions that had not been asked.

My father took the point that I was no scholastic genius with equanimity, being by now, immune to disappointment; Alec having only gone down with a Third while Henry had not taken a degree at all. He made mild noises, sometimes, between grouse drives, indicating that a job was what I needed in the not too distant future, for the simple reason that none of the acres over which we strode from dawn to dusk would be inherited by me. My mother, more direct as always, asked me, point blank, what I meant to do. I told her I was going on the Grand Tour with George Mercer Nairne, using part of the thousand pounds left me by my Aunt Isobel, my godmother. The rest of it I blew on a small Ford car.

This car stayed at home, however, when we drove in George's Humber Snipe through Germany and Italy and Spain, the furthest point south that we reached on our tour being Fez. He introduced me to a lot of architecture (animal and mineral) as well as the Prado and the Pitti Palace, and what interest I developed in those fields of art, in later life, before I married was in large part due to him.

Before the trip began, I had decided to embark on a theatrical career, since my bent seemed to lie in that direction and I needed money. Contrary to popular belief, the younger sons of Scottish peers are far from well-heeled, primogeniture, alas, being the rage in Scotland. Consequently each child of my parents – excluding Alec who cleared almost the whole jackpot – got £500 a year – no more, no less, until the end of World War Two when, at the whim of our solicitors in Edinburgh, that income was reduced by half.

While travelling in Spain, I memorized Romeo's balcony speech. On our return to London, I launched this unsuitable selection at the wilting head of Kenneth Barnes, Head of the RADA. 'Don't shout at me, Home,' he cried, after a few lines. 'We're alone in this room.' Muting my tone somewhat, I continued to the end which seemed, to both of us, to take a very long time coming.

'Oh, that I were a glove upon that hand, that I might touch that cheek.'

During the recitation, I got the feeling that romance had ebbed from my impassioned rendering as a result of Kenneth Barnes's interruption. In the silence that ensued, I looked down at him, as he winced at the impact of my heartiness. 'You've passed,' he told me, evidently relieved that the ordeal was over and, no doubt, making a mental note that it must never be repeated during the ensuing years. Nor was it, since whatever else he did for me – and he did much – he never cast me in the role of Romeo – rather the Doge of Venice, Bottom and parts of equivalent weight and responsibility. I cast myself as Romeo, however, in my own play, *Marry Bachelor*, which we did in my last year.

I learned a lot at RADA: voice production, ballet-dancing, make-up, how to stand still, how to listen, how, in Noel Coward's phrase, not to bump into the furniture. Towards the end of my time I was interviewed by Kenneth Barnes again. 'You're not a bad comedian,' he told me, 'if that's what you want to be. Or would you rather be a playwright?'

'Time alone will answer that,' I thought as I bade him farewell *en route* for Brighton, having been invited by a Mr Baxter Somerville to join the repertory company at the Theatre Royal at a salary of £3 a week. My first part was in *Anthony and Anna* and I still recall, without referring to the script, what must have been my longest speech.

'The creative artist, Mr Fair – I am a creative artist – does what you describe yourself as doing and his reward is partly pleased vanity and partly – well, pride in the sale of his work, but chiefly, it is intense satisfaction at his sense of power.'

While touring in *Anthony and Anna*, I received a letter typed in blue (a magic blue to me and many others of my generation) at a Bedford hotel asking me to go to London to the offices of H. M. Tennent in the Globe.

Behind a table in the attic office Binkie Beaumont sat with Dodie Smith, Murray MacDonald, the director, and the leading actor, Cecil Parker.

'Read this scene with Cecil, Douglas Home,' said Murray, handing me a script. I read it, putting on a blasé and conceited voice, in line with his instructions. When it ended, there was whispering behind the table and head-shaking. 'Thank you, Home,' said Murray. I made for the door. More whispering, then Murray spoke again. 'Come back and read it once more,' he said, 'but this time in your own voice.' This I did, and got the part. During rehearsals Murray said to one young actor in the cast from his seat in the front row of the stalls, 'I find it hard to hear a word that you're saying, James. You ought to go on the films.' The young actor's name was Mason.

After quite a modest run in this play I was cast, by Binkie Beaumont again, in a play with Ronnie Squire and Yvonne Arnaud. In the cast was Ronnie's daughter, Jacqueline, to whom I got engaged for a short period. This episode caused much unhappiness to both of us – but, ultimately, I decided that I was too young for marriage, too unsettled and, in short, too immature. This view, I like to think, was shared by Jacqueline.

This time James Agate was more friendly, giving both the juveniles a favourable notice in the *Sunday Times*. Apart from the emotional disturbances, resulting from our short engagement, I enjoyed the run of this play. Yvonne Arnaud was a splendid lady, fluttering her handkerchief in every scene, much to Ronnie's annoyance, since he thought that she was doing it in order to attract attention to herself. He could have been correct. She needed no such aid, however. Nor did Ronnie need to worry about his own impact on an audience, his charm and method of delivering his lines, with a dead-pan expression, being irresistible.

When Ronnie died, his widow sent me some of his cigars and, as I smoked them, I remembered evenings spent in restaurants, with sleepy waiters moving to and fro, switching the lights off one by one, until the candle on our corner-table shone unchallenged while Ronnie recounted to me stories of a long distinguished life spent in the theatre as a much loved, much gifted leading actor.

Once he offered me his car to drive his daughter into the country on a Sunday; 'It'll do you good to get some fresh air,' he advised us at the supper-table on the Saturday night. Next morning we went to the garage to collect the car, only to find that the ignition key was missing from the dashboard. 'Mr Squire's got that,' the garage man informed us. 'You'd best ring him.' So we rang him up. A sleepy voice came down the line, 'What is it, dear boy?' it asked.

'Where's the key of your car, Ronnie?'

'Ah,' said he. 'Where are the snows of yester year?'

Then he went back to sleep and we abandoned our drive in the country.

Up in Southport, on tour after London with that same play, in September 1938, we queued up for our gas-masks and read the press reports of Neville Chamberlain's brave but ill-fated efforts to avert the Second World War. Alec went to Munich with him, in his role as PPS, wearing a silk shirt lent to him by either Brian Johnston or myself. We shared digs in South Eaton Place at that time with Jo Grimond.

Later in that year, at the conclusion of the tour, I stood with Brian in a crowd on Lanark Race Course listening to Sir John Simon, with Alec at his side, telling us – we were in full agreement with him – that 'these last few months have not been easy months'.

'One day, William,' Murray had informed me, while rehearsing Dodie Smith's play, 'you can step straight into Ronnie Squire's shoes.' Managements thought otherwise, however. When the Yvonne Arnaud play came off, I had no further offers from the West End, or indeed, from anywhere else. I rested, which, in actors' parlance, means that I was unemployed. So I sat down to write another play. This left me busy until war broke out. It came on, early summer 1940, at the Q again, but got no further. In July, my call-up papers fell on to the mat, one morning, through the letter-box. I answered, pointing out that since, in my opinion, no tribunal would exempt me on political grounds, rather than religious, I was prepared to be conscripted, on the understanding, however, that, if my most strongly-held political opinions should be challenged by the Government of Winston Churchill to a point beyond endurance, I was not to be relied on. No reply to this letter came from the Labour Exchange. So I left South Eaton Place for Maidenhead and Kingsbridge, Devon, Worthing, Eastwell Park, near Ashford, Kent, Farnborough and Normandy, then Northern France and Ghent and finally, for Wormwood Scrubs and Wakefield Gaols.

# Chapter 4
# The Prison House

The strong political convictions that I held at that time have been dealt with since in many articles by many journalists, as well as by myself in my first book, *Half Term Report*. However, since the world is full of an increasing number of new readers, I feel bound to detail them again, though more briefly and with more detachment than I managed at the first attempt.

The war started with myself a near objector, conscientious certainly, religious much less certainly – rather political. Naïve I may have been but I was honest – simple-minded, possibly, but sincere. I felt that to go to war with Germany without a war-aim, other than clear-cut victory, was unimaginative. Had I had a seat in Parliament in 1940 and a platform from which I could have called for negotiation between those in Germany (and there were many in the German Army) who disliked their Government, I might have made some impact. As it was I was like a motorist who hears, as he exceeds the speed limit, the voice of that eccentric toy once purchasable in America: 'This is St Christopher calling – you're on your own now.' Out of step with almost everybody but myself I went to Maidenhead and joined The Buffs.

There, in a field across the Thames from Cliveden, I resumed the weapon-training I had undergone at Eton until Colonel Hills relieved me of my duties. This time there was no understanding fellow ready to repeat the process. Nor had Colonel Reid or Captain Anderson, his Adjutant, been notified about the contents of the letter I had written to the Labour Exchange. In their eyes, I was a conscript, just like any other, to be trained and disciplined and, maybe sometime in the future, sent off to learn to be an officer at an OCTU. So I learned again about the body-locking pin on the Bren Gun and heard again the sergeant retailing crude jokes about it and laughed dutifully, with the rest. I slept with other conscripts in a bell-tent, feet to the tent-pole and endured their jests about my social status, the details of which had been confided to them either by the Adjutant's clerk, who was privy to such secrets, or by the Post Corporal.

'How's the Honourable f—g Bill?' my colleagues would enquire of me on our return from swilling beer in Maidenhead pubs, 'How's his f—g lordship?' 'F—g well,' I used to tell them as I pulled my blankets round me and went off to sleep.

In due course, Colonel Reid sent for me. 'You're going to an OCTU, Home,' he told me. 'How do you react to that?' I told him that, as officer material, I might not be what he was looking for, in view of my political convictions which were, in a nutshell, a demand for peace-aims.

'Oh, to hell with politics!' he said. 'You're in the Army now, you bloody fool.' The Adjutant, who stood behind his chair, smiled.

'You're going to an OCTU,' Colonel Reid repeated, 'and if you pass out, God help the regiment you go to!' Then he smiled, too, little knowing that the regiment that I would go to, when in fact I did pass out, would be none other than his own!

At Sandhurst, after a short while, my company commander, who was a Scots Guardsman, told me that I was not wanted on the voyage by the Grenadiers, for which sophisticated regiment some optimistic but misguided friends had put down my name. 'We'll have you though, with pleasure,' he informed me. But his Regimental Adjutant, encouraged by another Scots Guards officer instructor, that same Hope who had shared digs with me in Merton Street, rejected my advances.

I was satisfied with this decision since, holding the views I did, I felt that I would not be even reasonably happy in the Army anywhere but in the unit to which I had first been posted by the Labour Exchange. Soon a letter winged its way to Kingsbridge, Devon, to my Colonel, in which I repeated my objections to an all-out war and asked for reinstatement in his unit. Back his answer came, still fulminating against politicians and, above all, would-be politicians, telling me to concentrate on being a Lieutenant rather than an unelected MP, and saying he would have me back with pleasure, not unmixed with resignation.

Back to Kingsbridge then, I went, with one pip on my shoulder, to face badinage from all my former colleagues who were still in the ranks. I have often heard it argued that I should not have allowed myself to be promoted. My reply to this has always been that, once I was conscripted, I was bound to do my best, at any rate until some situation such as I had outlined in my letter to the Labour Exchange came to pass.

'Trust you to find one, old bean,' Jakie Astor commented with his mother's bald outspokenness.

I soldiered on in Kingsbridge as a subaltern in charge of signalling and entertainment. So far, so good, till Sir Winston, then plain Mr Churchill, worked out with F. D. Roosevelt the policy of Unconditional Surrender. This stuck in my gullet. How, I argued, can those Germans who oppose the Führer attempt to overthrow him in the face of Unconditional Surrender? At about this time came Rudolph Hess's flight to Scotland, witnessed by my mother, incidentally, while she was brushing her hair before dinner.

'Charlie,' she said, when she came downstairs, 'I saw a funny-looking aeroplane low over the lake, flying towards Kelso '

'Oh, not towards Edith Trotter, this time?' said my father. His comment referred to a pre-war occasion when she had remarked to him at tea one afternoon that she had seen some wild geese flying over. 'Which way were they going, Lil?' my father had asked. 'They were flying towards Edith Trotter,' she had said – a friend of hers who lived a few miles north. The plane she saw that war-time night was flying in the general direction of the Duke of Hamilton with whom Hess, having parachuted out near Moffat, met up the next day. (Some say he walked towards a shepherd's house and knocked on the door, at which the shepherd's wife came out and said, 'Come away in and have a cup of tea, then, Mr Hess.')

There came a bye-election at Cathcart in Glasgow. I applied to stand. My Colonel snorted, but the Adjutant said, 'You can't stop him, sir – according to King's Regulations.'

Off I went and came second, after three days' campaigning, to a Tory. On the way to the bye-election, I stopped off at Hirsel with my parents, where I found my father's attitude lukewarm, to put it mildly. I was rocking the boat, in his estimation, though he never said so. Some years later, he confided to me that, during a dinner held in Glasgow shortly after my campaign, the Glasgow Chief of

Police had leaned across the table and called out, 'Was that your son, Lord Home, who stood in Cathcart?' 'Yes,' my father said, embarrassed and ashamed. 'My men were solidly behind him,' said the policeman, resuming his meal.

A few months later, Windsor lost its MP through death. I applied to the Conservatives to stand on their behalf, provided that they 'would respect my independent views'. No answer came. Instead, they chose Charlie Mott-Radclyffe, an old schoolfriend from my house at Eton, also in the Army. I stood as an Independent. There were just the two of us. He beat me by two thousand votes, but, judging from my seven thousand plus supporters, there were quite a lot of citizens who thought as I did.

When another bye-election loomed up at St Albans, I applied to stand again. Permission failed to come through this time, but I persevered, to no avail. I sensed antagonism both from my new Colonel and the Army Council. Then there came a day when the whole question of my standing in the bye-election nearly became academic. On a scheme, on the Downs behind Brighton, with live ammunition, I was ordered to accompany the infantry as a liaison officer, leaving my tank behind – myself, a sergeant and a wireless set. We reached a little wood and then the barrage started. To our consternation it fell all around us. We lay down beneath a tree and called the Colonel on the wireless. 'The artillery are shelling us,' we told him. 'Stop the guns. The infantry inside the wood are being killed.' The barrage went on, causing casualties and then abruptly stopped. The doctor came up from the rear to tend the wounded and lay out the dead.

Next day, I got a message from Lord Salisbury: 'Would I go to Hatfield for a meeting with him?' Off I went and, in his study, that distinguished elder statesman pleaded with me. 'Please don't stand,' he begged me. 'It will do untold harm. Take my word for that.' I fell for his persuasive charm, assuming something was afoot of which I had no knowledge, possibly a peace initiative. I withdrew my candidature and went back to my unit. When the seat was won by Raymond Blackburn as an Independent, I regretted my decision.

Just before the Second Front, I stood again in Clay Cross and lost my deposit. Back I travelled to the Regiment, declaring to the Press before I did so that a British officer with my convictions should not

The Hirsel

Douglas (now demolished)

The author's mother

The author's father, with A. E. Matthews, who played the role of the father in *The Chiltern Hundreds* – a part inspired by Lord Home.

The author, aged six, at the start of what was to prove a chequered military career.

The author as Romeo in the RADA production of his own play, *Marry Bachelor* in 1937.

A scene from *Now Barabbas,* the author's first West End success.

be required to fight and maybe die in order to impose a policy of Unconditional Surrender. This public statement was ignored by both the War Office and by the new replacement for my old and understanding Colonel, who had been declared redundant, due to his advancing age.

So to the Second Front, where acting-Captain Home sat brooding on his long political campaign, designed to make the Government of Winston Churchill see sense. Came a day, outside Le Havre, from which beleaguered town the German General asked to be allowed to evacuate the citizens, before the battle started. His request was ignored. For three days, a section of the British Army sat outside the town, with one near-frantic, non-co-operative acting-Captain asking himself hourly why the French civilians were not debouching from the doomed town through the lines to safety.

On the eve of the assault my Colonel told me I would be liaison officer between the tanks and infantry, but, this time, in my tank.

'No,' I said.

'Do what you're told, Home.'

'No,' I said again.

'Why not?' he asked me, angrily.

'Because we haven't let out the civilians.'

'That's no concern of yours.'

'I disagree.'

'Oh well,' said he, calming a little, 'I suppose I should have known that, in these circumstances, this was bound to happen.'

'That's right, sir.'

'All right, Home. Go and look after the transport.'

'No sir, I'm afraid not. I'm not taking part at all.'

Later, he sent me to the Sergeant Major who was looking after all the transport so that he could keep an eye on me. Then the assault took place – first, bombing, in which something like 12,000 French civilians were said to have been killed, and then by tank and infantry advance with, happy to relate, no British casualties.

At first, the Colonel made no disciplinary move. This did not suit me; not, as I have been repeating ever since, because I have a tendency to exhibitionism, but because I felt that such wrong thinking on the part of the misguided allied General who had rejected the German request, should be exposed.

So I sat down and penned a letter to the Press – to be precise, the *Advertiser* down in Maidenhead, where I had gleaned most of my votes in 1942. The publication of this letter stung the Colonel into action. With an escort officer, I left my regiment, now outside Calais, to conduct my own defence in my court-martial in Ghent. On arrival, I was shown my photograph in all the British papers.

On the morrow I was told that, when the German General in Calais asked permission to evacuate the French civilians, the Allies granted his request. 'Cause and effect?' as brother Alec charitably put it, in his book *The Way the Wind Blows* – 'We shall never know.'

Sir Basil Neald, Judge Advocate, pronounced the sentence: one year with hard labour. Back to Wormwood Scrubs I came, the would-be politician and the misfit soldier, harbouring no bitterness against the world in general nor, in particular, against my prosecutors, knowing, as I did, that they had no alternative.

If there is a moral to this long (and now most thankfully disposed of) tale, it could be that conscription, by its very nature, places far too great a strain on certain individuals, and that, from every point of view – the Army's and the individual's – the warning signals should be noted much more seriously and the individual declared redundant.

After some months in the Scrubs, I got a transfer to Wakefield, having asked for Edinburgh in my petition. Still, Wakefield was on the way and made a perfect compromise for the Home Office. One happy day, my father came to see me with my mother, travelling from Berwick to York station – thence by taxi down Love Lane to Wakefield Prison.

When our meeting was concluded, so my mother told me later, she climbed back into her waiting taxi and then turned to see my father walking down outside the prison wall towards a big house further down Love Lane. 'Where are you going, Charlie?' she called. 'Here's our taxi.' 'Hold on, Lil,' called back my father, marching steadfastly on, 'I'm just off to thank the dear little Governor for having William here.'

What it cost him to call on a disgraced son in prison must have been immeasurable. All his loyalties were on the side of law and order – all his instincts and his training told him that to rock the boat (although he never used that banal phrase) was wrong, that for an officer to be court-martialled and cashiered was the supreme dishonour. Yet in spite of this, he came to Wakefield Gaol, a little Lord Lieutenant in a bowler hat, because the love he felt towards his children came before all else.

'Wilkes was wrong, of course,' he must have told God on his private line, 'but the poor little devil knew no better.' And he may, perhaps, have added, 'I pursued a similar ambition in between the wars, when I fought hard to try to make the League of Nations a success. Once the balloon went up, though, I abandoned all my dreams of peace and international co-operation and put on my uniform again and kept my mouth shut. But Wilkes didn't. Please forgive him for that, God; I do.'

So, with forgiveness in his heart and goodwill towards all men, he knocked on the Governor's door, waited till it opened, then removed his bowler hat and shook the hand of that astonished man, and thanked him for his hospitality on my behalf. That done, he strode back to the waiting taxi, doubtless humming some tune ('Fill the sails and homeward', I would guess, 'across the dancing sea'), sat down beside his Lil, and travelled back to York, content with having done the best he could for his rebellious son and the dear little Governor.

My mother, I suspect, took everything in her stride, watching me for signs of stress, noting the state of my complexion, summing up the character of any prison officer she came in contact with, checking the gaol itself for dirt or otherwise, making no moral judgements, facing up to what had happened, wasting neither energy nor time in wishing that it hadn't.

She, of course, according to the form book, was much better fitted than my father to ride out the storm, for broadly speaking, Lambton blood means rebel blood, or anyway (to put it at its lowest and its least sensational) eccentric blood. Her Uncle George had, after all, become a racehorse trainer, and it may be that, in her mind, she considered that a blood relation who was ready to adopt so bizarre a profession, differed little from an equally eccentric son, who opted for a year in prison with hard labour.

I celebrated my thirty-third birthday with my friends in Wakefield Prison. Some of them were sentenced to stay there a long time, but this knowledge in no way inhibited their warm congratulations on my coming release.

Ethel Manning, who had written to me sympathetically, was the recipient of a last-minute request that she find me a constituency in which I could fight the coming General Election. In her prompt reply, she asked me to come down to Woodford (sitting member: W. S. Churchill!) when I came out, to discuss the proposition.

As I walked towards the station down Love Lane on a June morning, I was, once again, in public circulation. Contact with my fellow passengers was nerve-racking to start with, since they were the first free men and women I had seen – apart from visitors – for eight months. By the time the train reached London, I was getting used to rubbing shoulders with them, savouring the fact that I could walk along the corridor without seeing one supervising warder, go into the 'toilet' without wondering if it was one reserved for sufferers from VD.

Loneliness, however, was still with me, when I got to London. One old aunt, who lived in Brown's Hotel, received me coldly, and I got the feeling, as I left, that my rehabilitation period might well be difficult and fearful.

Then, one day in Regent Street, I met June Capel, now called Lady Hutcheson. She greeted me with undiluted warmth; then, over a drink, talked me back to life, without a trace of hedging in her conversation, no polite ignoring of the fact that I had just 'come out'. Instead, she asked me direct questions about my experience. With laughter in her voice and friendship in her eye, she faced the situation fair and square, and helped me, through her natural and healthy attitude, to face it for myself. We parted, and I walked down Regent Street more jauntily than hitherto.

A few days later Raymond Westwell, who had been a fellow officer, behaved towards me in precisely the same way, gave me a drink and took one in return, and then walked with me down to Covent Garden to seek out my batman, who had been a porter till conscription took him down to Maidenhead in the same draft as myself.

Sure enough we found him, and we stood there talking, Raymond in his uniform still, I in the grey suit that Mr Collingwood had sent to Wakefield pending my departure, and my batman, one Tom Josslyn, a Punch-like weather-beaten figure, in his apron, rolled-up sleeves and with his rugged countenance creased into a broad smile. We passed the time of day without embarrassment, then left him, commenting upon his good health and his cheerfulness.

A moment later we heard footsteps coming up behind us, then a nervous voice enquiring of my uniformed friend, 'Sorry sir, but would you be the Military Police?'

'No, nothing like that,' Raymond answered. 'Why?'

'Oh, well,' said my batman's boss, 'I just thought old Tom might have been in trouble.'

On the morning that I was to have met Ethel Manning a young serving soldier told the Press that he intended to fight Woodford as an Independent. Thinking that perhaps he had more right to do so than a cashiered officer just out of prison, I withdrew my candidature. Maybe this was just an excuse; maybe contact with my fellow creatures was not yet sufficiently established to enable me to contemplate a campaign, even though I had decided not to make more speeches than my rival, Mr Churchill, dealing as he was with affairs of state, intended to make on his own behalf. Maybe the fact that the war was now over, made the argument in favour of my standing less impelling. After all, the things I had been spouting in my uniform from platforms up and down the country in the past, were being said now by all kinds of politicians, freed at last from the inhibitive and democratically destructive party truce.

Sometimes, I still wake up at night, from a dream in which I beat Mr Churchill hands down, then resign the next day and allow him to resume his parliamentary activities much chastened by the lesson I had taught him. What they call a pipe dream? I dare say. But, none the less, an independent farmer with no policy that I could diagnose, nor any motivation for his candidature, took ten thousand votes off the chief architect of Unconditional Surrender. Could another independent and equally daft candidate with, on the form book, a consistent record of prolonged and active opposition to that policy, have polled the extra five, or six or seven thousand necessary votes, to enable him to bring down his old bête-noire?

Who knows? Stranger things have happened in this world. The betting against David knocking out Goliath, for example, must have been at very long odds if, indeed, a book was made at all on that encounter.

Be that as it may, instead of going down to Woodford, I went north to Berwick Station, where my father's chauffeur met me. He had met me there, throughout the war when I had gone on leave, save when petrol was low and I had had to travel on by train to Cornhill Station. This encounter differed in no way from any other.

'Morning, Mr William,' he said. 'Well on time, this morning.'

Home to Hirsel, to my parents, last seen from across a ping-pong table in the presence of a warder, down in Wakefield Prison.

Greetings from my father in the hall ('Hullo, Wilkes') flanked by Mr Collingwood, his faithful butler.

Upstairs to my mother's bedroom, through the window of which she had spotted the low-flying Messerschmidt of Rudolph Hess three years before.

Not much said, but a searching look over her spectacles, to see how her delinquent son was looking. Then, downstairs to breakfast with my father and my sister, Bridget, who had kept me up to date on family events all through my sentence. She had also written, with true sisterly devotion, to all those whose letters I was not allowed to answer due to the restriction on out-going letters (and incoming) – one per three weeks was the normal ration.

Breakfast conversation was conducted, largely, by my father. Roedeer, seen across the river last week from the drawing-room window; golden-crested wren still nesting in the fir tree in the middle of the rhododendron wood; Tweed low, few salmon coming up from Berwick; no use fishing on the Leet unless one was prepared to use a dry fly; Alec quite recovered from his operation now, conducting his election campaign in South Lanark; Billy, husband of my second sister Rachel, doing the same in Roxburgh and Selkirk; Henry with the Army still in Edinburgh, but coming home for the weekend; and Edward ('Ted') still missing.

Breakfast over, round the woods on foot, along the Leet, the brown trout darting under overlaying roots, the rehabilitation process swinging into action, slowly but inevitably, by-passing the foresters perhaps, to start with, since the nerves were still exposed and raw, but getting that much bolder and more sociable as each day passed. Although the prospect of impending visits from my relatives imposed a strain on my new-found morale.

When they finally arrived and made a joke about the shortness of my hair, or called attention to my ghastly pallor (due to nothing worse than eight months loss of whisky) we were quickly back on the old relationship. Yet always in my mind there lurked the thought that I was something different, a marked man who had been found out, punished and then, in the course of time, released. It took some years and quite a lot of thought before I finally decided that to be in such a situation might be put down as a kind of bonus mark in that it gave me, in some strange way, the same satisfaction as one feels on filing a receipted bill: the cost had been faced up to, and the payment made.

My Uncle Claud, of course, went further than the rest of my relations, wanting to know everything: why I had not been shot, why I had been sent to a civil prison rather than the Glass House, had I met a lot of murderers, what was the food like, could one drink or smoke, would I be asking any new found friends to stay at Hirsel or would they be coming uninvited, through the sky-light at night, what did I propose to do now, would I not regard myself as finished?

Tactless? My Aunt Olive, Claud's wife thought so anyway, and tried to stop her husband going too far.

'How's the gaol bird looking, Collingwood, do you think?' Uncle Claud asked as he left.

'Well, Captain Claud,' said Mr Collingwood.

'Come on, Claud,' said Aunt Olive, through the open window of the car.

'All right, old girl,' said Uncle Claud. 'Perhaps a stretch would do us all good, Collingwood, eh?'

'Could do, Captain Claud,' said Mr Collingwood, as my persistent but beloved uncle drove away.

He knew what he was doing. He was not a man for sweeping things beneath the carpet. He preferred to know the truth, and he liked everyone to share it with him.

When he left to go back to his farmhouse in the Cheviot Hills, I felt better, less on the defensive, more adventurous, and readier to breathe in the fresh air of my individuality.

One fine morning, I picked up a notebook and a pencil or two off my mother's writing-table, bicycled to Kinsham Dene, and sat beneath a small Scots fir tree in the middle of the young wood.

Stripping off most of my clothes to take advantage of the current heat-wave, I picked up the notebook, opened it, and started writing on the front page. This was what I wrote:

'The landing' as a heading, then 'scene outside backcloth'. Prison Clock striking seven. Officer King is standing beside the desk, looking up to the balcony.

KING: (he is cheerful, tubby) All mess men there?

VOICES: (off) Ten Mess missing, sir.

KING: (shouting upwards) Mess men, Ten Mess, Mess men, Ten Mess, get a move on.

SMITH: (upstairs) Comin', sir. Just comin', sir.

KING: No hurry, lads. No hurry. We like waiting! Will I bring your breakfast up?

SMITH: (appearing over balcony) Wot? 'Am and eggs – OK!

And so on. Every morning, every afternoon, for ten days, underneath that little fir tree and his close companions, I propelled my mother's pencil until *Now Barabbas* was completed. Then, Elizabeth, my sister-in-law, lent me her typewriter. In a fortnight I had a legible and fairly tidy script.

My sister Bridget read it first, and said it was well written. Mother read it next, and said how much she wished that I would not be vulgar. Father tried to read it, gallantly, but failed, remarking that he found plays quite impossible to read and that included all the works of my exalted namesake: William Shakespeare. *Now Barabbas* had two years to wait before production, at the Boltons Theatre in Kensington.

# Chapter 5
# A Proper Playwright

Meanwhile the General Election result came through. Billy Scott, my brother-in-law, won in Roxburgh. Alec lost South Lanark.

This news came to Hirsel in dramatic form. Lunch over one July day, Mr Collingwood came in to find my mother and my sister, Bridget, knitting, Father doing *The Times* crossword puzzle, William having a siesta on the sofa.

'Yes, what is it, Collingwood?' my father asked.

'He's lost, my lord,' said Collingwood, in gloom.

'Who's lost what, Collingwood?' my father enquired irritably, interrupted in his struggle with the puzzle.

'Lord Dunglass, my lord – he's lost South Lanark,' sobbed my father's stricken butler.

'Oh, is that all,' said my father, tackling his anagram again.

Poor Collingwood departed, Bridget and my mother went on knitting. I reclosed my eyes.

But, just before I went to sleep again, I had an idea. 'What about a play,' I thought, 'about a butler who is so devoted to the Tory party that he feels the loss of his employer's son's seat far more strongly than the family do?'

My mind then engaged another gear. 'And what about,' I added as a mental postscript, 'that same butler – if the son went Labour, for example, putting up against him?'

The siesta over, I picked up another notebook and a further handful of my mother's pencils, bicycled along the Leet, sat myself down beside the water and began to write *The Chiltern Hundreds*.

Some hours later, I was startled by a rush of wind past my ear, cocked an eye and saw, a foot from my face, on an overhanging branch, a kingfisher about to start his fishing operations.

For a second or two he remained there, then became suspicious,

H.P.H.–E

darting off upstream to fish elsewhere in some pool unencumbered by the presence of a pregnant playwright.

On I wrote and, in three weeks, the play was finished. In another week the typing, on Elizabeth's typewriter, was concluded.

This time, I believe, my father read the play, with some amusement.

Next, my mother. 'Must you be so vulgar, William?' asked she.

'Vulgar?'

'All those lords and butlers,' she said.

'But I've got to have a lord, Mamma, because he's Lord Lieutenant, therefore independent and resigned to being treated like a lunatic without a vote. I've also got to have a butler, otherwise I couldn't have the plot.'

'No; I suppose not, but it's so embarrassing for us.'

'It won't be, Mamma,' I said. 'Don't you worry!'

Sister Bridget gave me her considered support.

'It's quite funny,' she said.

'It could be that you've got something there,' I answered.

By now it was August and I took the boat to Jura. Michael Astor had invited me the moment I came out of prison, with his usual carefree, calculated kindness. This provided further rehabilitation, an extension of the treatment I had undergone in London, a release, but far more beneficial due to the fact that my stay at Hirsel had recharged my batteries effectively. Michael had been a Phantom captain in the European theatre of operations, his task being to gain information at Corps level, then relay it on the wireless in his scout car, or by any other means, to Richmond Park (site of the Phantom Regiment's headquarters) from where, if the contents of the message were deemed of sufficient interest, it was passed on to the War Office.

The fact that this bizarre regiment was in existence (boasting an impressive list of equally eccentric officers like, for example, David Niven) may mean that the most unlikely story of the D-Day pigeon is correct. This bird, or so the story goes, winged back from Normandy on D-Day morning and dropped at the feet of a distinguished group of officers, among whom could be recognized King George the Sixth, Montgomery and Eisenhower.

Forward stepped the signal officer, unrolled the message on the pigeon's leg, read it and blushed.

'Come on, man. Read it out!' rasped Monty. 'What does it say?'

Wishing himself anywhere but in the presence of his sovereign, the Supreme Commander of the Allied Forces and his Deputy, he carried out the order.

'I have been sent home,' the signal officer read out, 'for being naughty in my cage.'

The summer over, I came down to London with the two plays, *Now Barabbas* and *The Chiltern Hundreds*, in my suitcase. Where was I to live? A visit to the dentist solved this problem, since the dentist was none other than a fellow prisoner from Wormwood Scrubs, one Dr Sainsbury.

When I had been flown back from Brussels after my court-martial, I had spent one night in Scotland Yard, *en route* for Wormwood Scrubs, because of an administrative failure which resulted in no booking being made on my behalf. Next morning, I was taken out for exercise along Whitehall by a Guards Officer of my acquaintance called Jack Thursby, who had been seconded to the Military Police.

'We've got you a cell in the Scrubs,' he told me.

'Thanks.'

'You're going in tonight, and when you get there, please do something for me,' he went on. I squinted at him. What connection, I thought, could my blue-capped escort have with anyone in Wormwood Scrubs. 'My dentist's in there,' he continued. 'Had a fatal accident in his car in the blackout. His name's Dr Sainsbury – give him my love!'

'Of course,' I said.

Arrived in Wormwood Scrubs, I spent a few days trying to fulfil my promise. On the exercise ground I would whisper, 'Are you Dr Sainsbury?' to my companions.

'Who the f—k's he?' they would answer.

'He's a dentist,' I would tell them.

'So you think that I'm a f—g dentist, do you?' they would mutter, rolling up their sleeves.

'Of course not,' I would answer. 'My mistake. I'm sorry.'

'So you f—g should be!' they would say, relaxing as we passed the officer on duty.

Some days later, in the workshop, I observed a grey-haired man of

some distinction, driving an adjacent sewing machine. 'Are you
Dr Sainsbury?' I whispered, when the warder had his back turned.

'That's right,' answered my companion.

'Well, Jack Thursby sends his love.'

'Dear old Jack,' he said. 'Hasn't paid his bill for seven years!'

I took two rooms in Dr Sainsbury's house in Queen Anne Street,
a small bedroom in the attic and a larger sitting-room a little lower
down, with one chair and a desk and an electric fire of some antiquity.
From this firm base, I sallied forth to try to sell my plays. I also
started taking up again with my pre-war acquaintances and friends.

One day I lunched with Lady Astor. 'You're the greatest fighter
I know,' she informed me, with her usual candour. 'Fightin' not to
join the Army, fightin' to get out of it by fightin' to get into
Parliament, then fightin' to get into prison. What're you fightin'
at now?'

'Play-writing,' I told her. She laughed. 'Don't laugh at him, please,
Aunt Nancy,' said her relative, Elizabeth Winn. 'Why not?' said Aunt
Nancy. 'If I didn't laugh at him, I'd cry!'

I looked at her and marked a touch of moisture in those sapphire
blue eyes. 'What're you doin' after lunch?' she asked me.

'Nothin' – I mean nothing,' I said.

'Don't be cheeky,' answered Lady Astor. Then she smiled, and went
on: 'Come and meet a proper playwright! You come too, Elizabeth,'
she ordered.

Up the Great North Road she drove me, turned left just past
Brocket Hall, home of Lord Melbourne and his wild wife, Caroline,
into Ayot St Lawrence, and pulled up outside an unassuming villa.
Out she got, and rang the bell. A maid appeared. 'Is Mr Shaw in?'
Lady Astor asked her.

'Yes, my lady, but he's working,' the maid told her.

'Never mind that,' Lady Astor said. 'Come on, you two!'

We followed her in and walked through the house into the
garden, heading for a curious erection at the far end of it.

'That's where he works,' Lady Astor told us, pointing at a tall,
thin hut, more like a telephone kiosk than anything else.

As we drew near, I saw a pile of wood, an axe and a few neatly
cut logs. My pulse quickened at the sight, because I knew that my
great hero liked to do a bit of axeing when his Muse decided to take

time off. Sure enough, here lay the evidence before my eyes. Excitement mounted. 'In that elongated hut,' I told myself, 'sits Bernard Shaw, the greatest playwright of the age, and I am just about to meet him in the flesh – not only that, but see him working.'

Lady Astor turned the handle of the shed door, pulled it open, and I saw within a figure seated at a table working on a manuscript.

'Come out of there, you old fool,' Lady Astor said. 'You've written enough nonsense in your life!' The figure raised its head and, with its head, a long white beard – or was it faintly yellow?

'Go away,' it said. 'I'm working. Go away, and I'll give you some tea when I've finished.'

Lady Astor snorted, shut the door and walked us round the garden, while we waited for the Muse to knock off for the day.

She gave us some advice. 'Don't talk at tea, you two,' she said. 'He's very old, and doesn't want to listen. So let him talk.'

In to tea we went, when he came up the garden from his work, and no one talked but Lady Astor, anyway, until a certain memorable interlude.

'You're a lonely old man,' I recall her saying, 'since poor Charlotte died. You ought to come and live in London. I'll look after you!'

'I don't like London, Nancy,' he replied.

'Then I'll come and live down here,' she told him.

'Nothing,' he said, 'would move me to London quicker than that.'

And so the battle raged between these two old friends and sparring partners until tea was over. Then she rose to go.

'William writes plays,' she told him. 'No one wants to put them on, though, and quite rightly!'

Out we walked to the car and got in. The plus-foured figure opened the gate. Then, he came back to the car. As he leaned forward, I put down the window. 'Go on writing, my boy,' his voice advised me. 'One of these fine days, one of these London managers will go into his office one Monday morning and say to his secretary, "Is there a play from Shaw this morning?" And when she says, "No sir," he'll say, "Well, we'll have to start on the rubbish." And there's your chance, my boy,' said Mr Shaw.

With that, he stood aside and, as we shot out through the gate, I looked up at a pair of twinkling Irish eyes set like two tired old jewels amid a kind of bushy sheepskin hearthrug.

'Poor old man,' said Lady Astor. 'He won't last long. And he ought to give up writin' – he's too old! He only writes a lot of nonsense now. But still, he always did that. So perhaps it doesn't matter!'

'Good luck with the rubbish, William,' said Elizabeth, from the back seat.

My luck turned shortly after that as a result of meeting an old friend called Richard Longman who had been at Sandhurst in my squad and later, taken prisoner in Italy. He finished up in Germany where, having been a pre-war actor, he performed in many prison camp productions.

We had lunch together, and I told him about *Now Barabbas*.

'Let me read it,' he said.

'Naturally,' I said, 'that's what I've brought it for!' He took it to John Wise down at the Boltons Theatre, and Colin Chandler, his co-manager. At that time, they were in the process of preparing this new theatre for action. None the less, they found the time to read it, and agreed to do it as their second offering.

I went to see them one day. There was a small pond in mid-stage. Colin Chandler, on a step-ladder, was plastering the theatre wall.

'Hullo, cock,' he said. 'I like your play. And I'm going to direct it.'

Early next year, the theatre was opened. Came the first night, Richard Longman in the lead as the condemned man. The other actors excellent, without exception; the production inspired.

Critical reaction was astonishing. We transferred to the Vaudeville, and ran there from March to July.

'Would this be the new Galsworthy?' one drama critic asked himself.

The answer was not long in coming. *Now Barabbas* made way for *The Chiltern Hundreds*, starring A. E. Matthews. Although many of the critics found it funny, no one mentioned Galsworthy again. There was some disappointment, indeed, that so promising a young tragedian should have so soon retreated into trivial irrelevance, facetiousness and near-farce. The public took no heed of this, turning up in droves to watch the ageing A. E. Matthews out-Hawtreying Hawtrey. Even though my father was an unrepentant fan of Hawtrey's, he was ready to concede that Matthews played in the same league. Nor did he take exception to the thinly disguised portrait of himself.

'Dear old man,' he mused, after watching rabbits being shot from drawing-room windows, butlers standing as Conservatives and Lord Lieutenants entertaining Labour Ministers for the week-end. 'He knew what's important in life, and what isn't.'

This I took as a great compliment, because implicit in his criticism (and I use that word deliberately to illustrate the frequently forgotten fact that criticism need not necessarily be adverse) was an understanding of the fact that my portrayal of his character had not been false. Nor did my mother find *The Chiltern Hundreds* as vulgar as she had feared, though she still deplored the emphasis on peers and butlers which, as I explained again, was necessary to the plot.

The play ran for a long time, both in London and New York, and also in the country in the reps and with the amateurs. It is still running, as I write.

So, 1947 ended with the two plays I had written in the haven of my parents' home both successful. I believe my parents found the fact that I had hit on a profession and already found success in it, just three years after they had sat and looked at me across a ping-pong table in a Yorkshire prison, highly satisfying.

I was happy, too, and, on the strength of it, went out and bought a Bentley second-hand, and took a flat in Down Street, after Dr Sainsbury's electric fire had burnt itself out one day.

Then, in the first fine careless rapture induced by the royalties now flowing into my bank from the Vaudeville, I drove the Bentley up to Scotland and parked it outside the Hirsel.

From the window of her sitting-room, my mother saw it head on. 'Take that vulgar little car away, and put it in the stables!' she instructed me

'Vulgar, Mamma?' I said, 'It's a Rolls Bentley. Come out for a drive in it.'

She did so, and I drove her round the lawn, then put her in the driving seat and made her steer, to the astonishment of Mr Collingwood at work in his adjacent garden.

'Bless my soul,' he told me later. 'I thought I was seeing things. But no, I wasn't. Mrs Collingwood saw it, too. "That's her ladyship, George," she said. "Did you ever?" "No, I didn't," I said, flabbergasted.'

Nor did they again, although my mother let me drive her and her Charlie round the rides in the woods, holding tight and saying, 'Do be careful, William – no one's ever driven down this ride before!'

'It's all right, Lil,' my father would say. 'I've been down here hundreds of times on my horse.'

'Horses aren't cars,' my mother would reply, 'and it's high time you realized that.'

But, of course, he never did. He always looked on cars and horses as two forms of transport not at all dissimilar, except that one went, on occasion, somewhat faster than the other.

Indeed, when my brothers and myself, in youth, had asked, on his return from Edinburgh at lunchtime, for the loan of his car to go to some distant pigeon wood, he hardly ever granted the request.

'But why not, Dadda?' we would ask, in chorus. 'You aren't using it.'

'It's had a longish morning, going into Edinburgh and back,' was his reply. 'It's time it had a bit of a rest in the stables.'

As we trudged towards our distant pigeon wood, weighed down with cartridge bags, we visualized his chauffeur rubbing down his charge and then filling the rack with hay.

These pigeon shoots were fun. My brother Henry ran them, Alec being in the House of Commons or in his constituency far too frequently to be allowed the overall command, and our beloved father being basically averse to vermin killing. Anyway, he had a close affinity with pigeons, as he had with woodcock, and thought shooting them as they came in to roost, a shade below the belt. Instead, he strolled around the garden, with his Lil six or seven paces in his rear, commenting on the snowdrops pushing their way through the moss, or on the rising price of cartridges, hundreds of which he heard exploding in the distance, as the sun began to go down in the west.

'Why let them do it, Charlie, then?' my mother would enquire. 'Or, if you must, let them pay for their cartridges – '

'It's all right,' he would shout along the wind. 'It makes the farmers happy, and Strathern and Blair don't mind.'

Strathern and Blair were his solicitors in Edinburgh – watchdogs who never let him have a cheque book (as my brother Henry disclosed in his book *The Birdman*) but, it seems, took cartridge bills on their respective chins.

Some ten or twelve woods would be filled, according to their size, with one or more guns. Faces would be blacked, on Henry's orders, with burnt cork, or, during snow, sheets would be taken from my mother's linen cupboard to her great displeasure.

Massive bags were shot – fifty and sixty to one gun – sometimes a hundred, and the farmers gave thanks in due season, and Strathern or Blair, or both, sent off a cheque to Mr Forrest in the Square in Kelso.

On still afternoons, or with the wrong wind and/or too few pigeons in the area, the bag was sometimes only two or three apiece. But no one worried. Sitting on a tree stump, smoking one's pipe, well wrapped up, alone with nature, with a greater spotted woodpecker prospecting somewhere nearby for his next year's nesting site, or possibly a roedeer tripping daintily between the larches, is a pleasure in itself. So who minds if no pigeons turn up and, instead, a flock of long-tailed tits goes flitting through the bracken and the leafless saplings, like a troupe of ballet dancers, or an owl comes swooping down the ride and drops at one's feet on an unsuspecting vole?

The nearest that I ever got to nature was while working on a play beneath a beech tree. Suddenly, a dead leaf moved beside me, inches from my hip – a handful of earth surfaced, followed by another, then the head and shoulders of a mole appeared. He looked at me for a split second, then withdrew the way that he had come.

By now, my rehabilitation was complete among the family. Even Aunt Maimie – down in London, and too old, alas, to come north often now – had mellowed and no longer gave me the cold shoulder when I went to tea with her, nor could I find it in my heart to blame her for the cold reception she had given me the year before. She was the eldest of my father's sisters, married to Lord Guilford, who had suffered in the Camperdowne disaster in the year of my birth.

Blown out of the funnel, when two battleships collided on manoeuvre, Uncle Richard was court-martialled to elicit information, since he had been the Flag Officer on board. Although acquitted, it is my belief that he was never quite the same again. I think it likely that he took to drink. At any rate, my father always used to brush aside the questions that I put to him each time Aunt

Maimie came to stay.

'Where's Uncle Richard?' I would pipe up, in the drawing-room, little knowing that Aunt Maimie was behind the palm tree, knitting. 'Why is it he never comes here?'

'Let's go out and see if we can spot a rabbit in the garden,' said my father always, reaching for the rifle standing in the window-seat and, no doubt, tempted to direct it at his fifth and most inquisitive child.

Thus, although we often found a rabbit in the garden, I have not, to this day, found out the truth about Uncle Richard.

All I know is that he lived at Petrel Bank in Cumberland until, on his demise, Aunt Maimie moved to Draycott Place in London, thence to Brown's Hotel to sit out the war, shortly after which she went to join her unseen (by me) and intriguing husband in another world, leaving behind her Theodosia who got married at the age of sixty-three.

A sporting girl is Theodosia, now into her seventies, surrounded by a legion of adopted children and small dogs, besides her husband. As the eldest of my cousins, I looked up to her in youth because I was intrigued by her devotion to her mother, Russian refugees and small dogs, in that order. She was an eccentric, and I could and would have slipped her into any play, had not her mother had priority (as Lady Caroline, for instance, in *The Chiltern Hundreds*).

Alec gave her away at her wedding, but it was a close run thing. Elizabeth, while dressing, found him hanging round the house in Carlton Terrace when he should have been collecting Theodosia from her own flat.

'You'll be late for Theodosia,' said Elizabeth, 'if you don't get a move on.'

'Oh, I thought she'd meet me at the church,' said Alec. His efficient wife made certain that he thought again, and quickly.

Both my parents called Aunt Mary, Mary, and we children called her, to her face, Aunt Maimie. She was known throughout the family as Hairy Mary, not because she sported a moustache, but because a well-known salmon fly goes by that name and we, for what reason I cannot recall, thought that it suited her. She was a friendly lady, though somewhat equine in appearance and talkative beyond the call of duty. Maybe that was due to Uncle Richard not responding conversationally to her advances.

None the less, although my father used to mutter frequently, 'I'm glad I'm not a donkey. If I was, Mary would talk my hind leg off!' we loved her dearly, and looked forward to her visits, and we liked to go to tea with her in later years, in Draycott Place.

To her credit, too, she joined in the joke (if, indeed it was one) when my brother Alec got engaged and, learning that Elizabeth and he had both been bidden to tea with Aunt Maimie, I dressed as a woman and went early.

'Alec's been delayed, Aunt Maimie, in the House of Commons, so he told me to come on and introduce myself,' I informed Hairy Mary, in a high falsetto.

'How sweet of you,' cooed Aunt Maimie, 'and how brave of you to beard the family without Alec's support.'

We started tea, and thankfully I didn't have to speak again. Aunt Maimie launched into the history of the family, with all guns firing, told me how delighted Lilian was, according to a letter just received, and how thrilled Charlie was as well to see his eldest son so happy.

Where would be the wedding? And when? Who would be the best man? (I would, but I didn't say so.) Minutes went by, with my cousin Theodosia looking at me with affection tinged – or was it my imagination? – with suspicion.

Then the bell rang, and Elizabeth and Alec came in.

Dear old Hairy Mary – any other woman would have thrown the tea pot at me – but not her. She drew another chair up and plied me with scones and jelly and more cups of tea, and started again, without embarrassment, on her already once-delivered monologue.

A year or two before she died, my father got a letter from her. 'Lil,' he said, when he had read it, 'Mary's gone over to Rome.'

'You get on with your breakfast,' said my mother.

When my niece Fiona, Henry's daughter, asked me if I thought the family reaction would be adverse after she became a Roman Catholic, I told her this tale. I think it reassured her.

Hairy Mary had a younger sister, called Aunt Margaret ('Mouldy Margaret' to us), much more equine than Aunt Maimie but a lot less talkative. Her husband, Uncle Reggie, had once been a diplomat – or was it Consular official? He, unlike his wife, was grey-moustached and handsome, looking very like the White Knight. He was also a resourceful person.

Once, a large brown trout rose constantly in the Leet underneath an overhanging oak tree. Casting proved impossible from either bank, so Uncle Reggie laid his rod down in the field, then walked across the bridge, pulling out line, climbed out along a branch of the offending oak tree, fixed the fly to a leaf, and went into lunch. In the early afternoon, he went back to the river, recrossed the bridge and picked up his rod. Reeling it in carefully until the line was taut between the oak tree and himself, he jerked his Greenwell off the leaf and caught his fish.

One failing he had, was that he disliked the Duke of Windsor. Once I sat behind his chair while he was reading a newspaper, and delivered the Duke's farewell message to his subjects, learned by heart and brought, through constant repetition, to perfection.

'Charlie, turn that wireless off,' said Uncle Reggie irritably. 'I can't stand that fellow!'

Father was more tolerant, of course. He understood the Duke of Windsor's problems and, because he had been brought low, tried to find excuses for him.

'Chucked into the world too soon, poor little devil,' he would say. 'Knocked sideways by the First War – driven crazy by those tours in South America – upset by unemployment. Nobody to keep him straight, because the little king was far too busy. Can't blame the poor little devil, can you, Lil?'

My mother was a Whig, and therefore less inclined to find excuses for her erstwhile sovereign. Indeed, her whole attitude to monarchy was down to earth, though loyal. I recall that, when Prince Philip got engaged, my father, having heard the news, got up from his chair and walked over to a walnut cabinet, in which were displayed snuff boxes and other *objets d'art*.

'What are you doing, fiddling about there?' asked my mother.

'Looking out a present for the little girl,' my father said. 'We ought to give her something, as I'm Lord Lieutenant.'

Up my mother got to join him.

'What about this?' said she, taking out a scent bottle of some antiquity.

'It's cracked on the lid,' said my father.

'Never mind that,' said my mother. 'She can stick some plaster on it.'

Father's other sisters were Aunt Beatrice and Aunt Isobel. They had no nicknames, maybe because Beatrice was a strong, abrasive character, and might have given back as good as she got, while Aunt Isobel died young.

The latter was my godmother. I saw her in the summer house at Springhill, where she went to live out her last years. I knew that she was dying, having heard my father in his loud voice saying so to someone, although, mercifully, not to her. She sat on a white garden seat, on which was painted:

> The kiss of the sun for pardon,
> The song of the birds for mirth
> One is nearer God's heart in a garden
> Than anywhere else on earth.

That summer house is still there, and the seat with its inscription still intact and, in a bush a yard or two away, a long-tailed tit is wont to build its nest each spring. Sometimes, as I sit, hoping for a photograph, I think of my Aunt Isobel and of the youth who stood there years ago, tongue-tied and looking solemn, before holding out his hand to say goodbye to her, as casually as possible.

No doubt, my father touched his cap and hummed a great deal in the car that day on the way back to Hirsel, notifying God, that Isobel, his youngest sister, would be coming to stay with Him shortly, and suggesting that He keep an eye on her at least to start with, while his chauffeur and my mother, though embarrassed by the almost Muslim style in which my father broadcast his prayers, on this occasion held her peace.

Apart from my beloved Uncle Claud, my mother's closest relatives were Uncle Johnny and Aunts Violet and Joan.

Uncle Johnny was an interesting man, brimful of charm, eccentric, badly wounded in the 1914 war and thereafter interested in everything, active in nothing, except in the racing world, winning the Oaks with Light Brocade. In looks, Gerald du Maurier had much in common with him – rubber cheeks and rubber noses fitted to their faces with a pleasant and attractive disregard for symmetry. He married secondly my Step-Aunt Hermione, a cheerful comfortable lady with a stretch of racing luck which I have always envied. In one year, she had eight successive winners.

Uncle Johnny was a member of the Jockey Club. In his last years, he had a horse running at Goodwood called Snow Leopard. 'Is Snow Leopard going to win?' I asked him. 'Good God, is it running?' said he. 'What a prime example,' I thought as I hurried off to make what proved to be a winning bet, 'of the detached impartiality of the world's most efficient oligarchy.'

Violet, eldest of the family, was tall and willowy and always ready to absorb a juicy piece of scandal or, indeed, impart some with a relish that remained with her until her death at ninety-six. She married Uncle Brackley, a small, lively man with an outsize moustache who, like my father (possibly for the same reason), sent her up to bed at ten o'clock each night. He died when she was in her sixties and she, like my mother, spent her last long years without him opposite the television set.

The first time I came down to dinner as a youth at Douglas, I recall both Uncle Brackley and Aunt Violet, who were house guests, being late. On orders from my mother, Mr Collingwood held up his entrance to announce that dinner was served. Some time later, the door of the drawing-room opened, and Aunt Violet came in, followed by her husband who said, on the threshold: 'Violet, it could only happen to you.'

Later on that night, I asked my mother, when I went to say goodnight to her, what it was that had happened to Aunt Violet.

'Never you mind,' said she. 'Don't be so inquisitive.' I held my peace for more than forty years until, encouraged by a drop of Scotch, I put the question to her after dinner one night in her eightieth year.

'Violet broke her pot when she was sitting on it before dinner,' said my mother without hesitation, showing herself to be a rival to Queen Mary in her power of instant recall. 'Brackley had to bind her cut up with a face towel.'

Ah well, who shall say the mysteries of life do not reveal themselves if one keeps one's nose to the scent along the years.

Aunt Joan, the youngest of the sisters, was the quietest of the trio – grunting in a friendly way in answer to whatever comment one might aim at her, but with a ready sense of humour and an out-standing ability for carving little wooden animals, which much endeared her to her nephews. She it was who caught twenty-eight salmon one day on the Wark Dub (now sold), but it changed her not at all. She merely grunted her appreciation of the honour.

Uncle Hugh, her husband, was a placid man, extremely slow of speech, almost American in fact in his ability to spin out any phrase however short. Perhaps this quality in him accounted for his wife's habit of grunting, since the things he said, after much thought, were, so to speak, already documented and therefore did not require an answer.

Once, to my surprise, he shot a fox while standing in a pheasant drive beside the kennels where he kept his foxhounds.

'Uncle Hugh,' I said, at the conclusion of the drive, 'why did you do that?'

In his slow drawl, he replied, 'I'll tell you why I did it, my boy. That fox was disturbing my hounds.'

Olive, Uncle Claud's wife, was a portly, cheerful lady, with a laugh like gin cascading on to a tin roof. She loved her husband dearly, in spite of which he liked to call her 'you old fool', and pulled her leg unmercifully. She made him happy, none the less, and kept him to herself in spite of the opposition of a lot of local ladies, besotted by his good looks. When she departed this life he resisted all the sirens and remained unmarried, faithful to his 'old fool', till the day he died.

So much, then, for my uncles and aunts – all of them are dead now, buried somewhere in the Border land, both north and south of Tweed. But, in the memory of their now ageing nephew, they still live – eccentric, cheerful, full of character and charm.

## Chapter 6

# Rachel

One night, from my bachelor flat in Down Street, I went to a party given by Max Aitken in the Albert Hall. I saw a lovely fair girl, seated in the Aitken box and asked her to dance. On the floor, I noticed that she had a bandage round her upper arm. 'What's wrong?' I asked her. 'I got bitten by my horse this morning,' she replied. The music stopped, and we went back to the box. She went off to dance with someone else – a shade too frequently, I thought. Towards the end of the proceedings, I suggested that we went off to a nightclub. She refused. Later, I saw her go off with another dancing partner.

Back in Down Street, I retired to bed, making a mental note to keep in touch with her. When I awoke next morning, she was still on my mind. Other girls had been on my mind, I confess, during the past years; some of them a great deal too much on it. This time, I decided, unlike in the past, to play it cool.

We met again at intervals – at lunch in London – sometimes at a dance – at Goodwood Races for which she had asked me to her home, Mill Court, near Alton. There I met her mother for the first time, and her sister Tessa. Father was on business in the United States.

On the first morning, I was woken by the sound of Rachel's mother's voice calling across the garden from her bedroom window, 'Mr Roberts,' she was saying, with most penetrating clarity, 'I wonder, would you mind not cutting logs so early? You'll wake my guests up.' A direct result of this diversion was that I came down to breakfast early.

Other young men (if I may include myself among them) were among the guests, and I observed them closely at the races, watching their reactions to the elder daughter of their hostess, and hers to them. Neither gave me food for satisfaction. All seemed unashamedly attached to her, and who could blame them, since her beauty was outstanding, and her cheerfulness and sense of fun infectious.

The old bachelor became jealous, and assessed his prospects with misgiving. An old lag, court-martialled and cashiered, aged thirty-nine. What self-respecting girl would wish to marry him? A playwright, I daresay, but having hit no jackpot since *The Chiltern Hundreds* – nothing to commend him but an overdraft. However, I began to press my suit (if that is the right phrase) with more intensity and, for the first time in my life, felt calm and happy doing so.

In previous encounters with the opposite sex, I had always lost my head, behaving like a boiling-over kettle on the hob, screaming and hissing and indulging myself in ecstatic but entirely unprogressive and, at the same time, perspiring little jumps. This time, with a firm hand on the steam whistle, I was able to control the temperature. Meanwhile, her mother, for some reason best known to herself, decided I was brother Henry, and told Rachel I had had several wives. We straightened that one out, with the assistance of a book of reference.

The autumn turned to winter, winter to spring, with a new play (or, to be precise, a play that Colin Chandler had already tried out at the Boltons) coming on about King James the Fourth of Scotland, called *The Thistle and the Rose*. During rehearsals I learned, to my consternation, that Miss Rachel Brand had gone off in a motor car to Spain, accompanied by a male cousin and his sister, and a young man whose intentions I most heartily mistrusted.

Summoning my secretary, one Otto Herschen, for companionship, we jumped into the Bentley and arrived in Madrid two days later. There we sat in the car in the main square all day, looking for an English car containing Rachel Brand and her companions. No luck. Tired out by our vigil, we took the bridal suite in an hotel at which we had sat looking all the afternoon, for no romantic reason, but because the hotel was already bursting at the seams with tourists.

In the morning, I rang up the British Embassy. 'I'm looking for a girl called Rachel Brand,' I told the secretary to the Ambassador.

'We don't know where she is,' the secretary told me.

'That makes two of us,' I answered.

Some years later, I met Sir Jock Balfour, dining with my parents-

H.P.H.–F

in-law. He recalled the incident, since he had been, at that time, our Ambassador to Spain. 'I have to tell you,' said he, 'that it's not part of the duties of His Majesty's Ambassadors to look for young men's girl-friends in the country to which they have been accredited. However, I'm extremely glad you found her!'

Actually, I didn't find her. Instead, I drove back to Liverpool to see the first night of *The Thistle and the Rose*. Back in my room, in the Adelphi after midnight, lay a message pad with the inscription: 'Miss Brand rang'.

I slept well that night, although the first night performance of the play had scarcely been conducive to such peace of mind, its author having been left with the feeling that it had its shortcomings, not only as a play, but as a vehicle designed to sweep away my overdraft during its coming season in London. To the Vaudeville we came the next week. Rachel Brand came with me. In the narrow passage on the east side of the theatre, during the interval, I put drops in her eye to counter some infection she had picked up in Spain.

When the curtain fell, I had the same instinctive feeling that I had had up in Liverpool: that play, or cast, or both, had not quite come off. Jakie Astor shared this view, as did Tom Egerton and Ian Gilmour, each of whom had put £500 into the kitty (I had done the same) to raise the necessary £2000 to float the project.

When it sank without trace, Jakie told me he was not surprised. 'When that boy came on shouting "Mither, Mither",' he said on the telephone next morning, 'and his mither dropped a bucket full of water which splashed over me, and then a lot of men in armour rushed on to the stage in total darkness, I knew we'd had it!' Tom and Ian were more gentlemanly, forking out without a word of complaint, then or now. I say 'now', because even to this day, Jakie says at quite frequent intervals, 'When am I going to get my money back, old bean?'

'You're not,' I tell him. 'When I back one of your horses, and it loses, I don't ask you for my money back!'

'That's different.'

'In what way?'

'Because I don't ask you to back my horse,' says he, 'while you did ask me to back your play.'

We crossed the Strand, Miss Brand and I, to the Savoy, in which I gave a party, to which came the eligible young man who had been in Spain with her. With murder in my heart, I offered him cold chicken and champagne. He ate and drank, and then departed.

Some days later, at the Café Royal, in the smart restaurant just opposite the main door, in which Oscar Wilde was wont to dine, we got engaged (first table on the right, as you go through the door). My mother had sent down a ring from Scotland, at my urgent request, which I placed on Rachel's finger, temporarily. Off we went to Alexandra Park that evening to secure the necessary cash with which to buy my own ring for her. In a three horse race, I put the necessary on Charlie Smirke at odds on. He came in third. Thus, the ring I bought her became that much more expensive.

Down to Hampshire for the weekend to inform her parents. I dined with friends down the river from Mill Court. The plan was that, when she had told her parents privately at dinner, she would call me up to say if it had gone down well or ill. If well, I should stroll up the river to Mill Court in carefree mood. If ill, I should do the same, but reinforced by strong drink.

The reader may consider that this was a craven plan. I would not disagree with that assessment, only point out that I lived in awe of father and much favoured the idea suggested by his daughter, that he should be softened up by saturation bombing by his wife and my fiancée before I came in on my lone run to make the final assault.

Rachel rang up after dinner. 'Everything's all right,' she told me. 'Daddy's very pleased. Mummy and I are walking down the river. You walk up and meet us.'

Up I walked, to be met at the halfway point by Rachel and her mother. Mother was extremely friendly, but I still had father to encounter, father being Tommy Brand, a leading figure in a merchant bank called Lazards, with a pair of searching blue eyes and a most uncompromising mode of speech.

I dragged my feet along the river bank on that enchanted April evening, dreading the thought of the cross-examination to which I was about to be subjected. 'How dare you get yourself engaged to Rachel!' I imagined him exclaiming. 'An old man like you. A cashiered officer, and an ex-convict, what's more. Not to mention a dramatic author, so-called, with a new play on in London that won't

see the month out. Get out of my house, and don't come back unless
you want the contents of two twelve bore Purdey cartridges embedded
in your backside!'

Up the steps we went, into the hall. 'Tommy's in there,' my future
mother-in-law said, pointing to the sitting-room on the left of the
front door. I went in, shook hands, took a seat when he had taken his.
Silence ensued (if silence can ensue from silence). Squinting at him,
I could see his blue eyes, sickled o'er with the pale cast of thought.
Silence continued to ensue, till I could stand the strain no longer.

'Well, sir, this engagement – ' I began, in trepidation.

'What engagement?' answered he, his now clear blue eyes beaming
on me like two searchlights on a frosty evening.

'Damn it!' I thought. 'Rachel told me she had told the fellow and
that everything was all right. And yet, here he sits, pretending that
he doesn't know a thing about it – what's he up to?'

He was up to nothing, of course, only being perverse, out to capture
the initiative, a policy which is, no doubt, instinctive to all bankers.
Having captured it, he suddenly spoke. 'What's your overdraft?'
he said. I told him. 'I've known bigger,' he replied.

Then the door opened, and his wife came in. 'Thomas,' she said,
'I hate to interrupt, but there's a plague of greenfly on the pillow in
the spare room. Would you go and deal with it?'

He went, leaving his future son-in-law in total sympathy with
each and every greenfly.

When I left that night to go back to my friends' house, he came out
to see me off, the greenfly having been reduced to impotence, no
doubt.

'Good night,' he said, stooping down towards the window of the
Bentley (although how it got there, I shall never know. Perhaps my
host down river had delivered it in order to provide me with a get-
away). 'Good night,' he said. 'I don't think you'll make her a bad
husband.'

Nervously, I drove away and felt the back wheel of the Bentley
rise as though it had run over something. Was it his foot? If it was,
he never mentioned the fact, not in all the years I knew him.

When he went into White's Club next week, or so the story goes,
in answer to a fellow member who said, 'How can you let Rachel
marry that abominable fellow?' He replied, 'I like him very much.

I always have. I was his fag at school.' Apocryphal, perhaps, but none the less that story adequately indicates his dry wit.

Later on, he rose to be the Chairman of the bank in which he had served all his life with such outstanding success. Yet in spite of this distinction he refrained from mentioning my overdraft again in all the years I knew him, and he took my failures and successes in the theatre with philosophical detachment, although, sometimes, on the chin. Nor did he give his eldest daughter or myself financial advice, except on one occasion when he told us: 'If you look through your accounts and one week see an item reading "Eggs: £100", you ought to look into it.'

We have done that ever since.

He died in 1964, in the Middlesex Hospital. That evening, I was on a televison programme – 'Call My Bluff' – with Robert Morley. In his dressing-room beforehand we rehearsed a little, insofar as one can in a programme of that nature. In the interval before the show, I went round to the hospital to see my father-in-law, and they told me he had just died. In fact, I suspected this already, having seen, on my arrival, a van parked down in a side street which, some instinct told me, had been brought round to take his body to the chapel.

Back I went, to Robert Morley and the television programme, thinking only of the father-in-law who had stood behind me through many years of married life, without a word of criticism, praising my successes and condoning my disasters.

After Rachel and I got engaged her uncle and aunt, Dick and Sheila Talbot, gave a cocktail party, to which came every member of the Brand and Seely clans. Rachel's mother, before marriage, was called Leila Seely, which implies (to those who know their Nottingham-shire) some degree of eccentricity (my life seems cast among such people) not to speak of volatility.

Her father was a Liberal MP, her Uncle Jack a soldier. He it was (the story is attached to many people, but it fits him best) who recommended his batman for the VC, on the grounds that 'he's been everywhere with me'. Though neither got the medal, both may have deserved it, anyway my mother-in-law's Uncle Jack, since Seelys are notoriously carefree not to say foolhardy, ready to tempt Fate in many different spheres.

Several times, her brother Jimmy rode in the Grand National on his own horse, completing the course each time, though unplaced. One year he missed the race because his horse, whom he had dosed the night before with some invigorating brew, failed to wake up next morning and slept through the afternoon of the race in placid disregard of Uncle Jimmy's well-laid plans.

Hugh Seely (later Sherwood) was my mother-in-law's cousin, and could be described as perhaps the top-seeded member of the Seely family in the play-off for eccentricity. One eve of the poll meeting in Berwick-on-Tweed, which seat he represented as a Liberal, he ridiculed the accusation, voiced by an insistent heckler, that he had lost £1000 at roulette in Le Touquet a few weeks before.

'This charge against me,' said he, rising to his feet in outrage, 'is most damaging. It illustrates the way in which a politician's reputation can be soiled by innuendo. It was not Le Touquet, it was Monte Carlo, it was not roulette it was baccarat, and it was not £1000 it was £2000.'

Then he sat down to tumultuous applause, and I am glad to say the citizens of Berwick-on-Tweed re-elected him.

He lived in Brighton in his later years. Sometimes, I met him at the theatre when I had a play on there. He was recognizable at once, because of a large scarlet blanket he wore round his shoulders, in the front row of the stalls.

'Have a drink, William,' he would say, when interval time came.

'Thanks very much, I'll get them – what would you like?' I would ask him.

'No, no, my fellow'll get them,' he would say, turning to his companion. 'This is William Douglas Home who wrote this epic – get two whiskies, will you?' Off would go his butler to the bar, and come back with, as I recall, three drinks instead of two.

So much for Seelys, gay, eccentric, fond of wine and women, sometimes in that order, sometimes the reverse, but always, male and female, ready for a laugh. So much for the dam's side. What about the sire?

My father-in-law's family came from the Hoo in Hertfordshire, a house I never saw and which is now demolished. Mr Speaker Brand (later Lord Hampden) lived there – no relation to the fellow who signed Charles the First's death warrant – and the family remained there till the Second World War, when they moved to an adjacent mill house.

When my father-in-law's mother died, a few years after the war, 'Pop' as he was known, my father-in-law's father, came to live in Hampshire with his eldest son. He was the kind of character my heart goes out to always, being of my father's vintage. When they told him that I was engaged to his granddaughter, Rachel, he remarked to his son: 'I don't know the fellow, Tommy. A bit hard on dear old Charlie, wasn't he, though, in *The Chiltern Hundreds*?'

When we got to know each other, I explained that 'dear old Charlie' thought quite the reverse. He at once accepted this assessment of the situation even though, because of dear old Charlie's sudden death three weeks before my wedding, he could not confirm the matter with his old friend.

When he got engaged to Rachel's grandmother Pop's reputation left a lot to be desired. Being a dashing officer in the Hussars, somewhat impoverished at that time – his future father-in-law, the Duke of Buccleuch, quite wrongly, thought him not the kind of fellow that his daughter ought to marry. Therefore, when his Duchess told him at the breakfast table, one day at Drumlanrig, that the match was on, he raised his walking stick and struck the breakfast service (Dresden, some say) from the table.

Some years later, when another daughter, Connie, got engaged to a young man about whom the Duke was even less enthusiastic, his resourceful Duchess, just before she broke the news to him at breakfast, substituted kitchen china for the normal breakfast service. In consequence, her husband's flailing walking stick did much less damage than it had on the occasion when his eldest daughter plighted her troth to her 'Pop'.

Between the wars, Pop served as Lord-in-Waiting to King George the Fifth, and, so the story goes (in fact, he told me it himself) a mild attack of haemorrhoids sent him to hospital.

'I haven't seen Lord Hampden recently,' remarked Queen Mary at the breakfast table, to Lady Elizabeth Motion, her Lady-in-Waiting.

'He's in hospital, Ma'am,' said her Lady-in-Waiting.

'Oh, what's wrong with him?' enquired Her Majesty.

Evidently, not wishing to use the word 'piles' in the presence of her sovereign's wife, nor yet the word 'haemorrhoids' for fear that it might not be included in Queen Mary's repertoire, the resourceful Lady-in-Waiting thought fit to quote, instead, the phrase printed in those days on every packet of Bromo, with a view to emphasizing that lavatory paper's beneficial effect on the disease in question.

'He's got, Ma'am,' she said, quoting from memory, 'that most distressing and almost universal complaint.'

At that the conversation turned to other subjects.

Later on that morning, as Lord Stamfordham was writing letters in his room, King George the Fifth burst in. 'Stamfordham,' His Majesty asked his astonished secretary. 'Who's been going round telling my wife that Hampden's got VD?'

Needless to say, like everything else he did in life, Pop died in style. As my father-in-law left his bedside for the last time and went to the door, he heard his forebear saying, 'Tommy, I'll be leaving here today.'

'Yes, Father,' agreed Tommy.

'I'll be moving to the Ritz,' said Pop.

I married Rachel at St Peter's, Eaton Square in 1951 – on 26 July, a date much favoured in her family for weddings. The reception was at the Hyde Park Hotel. My best man, Michael Astor, sent our chauffeur-driven car away, telling the driver that he would put through a telephone call to him at the end of the reception. Michael then forgot the name of the firm from which he had hired the vehicle. He hired another car, however, which took us to Northolt, stopping at a pub *en route*, because we were ahead of time. There we played darts with Michael Beary, who was on our flight to Paris, having been engaged to ride at Longchamps the next day.

Arrived at the Royal Monceau Hotel, Rachel found a message asking her to call her mother. This she did, to learn that she had packed a valuable necklace, loaned to her by mother, for the wedding. We located it and sent it home, resisting the temptation to dispose of it and have a field day with the proceeds. Then we wandered down the Champs Elysées, in an ecstasy of happiness, and dined at Fouquets. Next morning we picked up the Bentley, which had been delivered earlier by Otto Herschen, and drove south. In Menton, I recall a minor motor accident. A policeman asked to see my papers and enquired what my profession was. '*Je suis un écritoire*,' I told him,

proudly showing off my French. He drove away in some bewilderment.

We burned ourselves, sunbathing, while in Menton to such a degree
that, on arrival, late at night, in Genoa we could not step on to the
pavement outside our hotel, because of the acute pain caused by
taking an upward step. So we walked along the street until we found
the entrance to a garage, inched our way up the ramp and arrived
at pavement level. Thence, into the hotel, and, by lift, up to our
bedroom. On arrival, we rang down for a bottle of white wine, which
we drank, standing up on either side of the bed. Having emptied it,
we fell back stiffly on to the bed-cover, waking at breakfast-time to
find a marked improvement in our health.

In order to prolong the honeymoon, I wrote a film script, while in
Italy, for an Italian director, whom I met in Genoa. I wrote it in
Amalfi, for an hour or two each day, while Rachel coped with the
thank-you letters for our wedding presents. Having left behind the
book recording them, she found it necessary to fall back on her
memory. To her eternal credit, she achieved this Herculean task,
in record time, with only one mistake – she wrote to Kathleen
Dewar, Michael Astor's mother-in-law, thanking her for a delightful
wedding present which 'has come in very useful on our honeymoon'.
We, later, learned that Mrs Dewar had been much amused on reading
this epistle since she had given us a grandfather clock.

The remuneration earned by script-writing enabled us to stay
abroad until September. Then, the Bentley, having safely traversed
Italy and France, came back to Cranshaws in the Lammermuir Hills,
a square biscuit-coloured house which I had taken in the year before
my marriage. It sat high up on the grouse moors, with a splendid
view, a peel tower, and a difficult approach in winter.

In a period of snow, the year before, a friend of mine called Robin
Fyfe had come to stay the week-end with his wife, who was in an
advanced state of pregnancy. His call from Edinburgh, inviting
himself, had been prefaced by: 'Is that you, Willy? Listen, Liz's
gynaecologist has gone to watch a football match in Newcastle.
He says we can come out to stay the week-end with you.'

'Does he?' I said, unenthusiastically.

'Yes, isn't it a wonderful idea?' said Robin. So I drove to Edinburgh
to pick them up, and brought them back to Cranshaws, where my

other week-end guest was Colin Chandler, the director both of *Now Barabbas* and *The Chiltern Hundreds*, recently become director of a Drama School in Glasgow.

Sure enough, at 3 a.m. on Sunday morning, Robin came into my bedroom (treading like a lion in ballet shoes – a phrase I made a mental and approving note of at the time), and said: 'The baby's started. Isn't it exciting?'

'Go and get dressed, you old fool,' I shouted at him. 'And get Liz dressed, too.' He went back to their room, a shade crestfallen.

Leaping out of bed, I ran to Colin's bedroom. 'What's the matter?' he asked sleepily. 'The baby's started,' I said. 'Oh, well, get an ambulance,' said Colin, turning over and going to sleep again. 'An ambulance,' I thought, as I dressed quickly. 'What's the use of that? And where from? How long would it take? And would it ever get here?'

I pulled back the curtains and looked out. The snow was drifting silently down, causing me to make a quick decision. 'Robin,' I called, as I hurried down the passage, 'I'll go and get the car. Be ready in two minutes!'

Out I went into the white night, ankle deep in snow, to get the Bentley from the barn. As I revved up the engine, I thought: 'Via Gifford over the hill road? Or, via Berwick, nearly twice as long, but safer?'

As I ploughed to the front door, the snowflakes dancing in the headlights, I decided on the latter – and when Robin and Liz got in, I told them so.

'If we went by Gifford, we'd get there quicker,' I said, 'if we didn't get stuck in a snow-drift.'

'Is that likely?' Robin asked.

'Yes, very,' I said. 'I got stuck on that road last week.'

'Well then, we'd better go by Berwick,' said Liz.

'We may get stuck there too,' I warned her, 'but it's not so likely.'

Down the lane I drove in trepidation, due south, in the opposite direction to my destination, and turned towards Berwick and the A1.

Two hours later I pulled into Edinburgh, wiping the perspiration from my brow, despite the Arctic weather. 'Where's the nursing home?' I enquired.

'Don't ask me, dear boy,' said Robin.

'Liz, where is the nursing home?' I asked my quiet, front-seat companion.

'Second right, first left,' said she.

'Oh, Liz,' said Robin's voice from the back seat. 'Thank God we had you with us, otherwise we never would have found it!'

Having dropped her there, I took her husband to the Caledonian Hotel and left him in the lounge among a lot of football fans in a worse state than he was.

Back at Cranshaws, just in time for breakfast, Colin came down sleepily. 'Well, did the ambulance get there in time?' he asked. 'Yes, thank you, Colin,' I said. 'Just.' The telephone rang later to report the birth. I went out to the barn, patted the Bentley on the bonnet, staggered back into the house and went to bed – determined never again to invite an unborn baby for the week-end.

Two years later, none the less, an unborn baby came to stay at Cranshaws for nine months. I took the road to Edinburgh again, this time in May, with Rachel at my side, and Jamie, our first-born, arrived in Randolph Crescent the next day. I went round to inspect the new arrival and saw Rachel, looking beautiful and frail and happy, lying back against her pillow with, clasped in her arms, a baby racehorse trainer. On the way back to the hotel, I dropped a note into the Bishop's letter-box, informing him of the birth of a new Episcopalian. The next day, there arrived at Randolph Crescent a pair of baby's pants, knitted by the Bishop's wife.

A fortnight later, we drove back to Cranshaws with our son and heir and Nannie West. It's often said that children brought up by Scots nannies develop strong characters. That may be so or not, but certainly Scots nannies have strong characters themselves, and Nannie West is no exception. Handsome, outwardly stern but soft-hearted as they come beneath, she brought our children up impeccably, in spite of an indulgent father.

If Jamie should send out the Derby winner one day, that fact will owe little to his father, much more to his mother, with her practical approach to life and knowledge of the subject, and a lot to Nannie West for bringing out her little charge's individuality.

I well remember walking down the platform at Boulogne, *en route* for Switzerland, behind Nannie West and Jamie, when he was about six. Suddenly, he took his belt off his shorts, put it through the handle of his suitcase and continued down the platform with the suitcase slung across his shoulders 'Jamie,' shouted Nannie at him, 'just because French porters do that, there's no need for you to copy them. Be yourself.' It is pleasant to be able to record that he has been that ever since.

# Chapter 7
# Peace-time Politics

The year before my marriage I had been adopted as the Tory candidate for Kirkcaldy in Fife. That was a turn-up for the books and quite a tribute to Conservative broadmindedness. Since two out of the three elections I had fought in war-time had been fought against the Tories (Clay Cross being the exception) it was quite a tribute to my own broadmindedness as well!

However, Mr Churchill having called for men of good will and of all political persuasions to serve under him, I was prepared to take him at his word. I saw no inconsistency in this. The war was over – might not Mr Churchill, in his new role of domestic politician as opposed to that of war-lord, be a reformed character and, therefore, worthy of my patronage?

I must confess that there are those – most notably my brother Alec – who make jokes about my constant changes of political allegiance – Independent in the war; Conservative, for a brief period in 1950; and then Liberal for two elections in the sixties, since when I have been a 'floating voter'. 'Well, what party are you in this morning?' he once said to me at breakfast, shortly after I had broken with the Liberals and climbed back on the fence. 'Wait till I've read the papers,' I replied, 'and I'll see if any of the parties has come up with something new.' I am still waiting as I write.

The truth is that my record in the field of politics is not so inconsistent as a superficial glance might lead one to suppose. The three war-time elections that I contested had to be fought as an Independent or not at all. The fact that I was a 'pro-war-aims', 'anti-Unconditional Surrender', 'pro-Atlantic Charter' candidate – to list the slogans I adopted in each bye-election – demonstrates that I could not stand for a party – as there was a party-truce in force. I therefore had to be an Independent or else ILP, and since I was an Army officer and Jimmy Maxton's ILP was pacifist, I opted for the former in the fond hope that confusion might be less confounded. Whether I achieved that aim, or not, is open to debate. I did, however, get a word of praise from Jimmy Maxton himself, who spoke for his party candidate in Cathcart. 'This young officer,' I heard him say, when I attended a packed meeting, 'has the right idea although he's in the wrong profession!' and at the conclusion of the meeting, we shook hands. He wished me luck and asked with affection after brother Alec, who was ill with TB of the spine at that time. I left him, conscious that I had been in the presence of a great and good man and a splendid orator, whose knees, as I remember vividly, bent as he spoke, like those of any golf professional preparing for his drive.

The other politicians of note I had met – but these I met before the war – were Baldwin, Halifax and Inskip. Mr Baldwin came to Douglas when I was a teenager (accompanied by Mrs Baldwin, who had played cricket for England in her day), in order to address the faithful gathered in the gardens below from the terrace outside Douglas Castle. At lunch he asked me to hold his macintosh while he was speaking, as my father had informed him that the weather prospects were uncertain. I accepted this assignment with misgivings as I had been looking forward to an afternoon among the roedeer in the Long Plantation far away across the valley opposite the house. However, when the platform party gathered in the hall, my father, sensing my predicament, removed the coat that I was carrying and handed it to Mr Collingwood. I slipped out of the back door, bicycled across the valley and submerged myself, most thankfully, among the birches and the scattered beech trees.

I remember sitting comfortably beneath one of the latter, watching a young roedeer feeding while the voice of Mr Baldwin, amplified by the loudspeaker, echoed through the valley, causing the little deer to raise its head occasionally in wonderment and then resume its feeding. 'William was too shy to carry your coat on the platform,' said my father to the Premier at tea. 'Indeed,' said Mr Baldwin, looking at me through the pipe smoke in which both he and my disapproving mother were enveloped. 'So he didn't hear my speech?' 'Oh yes, I did, sir,' I piped up. 'I heard it all.' The rugged face resumed its customary expression of benevolence.

Sir Thomas Inskip and Lord Halifax I met at Cliveden just before the war the first time Michael Astor asked me for the week-end. I came down to dinner rather early to find Lady Astor, in her evening gown, reading the Bible. I sat down and held my peace. Sir Thomas Inskip came in shortly afterwards and tripped over the standard lamp flex causing the lamp to fall over. 'Lift your feet up, you great hulk,' said Lady Astor and resumed her Bible reading.

After dinner when the ladies had retired, Lord Halifax engaged himself in conversation with a German friend of David Astor's (post-war Editor of *The Observer*) called Adam von Trott, who was to die at Hitler's hands in 1945 after the July plot. I still recall the deep intensity of feeling in the voice of this young anti-Nazi German, later to be martyred, and the cool almost detached replies of Britain's Foreign Secretary. Lord Halifax, so far as I could ascertain, gave no encouragement whatever to this envoy from the anti-Hitler faction in the Fatherland and, as we left the table to rejoin the ladies, I abandoned any hope of peace. 'Why could he not have said,' I asked myself and anybody who would listen, 'you encourage me when you say that there is an opposition in your country, and not least within the Army. I will therefore do my best to conduct foreign policy in the way which will be best suited to encouraging that opposition.'

Maybe he did say that, when I wasn't present. Possibly he even did it. Certainly, his leader, Neville Chamberlain, attempted such a policy, but when it was too late.

At all events, when Churchill formed his government in 1940, all such thoughts of compromise were jettisoned and no attempt was made to offer those in Germany opposed to Hitler's war-aims anything which might have encouraged them to overthrow the Führer – only 'Victory' and later 'Unconditional Surrender'. In this sterile atmosphere, I found myself embarking on the one-man crusade that I have written of earlier.

Then, when the war was over and the purpose of this lone crusade had become academic, I saw little reason why I should not join the Tories, who had been courageous enough to invite not only an ex-convict but a cashiered officer to represent them. I drove to Kirkcaldy in the Bentley and made my acceptance speech.

The honeymoon did not last long, however. Came a meeting that I was invited to in Glasgow during the Korean War, in which I spoke, with vehemence, against my leader's attitude towards the 47th parallel – which I regarded as being aggressive. Back at Cranshaws, I received an urgent summons to attend a meeting of my now fed-up Association. Tactfully, they told me that, although the fault was theirs for having asked me in the first place, I would have to resign there and then.

I raised half-hearted arguments in favour of my action, pointing out that Mr Churchill had specifically encouraged people like myself and that, with loyalty, I had responded to the call, until he got up to his militarist tricks again. They shook their heads in sorrow, indicating that they disagreed profoundly with such specious reasoning.

I then recounted the names of my companions on the Glasgow platform, pointing out that I had been in most distinguished company. I also listed those who had sent telegrams, with one exception. They were unimpressed. They rose and shook my hand, and showed me to the door.

In the car park, as I drove out, I encountered Major Black, Jo Grimond's brother-in-law and one of the Tory executive. He came up to my car, as I put down the window.

'Thank God that you didn't mention old Jo's telegram,' he said, 'I would have found it most embarrassing!'

I shook his hand, and left him standing there – a Tory with a sense of humour, married to the sister of a Liberal with one, too – an unusual double in politics.

A song was in my heart as I drove south towards Queensferry. I had always known that I was not cut out to be a candidate – only an instant fighter of elections with, if possible, the certainty of being beaten, thus eliminating any risk of earning an unwanted five-year sentence.

'Never again,' said I to myself as I drove through the Lammermuir Hills towards Cranshaws, 'will I join a party. I am not the man to undersign a party programme and adhere to it through thick and thin. There is bound to be some policy which, finally, will turn into a fruitful field of disagreement and compel me to denounce it from a public platform to the consternation of my Chairman and the faithful gathered in the hall.'

I held to this resolve for ten or fifteen years until Jo Grimond

came to stay one week-end, dangling a bye-election in South Edinburgh before me. 'Any man can rat once,' Churchill had said, in
youth, as he crossed the floor of the House for the second time.
'It takes a brave man to "re-rat", however!' None the less I did so.
By the time Jo left on Monday morning, I was booked in for a bye-
election in South Edinburgh. Independent, Tory and now, Liberal –
I had 're-ratted' to some tune.

And yet my conscience was at peace. Indeed, I flattered myself
that I was a pattern of consistency in my approach to politics – an
Independent when there was a party-truce and therefore no alternative; a Tory when the main bone of contention between them and
me had ceased to be an issue; and a Liberal when my approach to
foreign policy differed, once again, from Winston Churchill's.
Rachel gave me her support wholeheartedly, resigning from the
Chairmanship of the Conservative Association in East Meon and
thankfully returning to the party in which her maternal family
had always served.

Of course I am aware that members of the party faithful, whatever
the party, find such acrobatics unforgivable, being unable to appreci-
ate the motives which cause those blessed with less faith and more
impatience to indulge in party-swapping. To me, such action is
entirely natural and blameless if, by taking it, one gets a little nearer
to one's goal, just as a man who wants to go to Birmingham is
free to travel by whatever transport takes his fancy with a view to
getting there on time. Thus politics, to me, is not a party matter
but a means of getting somewhere by the most convenient route.
Nor does the fact that I have never got there, influence this philosophical approach in any way.

The goal that I was aiming at the week-end that Jo Grimond came
to stay was 'more fluidity in politics'. For some years, I had noted
with distaste the deadlock between Labour and Conservative, the
block-voting, the close-run General Elections and the consequent
political closed-shop. I knew of course that party politics had come
to stay in Britain. Indeed, I regarded them as an essential in a democratic state. Nor did I have a quarrel with the constitution – written
or unwritten – or the monarchy or any of the Three Estates. My sole
ambition – was to loosen up the system by the introduction of more
independent members. In the absence of the university MPs (such

H.P.H.–G

as Sir Alan Herbert), who had been a breath of fresh air in the corridors of Westminster, I looked upon the independent little band presided over by Jo Grimond as a useful substitute. I therefore hitched my creaking wagon, temporarily, to his star.

I lunched with Jo at the New Club in Edinburgh before I started on my campaign. There he listed, between sips of Burgundy, the headings of his party's policies. In most respects, they coincided with my own, notably regarding the strong emphasis he placed on individuality in politics; so much so, indeed, that I wondered, audibly, just how a party which was so emphatic about individuality could possibly be held together. I was soon to find out. Sometimes, during meetings in the campaign, I would listen to my chairman introducing me and voicing views with which I had no sympathy. However, when I later rose and contradicted him, no one seemed to notice. It was obvious that in this isolated party, individuality had come to stay and was indeed the linchpin that held it together, even though there was no linchpin.

Only in our opposition to the 'squeeze' in force at that time and in our demand for devolution did we stand together in the Party. Otherwise we jousted on our own against our own selected opposition and in favour of the slogan painted on our helmets. This, of course, was Freedom with a capital F – individuality without responsibility and party backing without any noticeable obligation on the candidate to push those points of policy of which he disapproved. I found it heady stuff. And yet I was sincere in my approach to the election. Here was the 'fluidity in politics' that I was seeking. Never mind the differences between my chairmen and myself. 'Let us march onward towards polling-day,' was my sole thought, 'and the impending victory for individuality and common sense.'

Occasionally I must confess, in mid-speech, I would think of a remark that Colin Tennant had once made to Rachel during dinner. 'Rachel,' he had said, 'when you and William drive to Scotland and stop in a stubble-field for lunch, would I be right in thinking that you look out of the window of the car and say to one another "This looks a nice place to stand for Parliament, provided that we've not already done so"?'

At the poll, I finished second to a friendly Tory called Clerk Hutchinson. As I shook hands I told him how, in Morningside, some front doors had been shut against us when we were out canvassing. 'You ought to civilize them,' I said. 'I prefer to leave them as they are,' said he, with a proprietary smile.

And with good reason! When the General Election came, he beat me into second place again. This time, I dropped my vote, one reason being that a play of mine called *Aunt Edwina*, with an *avant-garde* theme, came on at the Lyric during the election period. Another reason could have been an article in *The Times* on the morning of the poll, in which, in answer to a question from their Northern Correspondent 'What will you do if you win tomorrow?' I was quoted as replying, 'I'll be the first winning candidate in history to ask for a recount.'

One welcome helper that I had the second time I fought South Edinburgh was Sir Compton Mackenzie. Rachel made her maiden speech one night, supported by this legendary figure, then he spoke in his turn. When he sat down to tumultuous applause, a heckler spoke up. 'Sir Compton,' said this fellow, 'we've just heard you speaking for the Liberals tonight.'

'That's right,' Sir Compton answered, rising to his feet.

'Then how do you explain,' the heckler persisted, 'your appearance one night recently on television, speaking for the Labour Party?'

'Easily,' Sir Compton told him. 'I don't mind if Liberal or Labour wins, so long as the Conservatives don't.' None the less, they did.

My brother Alec came into the act in this election, too. One morning, shooting pheasants at the Hirsel, he was missing two in every three. 'What's wrong with you?' I asked, at the conclusion of the drive. 'I'm very tired,' he told me, 'after speaking against some damned Liberal in Edinburgh last night.'

'That Liberal,' I said, 'was me.'

'In that case,' he replied, 'I would imagine you've got nothing much to pick up either.'

Now, with five election defeats to my credit, I am running level with Disraeli's tally, just before the death of Mr Wyndham Lewis which gave him, in the short run, a good wife and, in the long run, immortality. At one time I supposed myself to be his natural successor. Now, at my advancing age, although I share the blessing of a good wife, I see little prospect of political advancement. Nor, in fact, do I desire it any more unless, of course, at some time in the future, one compelling issue crops up, which I feel impelled to bring to public notice. God forbid that it should ever do so, but it probably will.

None the less, I like to study politics as a spectator and, maybe, write a play concerning them from time to time. Indeed just such a play called *The Eleventh Hour* lies on my shelf as I write, patiently awaiting a production. Meanwhile, I enjoy the drive down to East Meon school on polling-day, assessing the shortcomings of each party and each candidate; deciding, finally, for whom to vote as I produce my polling-card and say 'Good Morning' to the village policeman. My conclusion seldom varies, though I sometimes find it quite an effort to be so conventional. I have my panaceas, still, of course – I want to see the Tory party much less arrogant, the Labour party much less doctrinaire, the Liberals prepared to give up all ambition to become a major party and remain content with being a small but effective nuisance group.

I heartily deplore the custom, practised by most politicians, of deriding their opponents by describing them as liars, charlatans and twisters. I regard this habit as being the most important single reason for the near-contempt in which most politicians are held by the public. None the less, the system works in spite of its short-comings.

How will my grandchildren fare, I sometimes ask myself, in this imperfect world? I see no reason to despair. One daily reads, of course, of the world ending, of democracy on its last legs, of Armageddon lurking in the wings, of riots, revolutions, flood and famine. But if one has studied history, one has read all this before. I have a certain confidence about the future. Men (and women, too, and this could be decisive) are receiving education from the media on an unprecedented scale. This leads to an increasing number of enquiring people analysing, for the first time, values by which, hitherto, society has lived. In international affairs, this happy trend was illustrated by the US Senate sittings, while the war in Vietnam was raging, during which participants spoke openly against the prolongation of the struggle without anyone accusing them of cowardice, disloyalty or treason.

This is a step forward, less dramatic possibly although no less unusual, than the first step taken by Neil Armstrong on the lunar landscape – holding out, as it does, the rich promise of a future in which governments who wage war will no longer be presented with a blank cheque, signed for the duration, by an impotent and voiceless people. Because of this, I have hopes that my unborn grandchildren may live in peace, provided they and their contemporaries are prepared to follow this new star in international affairs.

At home, however, I would like to see them doing the reverse – that is to say, eschewing a commitment to reform without first studying the workings of our age-old constitution and assessing whether we can fairly lay the blame for our shortcomings on the system under which these islands have survived for centuries.

The House of Lords is a case in point. One would assume that Tories stood, four-square, in its defence, demanding its retention as a vital link between the Commons and the Crown, which latter institution could be dangerously isolated from the people by the abolition of the Upper Chamber. Instead, they tinker with reform, negatively by allowing the hereditary principle to lapse through disuse, thus creating a split chamber composed of hereditary and life peers, which can only breed dissension and a House divided, ensuring, ultimately, the inevitable fate of all such houses. Had they left it as it was and seen fit to create hereditary peers instead of life peers, might it not have survived what would now appear to be its terminal affliction and restored itself to health?

What other things concern me in this royal throne of kings, this sceptred island, though no longer, hopefully, this seat of Mars?

One answer is, of course, the Unions. Nor do I write as an outsider. Since I am, myself, an intermittent member of a Union called Equity, I can understand their original aims and intentions while, at the same time, deploring their ungainly methods of enforcing new aims and less praiseworthy ambitions.

Sometimes, in the watches of the night, I ask myself what would happen in my own profession if we carried on in a like manner. The answer, unbelievably, is that we would demand that management continue paying us, although the play concerned were losing money. If management should dig its heels in, then we – actors, playwrights, stage staff – would come out on strike, sit on the darkened stage and thus effectively prevent production, in that theatre, of any other play.

If we did this the police would move in, we would be arrested and the management would sue us. The judge would find us guilty of a breach of contract and impose on us a hefty fine, in compensation for the loss of income that the management had suffered. If we could not pay the fine, then we would go to gaol, deservedly.

Not so with militant Trade Unionists, who behave with just such irresponsibility and get away with it, unchallenged and unpunished. This immunity – and that perhaps is what is most important – is destructive to morale. Any man who is above the law is, also, on a lower level of morality than a sneak-thief who has paid the penalty for his shortcomings.

As things stand at present it looks perilously like a confrontation between those in the Trade Unions who are determined to retain, if not enhance, their present power and those who wish to strip them of it. This, of course, if it should come to pass, would mean revolution but it need not come to that. The ultimate solution, as I see it, will be instituted by the members of the Unions themselves, when they can be induced to recognize injustice and to echo Robert Burns' prayer, 'O, would some power the giftie gie us, to see oursels as ithers see us.' Pending the arrival of that happy day, I hope my grandchildren will read, mark, learn, digest and broadcast these reflections, should it still be necessary when they come to maturity.

Apart from these required reforms, I find no fundamental fault with life as it is lived in Britain and, indeed, am prepared to stick my neck out and predict that it will go on much as it has always done. Of course, there will be superficial changes – golfing week-ends on the moon, night-clubs on Mars and all the rest of it, but, basically, as some wise Frenchman once remarked, the more things change the more they stay the same. Take the Corridors of Power – a phrase beloved of those whose politics are dictated by out-worn slogans and the kind of propaganda that sustained the Labour Party in its early days. One might suppose the brother of an ex-Conservative Prime Minister would wander down those corridors and profit in a big way from so doing.

Not at all – I can recall no single instance during Alec's tenure of high office, when a benefit of any kind accrued to me. In fact, quite the reverse. The family connection brought me nothing but embarrassment. Some drama critics reckoned me to be an automatic member of the Tory leadership, by virtue of my blood relationship with one of them. One even saw fit to discuss Rhodesia in a review of *The Queen's Highland Servant*, about Queen Victoria and John Brown, evidently thinking that Alec and I were one and the same person.

There are no grounds for that assumption, and none either for assuming that to be the relative of a Prime Minister leads to preferment. The truth is that Alec failed to take advantage of his eminence. He exercised what little power a democratic premier has, without fear or favour – save in one small instance when, I must confess, he did show fear and, at the same time, favoured me with a fraternal call for help.

My telephone rang, one fine morning, at about 10.30, down in Hampshire.

'Billy Graham's coming for a drink at half past twelve,' said Alec's voice. 'Elizabeth is going out, so I'll be alone.'

'Good luck to you,' I said.

'I want you to come up,' he went on, 'because if we're alone, he might ask me to get down on my knees and say a prayer, or something.'

Noting the panic in his voice, I got my car out, drove to Downing Street, and found him in his sitting-room. We talked of racing until Billy Graham came in. Alec poured some sherry and the conversation, due to Billy Graham's expressed interest, continued on the same subject.

After half an hour, we parted on the best of terms – playwright, prime minister and evangelist. I motored back home, vacating the corridors of power for ever.

## Chapter 8
# The Reluctant
# Debutante

Having been dismissed by the Conservative Association in Kirkcaldy, I sat down and wrote to Mr Churchill, saying I was sorry to have let him down. In his reply, he wrote: 'You have another profession no less interesting, and with no less of an impact on the public mind.' I wish that I had kept the letter from that most magnanimous of men.

We stayed at Cranshaws till the winter. Then, one night, an episode occurred which brought home to me that we would not be in residence much longer. After dinner, when we came into the sitting-room, my labrador jumped up on to the piano and lay down on the top, where he spent the evening. He continued with this strange behaviour all through the cold weather, notwithstanding that we sealed the windows up with tape and put rugs under the doors.

Since the piano top lacked space for the accommodation of myself and Rachel, Nannie West and Jamie, plus the labrador, I knew that, come next winter, I would have to give up either my wife or the Lammermuirs. I chose the latter, and we moved to Gamlingay, in Bedfordshire, to the Dower House (or cottage) of Jakie Astor and his wife Chiquita. There, we spent a warmer winter than the last one, with both Rachel and the labrador being much more relaxed than at Cranshaws.

I felt a shade circumscribed to start with. But with Jakie's park at our disposal (and his wood pigeons) I soon became acclimatized, reducing my horizon gradually from endless hills of heather to root fields and spinnies and racehorses out to grass. Thus, after some months spent in counteracting restlessness, one more Scot, travelling the high road down to England, threw away his return ticket and became a happy immigrant.

One morning, that first winter, I woke with a temperature of ninety-nine degrees. Rachel confined me to my bed, and then, at my request, brought up an empty notebook and a pencil. At precisely ten o'clock when she went off to Gamlingay to shop, I wrote the following:

*The scene is laid in the Broadbents' flat. Jimmy and Sheila Broadbent are at breakfast. Sheila is opening letters.*

SHEILA: (opening a letter) Lord and Lady Aspeth. Who on earth are they? July the seventh, the Hyde Park Hotel. (She puts it down and opens another) Mrs Arthur Milligan. I've never heard of her. (Jimmy covers his plate with his side plate)

SHEILA: What's the matter, darling?

JIMMY: My poached egg.

SHEILA: What's wrong with it?

JIMMY: I just don't like the way it's looking at me.

That morning, though less painfully and with less trepidation due to previous experience, I was, in my own small way, going through what Rachel had gone through in Randolph Crescent – giving birth to *The Reluctant Debutante*. I wrote throughout that week until my temperature went down, then came downstairs with two notebooks of dialogue but still unable to devise an ending for the play. I put it on the shelf, and promptly forgot about it.

In the year or two in which we lived in Jakie's Dower House, other plays came on and off. The promise of both *Now Barabbas* and *The Chiltern Hundreds* was not being sustained. 'Will he train on?' was the silent cry among my friends (except for Jakie, who, needless to say, gave voice to it). 'You may be a short runner with two arrows in your quiver which, once fired and having hit the bull, are all you have to offer!' he would tell me.

Winter turned to spring, spring to summer, and the question remained unresolved. The off-form horse still went on writing in the daytime, and then dining in the evening up at the big house on an increasing number of occasions.

'Come and have a hot meal tonight,' Jakie's voice would say to Rachel on the telephone.

'We have hot meals down here,' Rachel would answer.

'Yes, I know, old bean,' Jakie would say, 'but not as hot as mine.'

So, we would go, and Mr Hopgood, Jakie's butler (bless my soul – another of those prehistoric creatures) would announce 'Mr and Mrs Home', and one could almost catch the only just held-back word 'again'. Jakie jollied us along, parading all our secret doubts and worries, and inspecting them with wit and candour, reminiscent of his mother's clinical approach to life.

'The question that we have to ask ourselves is: "Have you had it, old bean"?' he would say at dinner. 'Have we got to face the fact that all your plays are boring like your conversation? What do you think, Rachel?' Rachel would smile tolerantly, knowing that his talk concealed a deep affection for his victim, and, therefore, forgiving it.

He charged us no rent, only heating. Because of his kindness, we got through that first year without any undue struggle in the field of finance. Not much came in, but at the same time, not much went out. In military parlance we were marking time.

There came an evening when we dined with David Somerset in London.

'Father's selling Drayton,' David said, as we arrived.

'When?' Rachel and I asked in unison.

'Tomorrow.'

I picked up the telephone and rang up 'Father'.

'Bobby,' I said. 'Is it true you're selling Drayton?'

'Yes, tomorrow morning.'

'Any chance for us?'

'Come down as early as you can.'

'Right,' I said, and put the telephone down.

Next morning, we drove down to Hampshire to the house to which both Rachel and I had paid many happy visits before marriage, she being a friend of David's, I of Anne's, his sister. Bobby met us at the door and took us in to Betty, his wife. There we left the ladies, while he showed me round the garden and the out-buildings. On our way back towards the sitting-room, a great rat ran out from a yew tree up against the wall of the house. 'Ah,' said Bobby, 'our tame black bird.' Back inside, his wife turned to him. 'Bobby,' said she, 'did you show William our rat?'

They sold us that enchanting house for practically nothing,

when compared with what it would go for these days, and we owe them an eternal debt of gratitude. The friendly, homely atmosphere that they created there remains still, as we like to think, although they never came back to it, such was their affection for it.

Often, when in our sitting-room, I think of the first time that I met Bobby, having driven down from London for the week-end. He was seated on a sofa in the corner of the room, having come home that morning after an Atlantic crossing in a small boat, with some Cambridge students.

'Lovely having you here, Bobs,' said Betty from her armchair.

'Nice to be back, Bets,' said Bobby, as he tossed his lighted cigarette end casually into the corner of the room over his shoulder.

I remember that he told me he had woken up one morning on that trip to find his boat surrounded by high mountains. As the light came up, he realized that they were whales. He kept quiet and in due course, they moved away without disturbance. Lucky, perhaps, that he wasn't smoking at the time.

We moved to Drayton in the autumn of 1953. Rachel was pregnant once again, and so was I, having decided to re-start work on *The Reluctant Debutante*, although it was not called that then, the name being suggested at a later date on Ashridge Golf Course by George Bishop of the *Daily Telegraph*.

'What's the new play about?' he asked me, studying the line of his putt.

'It's about a country girl who doesn't like the London season,' I said.

'The Reluctant Debutante,' he said, half to himself, as he stooped over his ball.

At that time, the play still lacked an ending, and was lucky to have been included in the junk we brought with us from Jakie's Dower House. But, since the overdraft was rising steadily, the Bentley sold to be replaced by a Volkswagen, and another baby on the way, I took the notebooks from the cupboard where we kept our suitcases, in one of which it had been lying fallow for some months, and read the dialogue aloud to Rachel who was in bed (why, I can't recall – maybe it was quite late at night).

She laughed aloud from curtain rise right through to curtain fall (the latter very premature). I felt that heady feeling which accompanies the knowledge that one's own opinion has been vindicated. As I closed the manuscript, I thanked her for her audience reaction, and apologized for failing to have mastered the dénouement. This, as those who have seen it may remember, concerns mother, unbeknown to her, inviting the supposedly immoral young man back to dinner with her daughter, having only recently persuaded father to dislodge him from the flat by force. 'That's easy,' Rachel said. 'He'll have to change his name.'

'How can he?'

'People do. When they inherit titles, for example, don't they?'

'My God, so they do,' I answered, leaping from my chair.

A few days' work sufficed to write in Rachel's ending. From the outset, it was clear to me that it would work and work well. I typed the whole play out and sent it off to E. P. Clift, an impresario of nearly eighty with a gentle smile and quite a flair for his profession. After some days, I received a summons to a meeting. Up to London I drove. With him in his office was a thin, cadaverous man called Jack Minster – 'My new partner,' Mr Clift said, 'and a good director'.

After shaking hands all round, we sat down. Minster had not spoken yet, but Clift discussed the casting. 'I suggest Celia Johnson, for the mother,' Clift said, 'Wilfrid Hyde White for the father, or Tam Williams or – ' followed by two or three more names. From none of them did I dissent.

'And now for the director,' said Paul Clift.

I looked at Minster, wondering what manner of man he was. Then he spoke for the first time.

'Is that fly undone by mistake, or by design?' he asked me.

Hastily I looked down and adjusted the offending button, then looked up again into his smiling eyes but still unsmiling face.

'And you'll be directing it?'

'If that's all right with you,' he said. It was.

I grew to love him during my association with him until his untimely death. He had the same integrity as Colin Chandler, nothing phoney, nothing for effect, truth only, the whole truth and nothing but the truth. The job he did on *The Reluctant Debutante* was flawless, and his handling of Anna Massey, in her first part, nearly so.

He took her on approval for rehearsals with no promise of a

contract, as, indeed, he had to, since, with no professional experience, she might have lacked ability. His only error was to keep her on approval, after her ability had shown itself.

At lunch one day he said, in his sepulchral voice, to Celia, 'I don't know about Anna.'

'What don't you know, Jack?' asked Celia.

'Well, whether she can do it or not. That's why I've not given her a contract yet.'

'Perhaps if you did give her one,' said Celia, 'you might find out.'

'Yes, I suppose so,' Jack said. 'I've been thinking that.'

And so he gave her her first contract; with such good effect that, on the Brighton first night, Wilfrid said to Celia at curtain call, 'Let's get in front of that precocious girl so that the audience can't see her – she's too damned good!'

Earlier, I quoted the first few lines of the play, as I had written them in Jakie's Dower House on my sick bed. Now, in Brighton, on the first night, Celia spoke hers, as always, to perfection. Not so Wilfrid.

'What's the matter, darling?' said she, as per script, noting that he had covered his plate with his side plate. Answer came there none. One could have heard a pin drop in the theatre. The seconds ticked on. Rachel and I turned to one another, thinking that Wilfrid, perhaps, had lost his nerve.

Then suddenly his voice rang out (as only his can ring out in a restaurant, for instance, although seldom on the stage):

'Come on, boy. Come along. Give me the line, boy, give me the line!'

'My poached egg,' piped up a voice from the prompt corner. 'My poached egg,' repeated Wilfrid, with a sigh of relief.

'What's wrong with it?' Celia enquired. 'I just don't like the way it's looking at me,' Wilfrid said, with total confidence, and, from that moment, never looked back, till the curtain fell with Anna in the forefront between Celia and Wilfrid, Wilfrid having generously granted her full status as a star.

During the only interval Jack, one of nature's pessimists, leaned over our seats in the circle, listened to the hum of talk among the audience and whispered 'Honeydew!' That, coming from a man whom I had always likened in appearance to an owner leading in his Derby winner, only to hear it had been objected to, was praise indeed.

We opened at the Cambridge Theatre a few weeks later, to good notices. 'The sun was shining when Home wrote this play,' John Barber wrote in the *Express*. Not strictly true, of course – not in the bedroom at the Dower House, anyway, when I lay fighting off a temperature of ninety-nine – but, none the less, felicitous. A lady came from Hollywood. She took me out to lunch at the Savoy Grill, and then bought the rights for MGM for a substantial sum. 'What do you want them for?' I asked her, with the contract safely signed. 'A play about a debutante, for world-wide distribution?'

'But it's not about a debutante,' she said, 'or if it is, it's only superficially so. It's about a mother's concern for her daughter's happiness which is a universal theme.'

The overdraft evaporated quickly, and to add to the enchantment of that summer, on July the fourth, our eldest daughter, Sarah, was born.

Next year, with the play still running at the Cambridge Theatre, I visited America for the first time. Rachel had been there in the war, at school, her father having been a lease-lend representative in Washington.

My first impression of America lived up to all my expectations, starting with the view of New York's awe-inspiring skyline, followed by a close view of that city's awe-inspiring Customs officers, and then continuing till that same view receded in the wake of our ship two months later. In the interval, we went to Philadelphia and Boston in the wake of *The Reluctant Debutante*, with Wilfrid Hyde White starring with Adrienne Allen and her daughter, Anna Massey, who had been replaced in London, as had Wilfrid himself and Jack Merivale.

In New York, after a brisk dress rehearsal in the Henry Miller Theatre, we went with Wilfrid to a Chinese restaurant for which he had a great and inexplicable affection.

'Better ring and book a table, my dear,' he would say to Rachel, 'otherwise we won't get in.'

Invariably, when we got there, we and Wilfrid were the only guests among a crowd of Chinese waiters, but in spite of this, he went on booking in the hope, no doubt, that New York's citizen would, one day, grow to love the place as much as he did. On the night in question, Rachel got into an argument with Wilfrid on the subject of some actor's method of work (possibly his own), which raged throughout the evening. On the way home, it became increasingly apparent that our leading man was going to lose his voice. Next morning I rang up in trepidation. My worst fears were confirmed when I heard a scarcely audible croak answering.

I made a lightning assessment of the situation and decided on an instant cure. 'We're taking you to Belmont, Wilfrid – Nassua's running in his last race!' Came another croak. 'Don't argue,' I said. 'We'll come and pick you up!' We drove to Belmont Park with Wilfrid still maintaining an unusual and disturbing silence. This persisted till the great horse passed the post in front, and Wilfrid gave voice to a loud 'Hurrah, I backed the bugger!'

Sure enough, the cure had worked. We returned to the St Regis Hotel, where we introduced him to Jack Kennedy in our apartment.

'Who's this fellow?' Jack asked, as he came in.

'Wilfrid Hyde White,' Rachel said, 'our leading actor.'

'Is he up to it?' asked Jack.

Later that night, in Wilfrid's dressing-room at curtain fall, he said to me: 'I saw that tousle-headed bugger in the front row when the curtain went up, and I turned to jelly – "Is he up to it", indeed!'

He was – and when Jack came into the dressing-room a moment later, with a broad grin and sincere congratulations, he and Wilfrid were firm friends thereafter.

I recall another incident in the St Regis Hotel. Wilfrid asked to use our telephone, and rang a number. 'Ethel,' he said, 'what're you doing tomorrow for lunch?' We missed the answer but we got the gist of it, when he said, 'I don't want to know what father's doing – just what you're doing.'

What she did, in the event, was lunch with him and, later, marry him.

The play's reception in New York gave me some pleasure, but it failed to satisfy MGM. They considered that the film script should be written, not by me, but by a writer more attuned to the American taste. Thus it came about that, though my contract held a welcome clause requiring me to spend a month in Hollywood at MGM's expense, they made it very clear that they did not need my services. In spite of this, we went to Hollywood and stayed in the Bel Air Hotel, almost entirely incommunicado with the studio, at any rate until I sent in the hotel bill which, to their credit, they paid.

We played golf a great deal, taking lessons from Joe Novak at the Bel Air Country Club. We drove for one week-end to San Francisco, via Pebble Beach and Cypress Point, on both of which delightful golf courses we tested Novak's teaching. When the month was over, we returned the car that MGM had bought us, and went back to New York on the Santa Fe Express, and thence to England, well-refreshed but unemployed.

A week or two before I sold the film rights of The Deb to MGM, I rang up my accountant David Barton to tell him that, with prospects of financial well-being ahead, I wished to buy a racehorse. 'You may buy a cheap one,' he agreed. The morning after £50,000 had been contracted as the price, I rang him again. 'Not a cheap horse, David,' I said, 'an expensive one after this windfall.' 'I'm afraid not,' he replied, 'in fact no horse at all.' 'What!' I exploded. 'You'll be paying taxes on that £50,000 for years to come,' he told me, 'so a racehorse is out.'

Sure enough, when The Reluctant Debutante came off in due course, both in London and New York, a deep depression loomed on the horizon, which took seven years to dissipate.

The two occasions when the sun came out, in that unhappy period, were when I went to Paris to rewrite the script of The Reluctant Debutante, and when our second daughter, Gian, was born.

The first occasion came about as follows. I was shooting pigeons gloomily one afternoon at Hirsel, wondering how I could carry on with my profession, having lost the chance of a remunerative income due to MGM's defection. Rachel drove into the wood and told me that a cable had arrived from MGM, enquiring if I would consider writing the film script in Paris.

Casually, I fired both barrels at a passing pigeon, to no visible effect. 'I thought it was already written,' I told Rachel.

'So it is,' said she, 'but evidently Rex won't do it as it is.'

'Sound fellow,' I said, recollecting certain passages from the American script MGM had kindly sent me, to rub salt into the wound of my dismissal.

The author's Bentley, vintage 1938.

Wedding day.

Collingwood, paragon among butlers.

Wilfrid Hyde White with Rachel in New York for the opening of *The Reluctant Debutante*.

Lord and Lady Hampden with Vincente Minelli, who was in Paris directing the filming of *The Reluctant Debutante*. Sandra Dee, who played the debutante, is on the right.

'See that horse?' the debutante had told Clarissa, her co-debutante, as they stood on the sidewalk in Hyde Park, watching the Life Guards riding back to barracks. 'See that officer's horse?'

'Yes,' replied Clarissa.

'Well, that's David Bullock riding it,' said Jane. 'And if it waves its tail from side to side he's going to take me out to tea. But if it waves it up and down, it means he's on parade.'

I thought of that unhappy false-tailed horse, while unsaluted pigeons flew upwind into the fir trees in my rear, and Rachel stood there, waiting.

'How much will they pay me?' I said, with the same note in my voice as Shylock, no doubt, used when asking for his pound of flesh. She told me. 'No,' I said, amazed at the authority in my voice, almost looking round in fact to see if someone else was speaking from behind me. 'Tell them I'll only do it if they pay what they originally offered in my contract.'

With a new-found admiration in her eyes, as I thought at least, she walked back along the ride, got into the car, drove to Springhill and dispatched my ultimatum. I remained *in situ*, killing pigeon after pigeon drunk with power.

'But what,' I thought, as I drove back to tea, with the boot full of pigeons, 'if they call my bluff? Am I to settle for the lower offer, if indeed, it is repeated, or hold out and maybe lose the whole thing?'

Next day came a cable, signalling surrender, and I breathed again. But not for long, since being a non-flier, the acceptance of my ultimatum hinged on whether I could reach Paris by Sunday lunch-time – it now being Friday – since the 'shooting' started at Joinville on Monday morning.

On the Sunday night, I drove to Dover through a snowstorm, left the boat at Dunkirk in the early morning, and ran out of petrol two miles from the harbour. Cadging half a gallon from a friendly motor-cyclist, I drove on, and, with the petrol gauge approaching zero again, found an early-rising garage.

With the tank replenished, I drove, singing loudly, towards Paris, till the sight of the ignition light on red silenced my voice. With gritted teeth, I drove on, never stopping, fighting ever more despairingly to keep the engine running, since I knew that, if I let it stop, the chances were that it would never start again.

I stopped, for the first time, outside the Royal Monceau Hotel in Paris, in which Rachel and I had stayed on the first night of our honeymoon. I took my suitcase in, bathed, changed my shirt, came out again to drive to lunch with Rex, to find the car immobile. Back I went to the Hall Porter, asked him to ring up a garage and get them to tow the car away, secured a taxi and arrived to meet Rex and his wife, Kay Kendall.

Laurence Evans, their joint agent and now mine, explained the situation during the meal. The American script writer had attuned his script to Walter Pidgeon who, due to an unexpectedly prolonged engagement, had had to call off. Rex was invited to replace him, with Kay. 'OK,' said Rex, having read it, 'if the script's re-written, since the script I've read bears no relation to the play I saw in London.'

'Right,' they said, 'we'll get that done, and we'll do the picture when you've finished *My Fair Lady* in New York, and had a holiday before your London run begins.'

'See you in Paris with the new script,' Rex had said.

His holiday completed, he arrived in Paris, read the script and found it unchanged. 'Sorry, I won't do it,' said he. Hence the telegram from MGM which broke into my pigeon shoot.

When lunch was over, I returned to the Royal Monceau for a sleep, then joined a conference at the Georges Cinq where I met Pandro Berman and Vincente Minelli, the producer and director. 'We just hope that you'll work quickly,' they said, 'as we start tomorrow morning.'

'Very quickly,' I assured them, with my plans already laid.

When Monday morning came, Minelli was not on the set but in a hospital. A kidney stone had brought him low, but as the French surgeon approached him, with a view to cutting it out, he miraculously 'passed it', and was in the studio by Tuesday.

Meanwhile, I had made good use of the time granted by his illness. New scenes, typed by Pandro Berman's secretary, were handed over to him in the studio.

'Amazing,' said Minelli, as he read them, 'how you write these scenes so quickly. They're just what we're looking for.'

I held my peace, refraining from informing him that every scene was copied from my playscript which I soon began to wonder if they'd ever read.

The shooting started, and the 'rushes' looked good. All that worried me was that, apart from Rex and Kay and Peter Myers and Angela Lansbury, the actors were American, including the reluctant debutante herself, since all of them had been cast in support of Walter Pidgeon.

Still, I did my best with dialogue adjustment, which pleased everybody but Rex. He decided, as he said, one night at dinner in the Market, that 'I'd sold myself to the Americans'. This irritated me acutely, since I had had no alternative but to accommodate the actors MGM had cast already, and I told him so with some heat.

This, in turn, infuriated Kay, who told me not to speak to Rex like that. A slanging match ensued. The other diners took note, exchanged glances, then politely ignored this display of Anglo-Saxon temperament.

Next day, Rex sent an azalea to Rachel with a card which read, 'Sorry you were there when it happened.' 'So was I,' I wrote across it, and returned it – not the plant, only the card. Henceforward we were firm friends, moving in to be beside Rex and Kay in the Lancaster Hotel.

Kay was enchanting, with a merry and outspoken attitude to life. The first time Rachel met her was when we went to have a drink one evening in Rex's apartment. Rex was in the sitting-room, and he remarked that Kay was bathing and would join us shortly. Then the telephone rang. Rex, uncorking champagne, let it do so. From the bathroom came Kay, in her birthday costume, waved a hand of greeting at us, and picked up the telephone.

The caller was Sir Gladwyn Jebb, then our Ambassador in Paris. We could hear his voice quite clearly at the other end of the line.

'Would you and your husband come to dinner at the Embassy next Saturday?' he said. 'How nice of you, Sir Gladwyn,' Kay replied, 'but we both work so hard at the film that we don't go out much.'

'Not on Saturday, I understand.'

'No, that's true.'

'Well then, after a good day's rest, surely you'll both feel like a nice dinner.'

'Well, Sir Gladwyn,' Kay said meaningfully, 'the truth is that Rex and I are both so tired by Saturday night, all we want to do is dip our fingers into a gin bottle, if you know what I mean?'

'I see,' said Sir Gladwyn, diplomatically.

Our hostess then replaced the telephone receiver and went back into the bathroom, waving to us once again, *en passant*, and rejoined us later, fully dressed on this occasion, but no less attractive than she had been in the nude.

Rex knew, of course, at this stage (as Rachel and I did not, nor she herself) that Kay had only a short time to live. One can have nothing but the deepest admiration for the courage he displayed in this most tragic situation, later to be dramatized, although disguised somewhat, by Terry Rattigan in a play in which Rex himself performed in New York with distinction.

When the film was finished, we returned to Hampshire, living on the proceeds for a while, until the taxman wrote in once again, to claim his pound of flesh. Soon, I was back where I had been when Rachel brought the message to the pigeon wood from MGM – no plays in prospect, no films, nothing but a third child, Gian, to mark down on the credit side.

This situation was not due to work-shyness, nor any lack of output on my part. The plays still rolled down the conveyor belt on to the desks of West End managers, who promptly sent them back whence they had come.

Rejection letters varied in their content, depending on how well I knew the manager in question, but the basic message was, 'Not in this day and age, old fellow – sorry, but time's passed you by, and you are out of fashion, full stop.'

One was more specific. Binkie Beaumont sent back the manuscript of a play called *The Secretary Bird*, with a *cri de coeur* as honest as it was disquieting to the recipient. 'I daren't do it with the butchers in their present mood,' he wrote. I have the letter still.

# Chapter 9
# Aunt Edwina

Here, let it be explained that what had prompted those responsible for buttering my bread to write such letters was the New Wave. This had surged up on the beach a year or two before, submerging writers like myself beneath the rollers.

No one wanted us, or, if they did, they paid the penalty. The arbiters of taste decreed that the renaissance had at last come – drawing-room comedies were washed away like any other old hat left below high water mark. In consequence, the pedlars of fashionable comedy ran, panic-stricken, for the shelter of the sandhills and buried their hatless heads. A few, foolhardy like myself, attempted, like Canute, to stem the tide. The rest, more sensibly, bowed to the storm and battened down their notebooks and their pencils, in the hope that one fine day the tide would turn and they would find themselves in fashion once again.

Meanwhile, I fought on in the knowledge that bank managers, like wolves, were snapping at my ragged heels while, in the distance, I could hear the howling of the Inland Revenue as they, too, moved in for the kill. To save myself, I wrote a play called *Aunt Edwina*, which turned out to be the worst thing that I could have done.

The plot concerned an ex-Guards Colonel MFH who went off to America on holiday, with, allegedly, his wife, leaving the hounds to be hunted by his son and the Hunt Secretary. When he came back, some three weeks later, he had turned into a woman.

Written in Gstaad, in two weeks, in my bedroom in the Station Hotel while the family were ski-ing, I was more than satisfied when I came to the final curtain. 'How can any play,' I thought as I sat reading through the manuscript, 'with such a "with it" theme and so unquestionably funny, possibly be unsuccessful?' I was soon to find out. When we took the Basle Express for Calais there lay in my suitcase not, as I imagined, future fame and fortune but a load of trouble. My eccentric Aunt was coming home to roost.

It must not be supposed that when I settled for the sex-change theme I was indifferent to the tragic implications of such abnormalities in real life, any more than any author of a murder comedy is unaware that, in real life, such subjects are, inevitably, tragic. In the theatre, however, with life in suspense, a playwright may legitimately deal with any subject tragically or comically, according to his whim. My whim in *Aunt Edwina* was to write a comedy and not a tragedy. Consider the position. A Guards Colonel in a sex-change, tragic? Possibly. A DSO? Perhaps. An MFH? I wonder. But a combination of the three? Impossible!

Back home, I took her out and polished her and posted off two copies – one to Minster and the other to Hyde White. The former, though perhaps a trifle overwhelmed by her ebullience and shamelessness, stood up to her. The latter turned her down. 'It can't be done, m'boy, you'll never get away with it,' he cried.

'With you I would,' I told him.

'Couldn't do it, dear boy. Think of me in that first entrance.'

'I have,' I replied.

Then, Minster sent the play to Robert Coote at Drury Lane, who was about to leave the role of Colonel Pickering in *My Fair Lady*. He not only turned *Aunt Edwina* down but criticized her violently. Words like 'disgusting' laced his letter of rejection. Shaken although still undaunted, I then gave the play to Roland Culver. 'Just the part for you,' I told him. 'It's about a Colonel, with a little trouble on his hands.' I left it with him for a week, and then went back to dine with him. He told me, while our wives were upstairs tidying, that, not only would he not do the part, but that he hoped that no one ever would. I left him with the feeling that he thought I had insulted him by asking him to take the role at all.

By now Jack Minster was discouraged, so I gave the play to Paul Clift, now installed in offices in the Strand Theatre and under his own management. A few days later, he invited me to luncheon at the Garrick, and informed me, with a twinkle in his eye, that he would do the play. I took my hat off to him metaphorically. Here was a seventy-eight-year-old Edwardian, not one whit shocked by my dear Aunt, but ready, in the true tradition of that robust period, to have a go. Yet one more proof, I thought, of how old age is sometimes more progressive, less inhibited; more gay, less doctrinaire; more humorous, less prim, than middle age, or even youth.

We called in Wallace Douglas to direct it. He, like Clift, found nothing in the least distasteful in the play. Nor did Miss Wiman, the American who had presented *The Reluctant Debutante*. The backing was secure. The management was active. The director was engaged. The stage was almost set. We sent the play to Henry Kendall. He agreed to play the lead.

Rehearsals started during August. Two days up in Scotland was the only holiday I got that summer, and then on a Monday evening in September, in the Devonshire Park Theatre in Eastbourne, we sat waiting for the curtain to rise for the first time on my *Aunt Edwina*. Rachel and I had assessed our prospects very thoroughly. We knew that, in the people who had met her privately, *Aunt Edwina* induced varying reactions. Here, for the first time, she was about to make her entry at a public gathering. The question was, would they accept the lady, and the answer, as we saw it, was a fifty-fifty chance.

The curtain rose. The scene between the children, having after-hunting tea, went well, but that meant nothing. No one knew the plot yet. Then, when Margaretta Scott came on, as Colonel Ryan's wife, the dialogue first touched the theme. We held our breath. The scene progressed until the point where mother was attempting to inform the children of their father's strange experience while on his holiday. 'I don't know how to tell you,' she was saying, while, the son, in his embarrassment, had wandered to the window. 'Mummy,' he cried, 'there's a woman by the goldfish pond.' 'I know,' said Peggy Scott, and then she paused for a split second. Here, or so I told myself, is *Aunt Edwina*'s moment of truth. On the reaction of this audience, composed of all types and all ages, hangs her fate.

The fateful words dropped one by one from Peggy's lips: 'Yes, I know dear,' said Peggy, 'that's what I'm trying to tell you: that's your father.' After a suspended silence, such as precedes an explosion, came a roar of laughter.

As the scene progressed, while Peggy tried to get the children to approach the subject of their father's change less selfishly, the laughs continued, thick and fast. When Harry entered, with his handbag, in his dreadful brogues, the clapping and the laughter echoed and re-echoed through the theatre like thunder. Then, when Peggy had rebuked the son for being less than civil to his father, and he had delivered the line, 'Smashing hat, Dad', pandemonium broke out again. Harry not only had the time to walk from centre to stage right to pick his letters off the desk, he also found time to peruse a few of them before he could continue with the dialogue.

The moment of truth was past. My *Aunt Edwina* had been taken to the public's heart; her future was assured. These comforting thoughts raced through my excited brain as Rachel and I watched the play 'gang merrily on' to its end. The curtain fell, then rose again with gratifying regularity. The audience filed out. The actors in their dressing-rooms allowed themselves a certain measure of elation. Wally Douglas seemed elated, too, and Mr Clift looked more benign than ever. The local paper, when it came out, gave the play a favourable notice, and we played throughout that first week to capacity, less something in the nature of £10.

The next week, down in Bristol, the reviews of *Aunt Edwina* cheered us further. That theatrical town's leading critic went so far as to predict that henceforward *Charlie's Aunt* would find herself upon the shelf. 'The play was very funny,' so he wrote, 'the treatment was extremely tactful and the taste impeccable.'

Next week I went to Edinburgh to fight the General Election. *Aunt Edwina* followed me. I left my meeting early on the Monday night of her arrival. Hurriedly we drove to the Lyceum, and surveyed the last scene from the back. I thought the play went well. My brother Henry criticized me mildly for selecting the Guards as the regiment in which my Aunt had served. 'Why not the RASC?' he suggested.

In the hotel that night our thoughts were theatrical, and not political. 'How would our dear Aunt go down with the public here?' we asked ourselves. 'Would they be as enthusiastic as in Eastbourne? Would the critics eulogize her as they had in Bristol?' From the Press next morning we soon learned the answer to the final question. Broadly speaking 'No'. I qualify the 'No' because the *Glasgow Herald* critic liked it, but the *Scotsman* didn't, and some of his colleagues in the evening papers claimed to find the play in questionable taste.

This was the first whine of the rising gale. Perturbed, I asked the critic of the *Scotsman*, Ronald Mavor, a son of James Bridie, out to lunch, and cross-examined him. I found him, as I had expected, to be one of the new school of critics; none the worse for that, perhaps, but chronically allergic to light comedy or farce, especially applied to such a theme as this, with all its tragic possibilities. I did not feel that his condemnation of my *Aunt Edwina* would affect her coming debut in the West End, yet I was disquieted. After all, the fellow was intelligent, and although much too serious, sincere. Could it be that there was some hidden failing in my Aunt, which I, perhaps too close to her, might have overlooked? To set my mind at rest I asked the box office to send two tickets to Compton Mackenzie. Should he come, I told myself, I will get a second opinion well worth having. He came on Thursday afternoon. In trepidation I awaited his emergence at the end of the performance. From his face I knew at once that he was on my side. He found no fault with *Aunt Edwina*. Further than that, when I took him round to meet the cast, he told them unequivocally that he was very happy to have seen a good cast in a good play.

Ronald Mavor's view of *Aunt Edwina* also had supporters. Dancing round with Laura Grimond at the Liberal Ball that year, she looked at me and said, 'William, next time you stand for Parliament in Edinburgh, please see that any play you have on during the election is more edifying than your *Aunt Edwina*.' What prompted this remark, no doubt, was the fact that my General Election vote, with *Aunt Edwina* at my elbow, had dropped by two thousand from my bye-election vote when she had not been present.

After Edinburgh we went to Dublin. I went over on the ferry with a sword for Henry Kendall, lent me by a great friend, Billy Straker Smith, late of the Coldstream Guards, complete with ceremonial ribbons and sash. 'Is it for ceremonial, or normal wear?' Billy had asked me. 'It's for a Guards Colonel, in an evening gown,' I told him. 'Ah,' he nodded, with true Brigade impassivity, 'then ceremonial it is.' The Customs man in Dublin asked me what the sword was for. 'An actor,' I replied. 'Oh, well,' said he, 'I hope that he won't do himself an injury.'

'*Aunt Edwina* succeeds with farce formula,' headlined the *Irish Times*. Then, as in Bristol, their reviewer went on to compare the play to *Charlie's Aunt*. 'No dramatist since Brandon Thomas,' he wrote, 'has ever come so near the pay-lode with a farce of sex changes.'

Only when I reached the Fortune Theatre in London did I start to get cold feet when watching *Aunt Edwina* at the dress rehearsal. As I sat there, in the tiny circle, seeing her at what appeared to be the range of a few feet, I found her overwhelming. I gained comfort by convincing myself that with a full theatre this feeling of undue proximity would disappear. In fact, it never did.

One night at the beginning of November, *Aunt Edwina* stepped on to the boards, for the first time, before a London audience. Somewhere in the first scene, my father-in-law laughed, and for his pains got labelled the next morning by one critic as a bovine hunting type. (In fact, he was a riding-boot-less banker.) There were scattered laughs from other quarters, but in general *Aunt Edwina* failed to roll them in the aisles. Here was no second Eastbourne, no repeat of Dublin. 'Why?' I asked myself. One possible solution could have been that out of something like two hundred stalls no less than forty pairs were occupied by critics and their friends.

As *Aunt Edwina* strode that midget stage, and swung her corsage to and fro, almost above their heads, it was her final taste of freedom. By the time the morning papers came out, she was on the rack, and ultimately she was broken. Not, however, till her author was broke, too.

I don't know what it was that made me fight the critics over *Aunt Edwina*. Never, perhaps, did a lone crusader spur into a battle with a less suitable weapon, but the fact remains that *Aunt Edwina* was the only weapon that I had to hand. In any case, whatever the incentive, with a thundering of hooves, with Aunt Edwina's name emblazoned on my standard, with 'For art and freedom' as my war cry, I, the captain of a one-man army, plunged into the fray.

The battle started with a barrage from the critics. Almost every paper in the London area was outraged. 'Sick, sick, sick, sick,' was one headline. 'Bad taste,' was the slogan of the others. This, of course, made me see red. Had I not some weeks earlier turned down an offer to write the *Lolita* film script at a salary of £20,000 because I thought the film might do harm to the young? 'Just how many,' I thought, 'of those who now accuse me of bad taste would let that prospect stand between themselves and £20,000?' One editor called up to ask how I reacted to all this adverse criticism. I answered that I didn't write plays for the critics: there were not enough of them to make it worth my while.

By Saturday, the management had lost its nerve, and Mr Clift rang up to say that he was putting up the notice. This meant that the last performance of *Aunt Edwina* would take place that night. I hurried up to London. When the matinee was over, I went on stage and announced that *Aunt Edwina* was to be withdrawn that night. Encouraged by some cries of 'Shame' I asked the audience point blank to give their verdict 'for' or 'against' *Aunt Edwina* by a show of hands. The voting in her favour was, so far as I could estimate, unanimous.

I hurried from the stage and called up Equity, without whose blessing changes in the management cannot be made, and hastily arranged that I myself should replace Mr Clift. So far as I recall it was agreed that I should cover all expenses such as artists' salaries, while Anna Wiman, Mr Clift's co-manager, and lessee of the Fortune Theatre, should pay the theatre expenses which, in any case, were her responsibility. Thus I was able, when the final curtain fell that night, to go on stage and tell the audience that *Aunt Edwina* was alive and kicking, and would run. The cheers were heartening.

Encouraged by this, I dispatched telegrams to all the London critics, asking them to join me on the stage, and, from this vantage point, debate our different views about the play, then put it to the vote. I planned to read aloud each critic's review to the audience, and ask him, if he so desired, to amplify what he had written. How instructive such a session would have been. The audience, for once, having just seen the play, unlike a critic's normal readers, would have been enabled to assess exactly how correct or otherwise each individual's review had been. The critics would have found their verdicts criticized in open court by those who knew the facts as well as they did, and the playwright would have felt that he was being fairly treated.

This salutary experience was destined never to take place. No single critic would accept my invitation. Each preferred the safety of his normal role. And can one blame them after all? Yet I felt that I had gained a bit of ground when my opponents failed to respond to my challenge to debate the issue. Nightly I strode on stage, and informed the audience about the progress of the struggle. Sometimes I selected some review: read extracts from it; laid into the writer; made rude jokes about him; jeered at him for not making himself available to answer back; then, always put the matter to the vote and always won.

One evening a dramatic critic came from Dublin to investigate what had gone wrong with *Aunt Edwina* since she crossed the Irish Sea. He had been most impressed by her in Dublin and the furore that attended her debut in England had intrigued him so much that he flew across to take a second look at her.

That night in my speech, I informed the audience that he was somewhere in the stalls. They gave him an enthusiastic round of applause. Then once again I put the matter to the vote – the Irish critic as against the London critics' view. The Irish critic won hands down, and wrote an article about this most unusual evening in a critic's life when he returned home

Box Office returns were rising slightly. Naturally, the Press attributed this fact to my speeches: 'Audiences think Mr Home's remarks at curtain fall much better than his play,' and so on and so forth. Not all the Press spoke in this vein. The *Daily Mail* permitted me to write an article describing *Aunt Edwina*'s career up to date.

Throughout all this the cast had been behind me to a man and woman. Actors as a breed, are not inclined to favour demonstrations against critics. Being peaceful, philosophic folk they take the view that it is better to be uncommitted than to run the risk of being victimized. This cast, however, gave me every backing. Only Cyril Raymond took me aside one night and expressed his doubts about the wisdom of my actions. 'After all,' he said, 'if every actor made a speech after a bad press. . .' Yet in spite of being morally opposed to my intransigence, he compromised by slipping off the stage each night before I came on. Thus he registered his disapproval and at the same time remained a loyal member of the cast until we left the Fortune.

Meanwhile, trouble hit me from another quarter when Miss Wiman, growing tired of *Aunt Edwina*'s caperings and longing for a quiet life, started toying with the idea of replacing her with something cheaper and less controversial. To restrain this tendency I went to see her and announced that I would shoulder the expense of running *Aunt Edwina*, not only the running costs but theatre expenses too, if she would let me stay on in the theatre. To this she readily agreed.

Elated by this new arrangement, I began to plan the nursing of my *Aunt Edwina* through a prolonged period. I worked out just how much, at present takings, she was going to cost each week and how long, if she stayed at this low level, I could carry on. I came to the conclusion that, with my father-in-law's help, I should just be able to continue at the Fortune till her convalescence ended and she settled down to a long life.

That night I went on stage and told the audience that *Aunt Edwina* would be staying at the Fortune Theatre indefinitely, and that if they and their friends continued to support her, she might settle down into a long and healthy run. Again the cheers encouraged me. Then, I received a letter from one of Miss Wiman's partners, telling me the notice was to go up next Saturday – the letter came on Thursday. I protested on the telephone against this ultimatum, pointing out that Anna Wiman had agreed to let the play run on at my expense. The writer of the letter remained adamant. Miss Wiman had reversed her previous decision and the play must close on Saturday.

I called up Michael Rubinstein. He, in his turn, called up a lawyer friend of mine, Robin McEwen. Both decided to seek an injunction from a Judge in Chambers, to restrain Miss Wiman from closing on Saturday. On Friday morning, thirty-six hours before *Aunt Edwina*'s death sentence was due to be pinned on the Fortune's Stage Door notice board, we stood in front of Mr Justice Salmon seeking a reprieve. I watched this neat, imposing figure listening to Anna Wiman's lawyer and Robin McEwen as they laid the facts before him. After a few comments, which included an enquiry as to my financial resilience, he granted an injunction on the understanding that I would produce the necessary sum to cover losses during the next week. *Aunt Edwina* was reprieved again. The Press, of course, reported this with relish. After all, how often had a Judge been called upon to intervene in such a matter? Would this second reprieve help the poor old lady to survive these constantly recurring crises? Would the takings rise in the ensuing week? And would the Judge continue the injunction when we met again?

Next week we stood outside his Chambers once again. The opposition, I suspect, had thought we wouldn't face it. Now, with half an hour to go, the lawyers started on a conference. With five minutes to go the terms of an agreement were approved. With one minute to go both parties reached a compromise. We went before the Judge and Robin told him that both sides had reached agreement. He expressed his satisfaction, then smiled. 'How is *Aunt Edwina*?' he asked Robin. 'She'll be all the better for seeing you, my Lord,' said Robin.

We watched the Box Office returns with added interest. Could we each week reach the figure that had been agreed upon? Would audiences, having heard *ad nauseam* about my *Aunt Edwina*'s illness, come round to the view that she might give them a good laugh? I kept a watch on booking agencies. I called up sometimes, posing as an entertainment officer for some fictitious factory and asked about seats for the Fortune. Peggy Scott did the same. Sometimes they told us that the play was coming off. At other times they told us that the house had sold out. The latter, of course, was far from accurate, the former questionable.

That week, we failed to reach the figure that our compromise agreement called for. *Aunt Edwina* was to leave the Fortune Theatre at last. Two days before our demise, Baxter Somerville called from the Lyric, Hammersmith, and offered me a home.

'How long for?' I enquired, with palpitating heart.

'A month and then a week at Brighton.'

'What about the money?'

'The same as the Fortune, broadly speaking.'

'I'll let you know as soon as possible.'

Up to London I sped. Could I raise the money for the transfer? Could I replace Cyril Raymond, who was leaving, thankfully, to take a new part. At the matinee on the last Saturday, I started up my speech-making again. I told the audience that £1500 was needed to ensure my *Aunt Edwina*'s transfer to the Lyric, Hammersmith, where she would stay till she came back to the West End. They cheered again. From one of that small audience I got that very sum. I got, too, Geoffrey Lumsden, an old friend, to replace Cyril Raymond. That night I informed the audience about the old girl's last reprieve. Again they cheered her to the echo. Poor old *Aunt Edwina*, bruised and battered, saddled with an evil reputation from the start of her career, loved by the few, hated by some, and unknown to the many save as a dishonoured name, was heading down to Hammersmith, and then to Brighton for a week.

Unfortunately nerves were much on edge among those nearest to her. When rehearsals started at the Lyric Theatre on Monday, we were told that Anna Wiman's lawyer had forbidden us to use the set and furniture, although we offered £50 a week in rent, unless I agreed never to invoke the law about my *Aunt* again. This I refused to do. The Lyric staff began to work, encouraged by my admirable stage director, Brian Shiner, Ronald Shiner's cheerful, charming and incredibly efficient and hard-working son. They made a set. They hired some furniture. The costumes, in most cases, were provided by the cast and their friends. This last item led to the director walking out. A note in the new programme, thanking many people who had lent equipment – this included Rachel's fur coat – upset Wallace Douglas, for some reason, and he left us. Harry Kendall carried on.

On the first night the curtain rose and, in this larger theatre, and this time at a safer distance from my formidable aunt, the critics found her less disturbing. In my curtain speech I hoped the past had been forgotten. Next day, the majority of critics, although sticking to their view of *Aunt Edwina*, did record the fact that audience reaction was entirely in her favour. Yet the takings each night were unsatisfactory. The faithful came – the curious too – but as a whole the public stayed away. Perhaps this was because the subject shocked them, or, more likely I suspect, it was because they had been told the subject shocked them. Anyway, no miracle took place. Instead, another crisis intervened, when Harry Kendall, who had been asked to direct a new play, was forbidden by his contract to continue acting at the same time. This meant that our closing date in Brighton could not be fulfilled unless we got another actor to replace him. Baxter Somerville, who had employed me in the pre-war years, suggested I should do the part.

My nerves were strained as I sat in my dressing-gown at Brighton, being made up by an admirable make-up artist under Rachel's supervision. As I dressed for that first night there hung, around the walls, my props – most notably – the evening gown which Rachel had bought at Dickens and Jones. In spite of first-night nerves the recollection of that purchase made me smile, as I sat waiting for the call-boy to announce the half hour. We had gone together to the shop.

'I'm looking for a large sized evening gown,' said Rachel to the sales woman, who looked at her in some surprise. She chose one.

'Better try it on,' she said to me.

'Of course,' I said.

'This way,' the shop assistant said.

Once in the cubicle, I took my coat and trousers off. The shop assistant, bearing the selected gown, came in to find me standing there in shirt and pants and socks and shoes, smoking my pipe.

'This gown is for my husband,' Rachel said to the bewildered lady. Then, in order to banish the thought that might be lurking in her mind that I was a transvestite, added, 'For a play, you know.'

'Ah,' said the sales person, relieved. 'He is an actor, then.'

'That's right,' I told her, fixing her with a stern, masculine look. 'Will it fit me?'

'We'll soon find out,' she said, advancing on me with a pin-filled mouth, at times obscured by the smoke from my pipe.

My nerves returned at curtain-rise. I tottered to the wings, on high-heeled shoes and waited for my cue, only to hear a stage hand whisper to his colleague, 'She's the prettiest girl in the f—g cast.'

I went on, filled with new-found confidence. The first night went extremely well and all the week we played to happy houses. Brighton had at last revived what Eastbourne had begun. Even the money rolled in. In that week we took as much as we had taken at the Fortune in a whole month. Letters came in. One, I treasure, from an old age pensioner.

Dear Mr Home,

I cannot begin to tell you how very much we enjoyed your *Aunt Edwina*. We found it one long laugh. We cannot understand at all why it was a flop in London, but I should think that after Brighton it will go back to London and be a great success. We wish you all the luck in the world, you deserve it so richly. We have even been twice to see it. Would it be too much to ask you for a signed photo of yourself. We would like one in remembrance of two happy days with *Aunt Edwina*, and may God prosper you and your wonderful play.

She also enclosed a ten shilling note to help *Aunt Edwina* return to London. When I wrote and told her I could not accept it she wrote back:

Rex Harrison opening the church fête at East Meon.

The author as Aunt Edwina

Henry Douglas Home bird watching.

Rachel with, from left
to right, Gian, Dinah
and Sarah.

With brother Alec on
a picnic.

Darling *Aunt Edwina*, please do not ever consider returning that tiny mite as you suggest in your note today. Whether anything happens to darling *Edwina*, or not, you must keep it and get some baccy. You will offend me if you return it. Yours – all for your success.

When the curtain fell on the last night, and in the bar beside the stage we said goodbye to that supremely faithful cast – the indefatigable Peggy Scott and all the rest of them – I felt the magic of the theatre more strongly than I ever had before. There we all were, together, after five or six months' battle against hopeless odds, in total rout, our theories concerning the potential popularity of *Aunt Edwina* all disproved, or anyway non-proven – six months wasted, fighting in a hopeless cause, defeated, spat at, unemployed and in my own case anyway, insolvent, and yet happy. As we left the theatre and drove home across country on that Sunday night, Rachel and I, run down as we were after the long, punishing campaign, both somehow felt that it had all been well worthwhile.

And so it proved. As I had always thought, my *Aunt Edwina* turned out to be indestructible. Years later, a press-cutting told she had been performed successfully by amateurs in the West Country – the employees of a highly reputable bank.

'She's on her way back,' I thought, as I read it. Sure enough, my telephone rang one day last year, or the year before.

'Would that be Mr Home?' a voice asked.

'Yes.'

'I'm the Head Mistress of North Foreland Lodge,' the voice went on. 'The girls are doing one of your plays next month.'

'Ah yes,' I said, thinking it would be *The Deb* or *Lloyd George Knew My Father*, 'which one?'

'*Aunt Edwina.*'

I could not accept the invitation to attend, being away in Scotland, but it went well, my informants told me. With new-found respectability, perhaps, my *Aunt* will come into her own – more amateur productions, followed, in due course, by repertory productions, followed, who knows, one fine day, by a revival in the West End, thus allowing her to take her rightful place beside her, so far, more successful, much less persecuted predecessor, *Charlie's Aunt*. Dear *Aunt Edwina* – your good health.

H.P.H.—I

## Chapter 10
# Rome, Rewriting and Rhythm

Exactly a week after *Aunt Edwina* closed in Brighton we were on our way across France in the Rome Express, but not on holiday. Although we needed one, perhaps more than at any other time in our lives, the financial situation did not warrant such escapism. I had been summoned to a conference with Dino de Laurentis on the subject of a film he was about to make. The conference concluded, we returned home. I sat down and wrote a full-length treatment, sent it off to Rome, then waited the great man's verdict which, in the event, was favourable. This was followed swiftly by the contract, much to my relief.

Since the *Reluctant Debutante*, this was my first assignment to a picture outside England. Looking back on it, it seems I was selected because I had written the script of *The Colditz Story* some years earlier with Ivan Foxwell and Guy Hamilton. I had, too, done a minor stint for de Laurentis in a film adapted from the German, my task being to add colour to Charles Laughton's dialogue in the role of a British admiral. Dino and Laughton evidently had been pleased by the result.

Guy Hamilton had charge of this film, which was called *The Best of Enemies*. The stars were David Niven and Alberto Sordi, and the theme the war with Abyssinia in Mussolini's day. I took this seriously while both Dino de Laurentis and Guy seemed to find it funny. This caused friction from the start.

However, it was not the script which was the trouble in the early stages. The main problem when I arrived in Rome, was the location. No one seemed to have the least idea which country would accommodate the film unit. 'I'm off to Spain tomorrow,' Guy would say to me at dinner. 'Won't be back for three days.'

Then, when he came back, with de Laurentis that much poorer, having paid for two or three air liners (just as he was paying for our dinner) he would say again, at the conclusion of the meal, 'Won't see you for three days.' 'What country this time, Guy?' I would enquire, and he would say 'Bulgaria', or 'Portugal' or 'Libya', according to the latest command from on high.

None of these countries would do and one evening, after an inspiring Strega, I heard myself saying, 'Guy, it's just occurred to me – why don't you go and have a look at Abyssinia?'

'Good idea,' said Guy. 'After all, the film is set there.'

'Right,' I told him. 'That's what made me think of it.'

So, off to Abyssinia he went, the same old aeroplanes, the same old camera crews, that's to say the same old circus, followed by the same old dent in Mr de Laurentis' bank balance.

'Well,' said I, the night he came back, as we dined, 'how was it?'

'No good,' said he.

'No good? But why not?'

'Because it doesn't look like Abyssinia.'

They finished up in Israel, but I was out of it before that, having just been sacked and then replaced by Nigel Balchin, only to be called back later, much to Guy's amusement.

'Don't think that I asked for you back,' said he. 'You're too damned obstinate.'

'I never thought that for a moment,' said I.

'Then why come?'

'Because I like my dinners with you. And I'm not averse to Dino's money. Nor have I abandoned hope that he may do the script I've written rather than the near farce you both seem to favour.'

'Niven's doing it, and Sordi, don't forget,' said Guy.

'I don't forget that.'

'You forget they're comedians.'

'No, I don't,' I said. 'Clowns are just the ticket for a tragedy.'

And so the battle raged – until they sacked me for the second time, with no hard feelings, and the warning that they might require my services again one day, which indeed happened some years later, though it never came to anything.

One reason why the battle raged for so long was that Dino de Laurentis had a deep attachment to script conferences. Every Sunday he would summon his '*Autori*' (there were one or two Italians to deal with Sordi) and discuss the coming week's work.

'Listen,' he would say. 'All this week, you will write this scene and that and then the other.'

'Yes, sir,' I would say.

'And when will you deliver all this?'

'Sunday.'

'Good.'

Come Monday morning, I would take my notebook and my pencil, and start work. Ten minutes later, Rachel would come in and say, 'The studio's just rung to say that there's a conference this morning.'

Notebook closed, pencil in pocket, I would drive to Rome, arriving at the studio, or Dino's villa in the Via Appia. If at the former, Dino would turn up in a magnificent Mercedes, highly polished, and leap out while someone with a hose began to wash the car down on the instant, almost spraying his dynamic master with cold water as he hurried to his office.

Minutes later, having heard the cry '*Autori*' ringing through the corridors, my colleagues and I would proceed towards his office and sit down, across the desk from a now sheeted figure, being shaved by a Rome barber.

If the venue was the villa, Dino would be seated on the lawn surrounded by '*Autori*' and Guy.

We would then be treated to a résumé of all the ideas that had come to Dino in the watches of the night, and now, in their turn, came to us to be transferred into our notebooks.

Briefing done, I would drive back to Anzio in time for a short swim before lunch, and, thereafter, a siesta, after which I would begin on my revised week's work. But seldom did an hour go by before one of the children, dispatched by its mother, burst into the room announcing, 'Mummy says that Dino de Laurentis wants you for a conference at five.'

'Where?' I would ask this sun-tanned envoy, shutting up my notebook, 'Studio or villa?'

'Villa,' it would say, as it skipped down the stairs again towards the cooling ocean.

Back along the Appia Antica I would drive, to join the group beneath the cypress tree on Dino's lawn, already chewing over the ideas that had come to him during his siesta.

Same again the next day, early in the morning maybe – and again at sundown – likewise for the rest of the week – conference on conference – idea upon idea – kilometre after kilometre.

Switch the scene to the next Sunday conference; *Autori* ranged before their master, empty, or near-empty notebooks on knees. 'William,' says Dino, 'the work I give to you last Sunday to do. It is done?'

'No, Dino,' I would answer.

'And why not?'

'Because we've had too many conferences. Two a day, since Monday, or more. I've been taking notes and driving all the week, and I can't write and drive at the same time.'

'You are the obstinate *autore*,' he would say. 'Next week let it be different.'

But it wasn't and he fired me ultimately, not because I didn't do the work (which I did manage to get done, though under great stress) but because the script I wrote had tragic overtones (befitting, as I thought, a tragic war) little resembling the soufflé that both Dino and Guy wanted to produce and, needless to say, did. I have my script still, and I like it. Whether in the finished product anything remained of my brain-child I cannot tell, because I never went to see *The Best of Enemies*. One day, perhaps, I'll go and try to spot a line or two from my script (as opposed to Nigel Balchin's or whatever other *autori* Dino called in before the film was in the can).

No wonder, while engaged in trying to jump through whatever literary hoops Dino instructed me to jump through, I began to seek another outlet, less frustrating, more constructive and, above all, more creative. This I found as a result of meeting Robert Morley in a bar in the Via Veneto. As we savoured our Americanos, the talk turned to Wilfrid Hyde White, who was Robert's greatest friend at that time. I told Robert that I had an idea in my head, concerning two old diplomats with their pasts coming back on them. The play would be set in Rome; the two leading parts, Sir John Holt and Sir Lionel Hibury – the former, British Minister to the Vatican; the latter, visiting Head of the Foreign Office.

'Which will be the best part?' Robert asked at once.

'They'll both be equal,' I informed him.

'Oh,' he said with disappointment in his voice.

Then, I outlined the plot. It sounded good to me and all the better as I visualized him playing each scene with his crony.

'Have you written it?' asked Robert.

'No, not yet,' I told him, 'but I'm going to start tomorrow morning.'

'Good,' he said, 'I'd like to read it when you've finished,' which I took to mean I had him in the bag already. When the play – *A Friend Indeed* – was finished, Robert would not do it. Neither would his old friend, Wilfrid – not unless his old friend, Robert, would.

'I think that this is it,' wrote Robin Fox, Robert's attractive agent, whose sad death a few years back brought so much sorrow to a host of friends.

But it was not. Wilfrid and Robert brought up every argument in the book against doing it. 'If you let me re-write it, maybe I'll do it,' Robert used to say.

'Not on your life!'

'Well, let me make some notes.'

'If you must,' I would say. And so he did, but they lacked all appeal for me.

He even took me out to lunch with Wilfrid at Bucks Club to talk it over. We sat at a little table flanked by other tables at which sat young, well-behaved Guards Officers. Wilfrid, as I remember, started talking as we sat down in a very loud voice. This embarrassed Robert – after all, Bucks was his father-in-law's club and it was surely up to him to see that the proprieties were observed. 'Lower your voice,' Robert hissed at Wilfrid, as he bellowed on. 'This is a gentlemen's club.'

Wilfrid paused in thought a moment, then said, 'Is it? Nothing written up to say so anywhere.'

As I left Bucks that afternoon, I knew that I had missed a golden opportunity. As I drove home, I tried to pin-point where things had gone wrong. Perhaps, I had been unwise to tell Robert that the parts were equal. Should I not have said his was the best and, then, on my return to England, told Wilfrid the same regarding his?

Misfortunes in the theatre fall off one, normally, as easily as leaves fall off the shoulders of a macintosh in autumn. But the memory of this misfortune lingers still. The play went on, of course, but not with either of the stars I wrote it for. Yet still, I live in hope, since actors, in my view – a view that I have held with strong conviction since my eighty-year-old hero, Matty, acted for me in the *Chiltern Hundreds* – come late to maturity.

It is not my intention to recount a chronicle of plays, a blow by blow account of all my failures and successes. That would be as tedious for me to write as for the reader to read. *A Friend Indeed*, however, was a prime example of 'the one that got away' and, as such, worthy of inclusion.

Most plays I have written have been acted by the actor and/or actress that I wanted. My relationship with that branch of the profession, in consequence, has almost always been unruffled. Not so, always, with the other branches. Naturally, the situation varies with each play. In some, the rapport between all concerned is idyllic, but this is the exception rather than the rule. In most productions, there is friction; sometimes due to management (mis-management?); at other times due to the character (or lack of character?) of the director; much less often due to bloody-mindedness among the cast and, on occasion, let it be admitted, the shortcomings of the playwright – not so much his obstinacy, as, strangely enough, his lack of it.

Let me explain this if I can, by saying that, in my opinion anyway, the playwright has a sacred trust. He it is who, starting from nothing – that's to say, without assistance, without training, without any in-bred form on which to base his prospects and his hopes - becomes a playwright.

Maybe in his youth, as I did, he attended RADA, or some other equally efficient drama school – but not to learn to write plays, only to absorb, through any acting that he did there, basic facts about the theatre: the way an actor makes his exits and his entrances, for instance; what the human voice can compass when delivering a line of dialogue, and what it cannot.

Otherwise, regarding the profession he has chosen, he is nothing but a learner driver with an L plate on his car and no instructor. All that he can do is either, if he is an imitator, emulate the other drivers, past and present, he has seen progressing down the highway, or, if he should be an original, attempt to travel alone. The decision is, I submit, the first that a playwright has to make in life. 'Is it to be dual control or single?' 'Am I going to drive alone, or with companions – play-doctors, directors and the like?'

Yet his response can only be a general submission of intent because, in fact, he has little choice to start with. Play-doctors will be around him in his infancy like wasps around a jam jar, and so will directors. If he wants to get his first play produced, he will find himself submitting to the dictates of one or the other, or, more likely, both.

I followed this road in my early days, my mentor being the benign and charming Archie Batty, play-reader for H. M. Tennent, who advised me to write extra scenes into the *Chiltern Hundreds* which I did and, some years later, extra scenes into the *Deb*, which I did not. This later independence meant, of course, that as a playwright I was growing up, becoming much more confident of my ability to cope with play construction, standing, in fact, on my own feet.

At this point, I would suggest to any learner playwright, ask yourself: 'In spite of the inevitable limitations on my independence, am I still for single control as opposed to dual?' If his answer is 'single', he may have a happy life, because, in my experience, each time one settles – in one's weakness, or in one's desire to get a play on – for dual control, it results in a feeling that one has betrayed one's trust. Worse, much worse, one suspects that, when one sets out to write one's next play, the Muse will very likely not co-operate, or, anyway, will go slow. Ultimately, should the insult be repeated once too often, it may go on strike for ever.

Therefore, having shaken off the play-doctor, like some young zebra which, learning its strength at last, scrapes off the lioness, clawing at its flank, by galloping beneath an overhanging branch, let the enfranchised playwright emulate that zebra and continue galloping, because there lurks another predator, stretched out perhaps along that very same overhanging branch – a leopard, in the game park; a director in the theatre; both out for blood, determined to pull down their prey.

The golden rule for playwrights is: 'If your director wants to change your play, change your director.' It's as simple as that, but a lot more difficult to practise. After all, imagine the scenario . . .

Play written – agent places it with impresario – said impresario engages a director who would like to do it ('mad to do it' is, in fact, the phrase used by most impresarios). Next stage in this eventful history: impresario gives playwright and director lunch. Maybe they've met before, maybe not. Casting is discussed and settled. ('So and so has read it.' 'What did he think?' 'Oh, he's mad about it. He suggested so and so.' 'And is she mad about it?' 'Mad about it, too'!)

Glasses are raised, toasts drunk. In this euphoric state the impresario calls for the bill and passes it to the headwaiter with a friendly smile, denoting that he's happy to observe that service is included.

'Right,' he says, replacing his pen in his pocket. 'When are you two going to meet to talk about the script?'

'Oh, any time that suits,' the playwright answers gaily through a screen of claret, as his heart goes plummetting to his boots. 'Any time at all.'

'Well, no time like the present, is there?' says the impresario, then turns to the director. 'How about this afternoon?'

'OK by me,' says the director. 'Where shall we go?'

'My flat,' says the playwright quickly, trying to assert himself, if only by selecting, at least, the terrain for the impending massacre.

'OK, your flat,' says the director.

The impresario shakes hands and thanks them both for their co-operation, with a look of satisfaction on his face such as a snake charmer might wear, having succeeded in bringing to bed, for mating purposes, a grass-snake and a boa-constrictor.

Parked as near the flat as possible, our twin souls take the lift up to the chosen slaughter house. The playwright's wife, if she is present, makes some coffee and, while doing so, sums up the character of the director. She decides that he is going to win the battle, if indeed it's even joined, which seems unlikely, since she has detected in her husband's grovelling demeanour, what can only be the seeds of unconditional surrender.

Having poured the coffee, she shakes hands with the director, makes excuses about having to go shopping, waves with profound but well-concealed contempt towards her craven husband, and departs for Peter Jones, leaving her coffee-drinking lord and master to unfurl the white flag at his leisure.

For, when all is said and done, what other action can he contemplate? Refuse to be dismembered? Dig his toes in? Say to the director, 'Listen, pal, I wrote this play with the co-operation of my muse. Each word, each line of dialogue is, therefore, sacred to me. If, you want it changed, or your star actor does, or both, you're crying for the moon, because this playwright isn't going to do it. Full stop. I suggest you finish up your coffee, hand me back my script, and bugger off!'

Of course, he knows full well he can't say any of this, because if he does, this obstinate director will accept him at his word, hand back his script, and leave the flat on course for some alternative production. Should that happen, while he toys with the idea of suicide, the telephone will ring and he will hear the impresario's voice – on a very different note from that which he employed at lunch-time – telling him that he has lost the best director in town, not to speak of some of the best actors, and that the production's off because both the director and the actors have already transferred to the next play on his schedule, and because the playwright's flimsy, ill-constructed little play will stand no chance with anybody else – assuming anybody else will look at it!

So, as the playwright's wife approaches Peter Jones, he runs up the white flag, without a shot having been fired in anger – takes his notebook and his pencil and writes down his gaoler's recipe for the improvement of his script: the star's requirements for re-writing if he is to sign his contract; plus suggestions as to how to calm the leading lady's worries about age or changes between scenes. All that he can do is fight a rearguard action, trying to save something from the wreckage – change a line here, let a cut through there, then take it back when no one's looking, with a bit of luck; swing the director round in favour of some passage queried by the star, and get him to support a bid for restoration, or alternatively at rehearsal, if he is so foolish to attend one, swing the star in favour of some cut that the director ordered prematurely.

Best of all, perhaps, have the script retyped, leaving out the cuts made by the star and the director and then later, at rehearsals, say, 'There's something missing here, I think, don't you? I'd better write in something,' and restore the cuts which those who made them have now mercifully forgotten.

I remember once using a different ploy with highly satisfactory results. The play was called *Master of Arts*, the plot concerned a house master in some anonymous school in which all the boys wore tails and top hats, and the part was played by Roland Culver – a delightful actor of outstanding charm both on and off the stage.

Rehearsals started before Easter and, in the first week, as many actors do because of frayed nerves at the prospect of embarking on a new production, Roland began to worry about one short duologue (towards the end of the first act) between himself and the attractive sister of one of the most unpleasant little boys in his house.

'But it's all right, Roly,' I kept saying to him. 'What's the matter with it? It looks perfectly all right when you're doing it on stage.'

'Well, it doesn't feel right,' Roly argued.

'How do you expect it to. You hardly know it, either of you?'

'It's not that, it isn't right. Where are you spending Easter?'

'Scotland.'

'Well, re-write it when you're up there,' he commanded.

'I'll look at it,' I said, to keep him quiet.

What's more, I meant to do just that. But what with finding myself stuck into the salmon on the Tweed on Easter Saturday and Monday, I forgot about it. Only in my sleeper, during Monday night, did I recall my promise, just as I was dropping off to sleep. I turned the light on, got my script out of my suitcase, read the scene through, found that it was good, and made a snap decision. Sitting up in bed, I copied out the whole scene (at the most three pages) on some sheets of foolscap paper, left them in the script, turned out the light and went to sleep.

Arrived at the rehearsal on Tuesday morning, I went up to Roly. 'Here's your new scene,' I said, handing him the sheets of foolscap. Roly read them through with satisfaction.

'That's much better,' said he. 'Thanks.'

'No trouble,' I said, as I stood and watched him stick the foolscap pages in his script over the pages I had copied, word for word, the night before, as the train slid through Morpeth.

A few pages back, I wrote a passage indicating that I think it foolish for a playwright to attend rehearsals. This, in fact, I seldom do and for good reason. If a playwright does go to rehearsals, he presents a sitting target to the actors and director. 'Willy,' I have heard called from the stage, waking me abruptly from a dreamless sleep at the back of the stalls. 'Can I change this?'

'Change what,' I ask the fellow, swaying down the aisle, still semi-conscious. 'What's the matter with it?'

'It just doesn't sound right,' he says, holding out his script, while the director lights another cigarette, displeased at being left out.

I recite the line. 'It sounds all right to me.'

'Well, not to me.'

'What do you want to say instead?' I ask the actor, weakening already.

'What about this?' he says, reading aloud something pencilled in his script.

'It knocks the rhythm arseways.'

'Rhythm?' he says, with brow furrowed.

'Yes,' I tell him. 'Rhythm – R-H-Y-T-H-M, Rhythm.'

'Nonsense,' cuts in the director. 'It sounds perfectly all right.'

'So now you've turned against me, too, you bastard,' think I. I don't say it, though. I merely say, 'I don't agree.'

'What are we going to do about it, then?' says the director.

'Leave it till we open,' I say, moving back towards my back stall.

'But it's not right,' protests the actor.

'Willy thinks it is,' says the director, 'and he wrote the bloody line.'

Needled by this, I turn and say to the actor, 'All right, change it if you want to, but I claim the right to change it back after we open.'

'Why should I learn two lines?' says the actor.

'You're lucky to have two to learn,' I say, 'the way that you behave.'

'Now, Willy, Willy, that's not nice,' says the director to me and, to the complaining actor, 'Let's get on.'

'With which line?' asks the actor.

'Willy's, I suppose,' says the director, 'if he's going to go to law about it.' Laughter all round.

That is why I don't attend rehearsals; not that such things happen often, but there is the ever-present danger that they might. Whereas if the playwright avoids rehearsals, actors and directors will be better able to avoid temptation.

My own opposition to script changes – quite apart from changes in the rhythm – is based on a simple calculation; namely, that the play is likely to be better as I wrote it first, until proved otherwise by audience reaction. If any line is changed before an audience has heard it, I am worried by the thought that, had that line been spoken, it might have proved itself to be better than the substitute. In such a case, I am prepared, indeed inevitably forced, to argue for its restoration, thus infuriating everybody.

To sum up, I repeat with feeling, 'If directors want to change your play, change them,' and add the rider, 'if you dare to,' continuing cynically but sadly, 'which of course, you never will.'

A word about the rhythm that I mentioned earlier, which makes me even more allergic to script changes than most playwrights. Writing as I do in such a rhythm, means that any paraphrasing of the lines or unadjusted cuts imposed by the director damage my play. Jack Minster, to his credit, noted this in his preface to the published version of the *Deb*.

'When we were first rehearsing the play,' he wrote, 'the author pointed out that, in writing the dialogue, he had intended a certain rhythm, a beat, and this is by no means as unlikely as might appear at first glance – as, no doubt, will be seen by good players.'

Let me try to analyse that beat. It is, I think, a rhythm the use of which somehow sets the play in a distinctive mould – permits the dialogue to flow uninterrupted and cuts out 'air pauses', to use an expression of my own invention.

If a line of dialogue is written in a style and in words which require an actor to pause a split second before speaking it, or speaking what comes after it, that is an 'air pause' and, in my opinion, an unnecessary hold up to the progress of the play. It creates a minor vacuum, in which the audience may lose its concentration and, instead of following the play, begin to think of dinner, times of buses, Mabel's measles, seat discomfort, chocolate boxes and the like.

In order to avoid this, a dramatist must keep things moving smoothly and continuously through each scene. I am convinced that the use of this rhythm makes my plays (whatever their short-comings otherwise) act better than they would if I did not employ it. Thus, my better plays flow pleasingly and without interruption to the final curtain, while the rest are better able to disguise whatever shortcomings they have.

A few examples of this 'rhythm' might not come amiss. They may help to explain, without undue profundity, how such a process works and what I mean by 'air pauses'. Take certain lines from *The Reluctant Debutante*, as spoken by Hyde White and Celia Johnson, with Wilfrid speaking first:

'Hullo, the Duke of Positano's dead.'

'Who cares?'

'The Duchess probably. Oh, no, she's dead as well.'

To anyone who cares to read those lines aloud, the beat – as Minster called it – instantly becomes apparent. Paraphrase them, and the beat takes flight at once.

'Hullo, the Duke of Positano's dead.'

'Who cares?'

'Probably the Duchess. Oh, no, she's dead as well.'

See what I mean? The transfer of that lone word 'probably' at once creates an air pause, because after 'Who cares?' a split second must elapse before the actor can say 'probably', the rhythm having been destroyed.

One other illustration out of *Lloyd George Knew My Father*:

'What's that?'

'Heber, father.'

'Heber-Percy, do you mean?'

'No, father.'

'He commanded my Brigade in India.'

'No, not him, father.'

'Why the devil bring him up, then?'

'I said Heber, father, without Percy.'

'No, not Percy – Walter was his name – not Percy.'

Anyone who cares to read that passage aloud, cannot fail to get the message from the rhythm, or what Minster, in his wisdom, called the beat. Whereas, the rhythm goes to pieces if one single word or phrase is altered. For example:

'What's that?'

'Heber, father.'

'Do you mean Heber-Percy?'

It is clear that there must be an air pause after 'father' before any actor can voice 'Do you mean Heber-Percy?', and another one before his colleague can reply, 'No, father'.

The moral of this is that the more economical the dialogue, the more austere the rhythm, the more definite the beat, then the more likely is it that the audience will respond – in a comedy, with clear-cut laughter, in a tragedy, with tears.

'Oh, Hamlet, thou hast cleft my heart in twain
Oh, throw away the worser half of it
And live the purer with the other half.'

Adjust that jewelled dialogue by taking out the second 'oh', and what is left?

'Oh, Hamlet, thou hast cleft my heart in twain
Throw away the worser half of it
And live the purer with the other half.'

The beat is gone, the air pause introduced in place of the 'oh', and the beauty of the passage undermined.

Of course, one could adjust it – since adjustments can be made to almost anything, even perfection, but it must be done with care and even then is most unlikely to live up to the original.

'Oh, Hamlet, thou hast cleft my heart in twain
*Then* throw away the worser half of it.'

Or, if one wants to be ambitious, one could write:

'Oh, Hamlet, thou hast cleft my heart in twain
*Then*, *rather*, throw away the worser half
And live the purer with the other half.'

But Shakespeare did it better. Why then, when it comes to lesser mortals, who pay tribute to that great man's application to the smallest detail by doing the same, in their small way, do actors and directors try to make improvements in a sphere in which they are not expert?

It is my profound conviction that if every worker in the theatre did his own job to the full limit of his powers and left his colleagues likewise to do theirs the theatre would be a better place in which to work. In saying this, however, I am well aware that I am crying for the moon since, after having written more than thirty plays, I still find actors and directors who are more than happy to attempt to do my job for me, and this in spite of Somerset Maugham's tribute to my skills.

I sent a play to him once after meeting him at dinner in the

Dorchester with Lady Cunard, who had taken me up after *Now Barabbas*. Ten days later, it came back. Pinned to the cover was the following note:

'Very clever – quite worthy of Agatha Christie herself. Yrs, Willie Maugham.
P.S. You might do worse than marry her.'

## Chapter 11
# Survival

In the aftermath of *Aunt Edwina* and the de Laurentis film, I reached the nadir of my playwrighting career. Although by nature optimistic, I could see no future in it. The New Wave had finally submerged me. Even though Ben Travers, in a letter that he wrote me some years later, said 'You have been holding the fort for years when all the rest of us gave up,' I gave up, too, at this point. 'No one wants my plays,' I told myself (the impresarios told me, as well, in no uncertain terms), 'so why write any more?' I sat in my armchair, an open notebook on my knee, and gazed at the blank page. How long I would have sat there I don't know had not my father-in-law, noting my depression and my lack of income, given us a free trip to South Africa to stay with Julian and Tessa Thompson (Rachel's younger sister). On the voyage, I was moody, so much so that Rachel diagnosed a change of life. This pessimistic forecast was frustrated by the sea air. The improvement in my health enabled me to win the Deck Bowls Championship. On arrival at Capetown, I was a new man.

Restored in health, we travelled home, again by boat, and reassessed the situation on arrival. There was no change – apart from a few more letters, lying on my desk, from impresarios, rejecting my advances. When *The Secretary Bird* had been turned down by no less than thirteen managers I sent it, in despair, to Wilfrid Hyde White, in the hope that he might be prepared to flout public opinion. I told Rachel this.

'Well, get it back from him,' was her advice, 'he'll never do it. He's already said he's too old for it.'

'I know,' I said, 'but I've told him that he isn't, even though he will be if he goes on dithering much longer.'

'He'll never do it,' she repeated, 'in the present climate.' I remembered Binkie Beaumont's letter. Sure enough, Wilfrid's reaction after reading it was that the first scene was well written but the rest a let-down.

'Let me have it back, then, you old fool,' I told him on the telephone.

'All right, my boy, come in and pick it up one evening at the Haymarket, and I'll give you a drink,' he said.

'I'll do just that,' I told him.

Next day my telephone rang. 'Hullo, my boy,' said Wilfrid. 'Gave your little play to a mad fellow called Roye – in the play with me, you know. Plays a part in the ballroom scene. Ever heard of him?'

'No,' I said.

'Funny little fellow,' Wilfrid told me. 'Acts in London in the winter and does summer tours in Devonshire, wherever that is – told you he was crazy, didn't I? Well, he came in to have a drink last night and saw *The Secretary Bird* lying on my dressing-table. Asked me could he take it back to bed with him. Just rung to say he's read it and he wants to do it. Told the silly bugger I'd tell you. Come to lunch tomorrow at the Chop House, opposite the Comedy. I'll introduce you to the silly sod.'

I drove up next day and met Anthony Roye, short and tubby, reminiscent of the Duke of Norfolk of that era. We sat down to lunch.

'The fellow wants to do your little play,' said Wilfrid. 'God knows why.'

'Because it's a good play,' said Anthony.

'Just listen to him,' Wilfrid said. 'I told you he was mad. What does he know about plays, good God. I've already told him if he's going to do it, he'd better do it in one of those Cheddar Gorge caves, if he's fooling round in the West Country.'

'I'll open it in Swanage,' Tony Roye said.

'Swanage – there's no theatre there, my boy.'

'Yes, there is. A new one called the Mowlem. I'll direct the play, and play the lead myself.'

'And be the audience as well,' said Wilfrid.

'Then I'll go to Ilchester and Plymouth,' Tony Roye went on, 'and Street, and Weston-super-Mare and Scunthorpe, with a week out in between the last two.'

'You've not got the play yet, boy,' said Wilfrid.

'Yes, he has,' I said.

'Well that,' said Wilfrid, 'makes two lunatics!'

A few weeks later I went down to Wimbledon to meet the cast. I sat through a rehearsal in a small room in a YMCA building. They had scarcely started on the first scene – Tony and his leading lady – when I found myself intrigued by their interpretation of it. No frills and no affectation. No attempt from either of them to exploit the laughs – straightforward, sincere acting in what I began to think might well be a straightforward, sincere play. The rehearsal over, I congratulated the five members of the cast on their performances, and told them I looked forward to our meeting next week at the Mowlem Theatre in Swanage.

Then I left the room with Tony Roye. 'I like you, both as actor and director – and I like your cast,' I told him, as we stepped into the street. 'I also like the play. But what about the set?'

'Come back and have a glass of sherry in my flat,' he said, 'and you'll find out.'

Down the street we went, towards a block of flats. He showed me into a large room, devoid of any furniture, apart from a bed, with no carpet on the floor.

'Well, that's the set,' he said, 'or rather, where it used to be, because it's in the bus we've hired for the tour – two rows of seats in the front for the cast, rest of the space for all my furniture and lamps and carpets. Sherry?'

In that empty room, we drank a toast together to *The Secretary Bird*, and a second to the manager – director – leading actor standing by my side. 'See you in Swanage Tuesday night,' said he.

Rachel, her mother and I drove to Swanage on the Tuesday afternoon. We dined with Tony in a hotel opposite the Mowlem Theatre.

'How did the dress rehearsal go?' I asked him. 'Very well,' he said, taking a tranquilliser. 'But before that, all hell broke loose. Couldn't get my furniture in.'

'Why not?'

'Because there's no bay. We had to park it on the shore and lift it up on ropes. I might have lost my whole flat if the tide had been in.'

Shortly afterwards, he left us. We concluded our meal and then took our seats across the road. The house was thin – the reason being, as I found out later from my leading actor that it was the first performance ever to be given in the Mowlem Theatre, which was not due for an official opening until the Thursday.

'It seems the inhabitants of Swanage,' Tony said, 'are chary about going to a theatre on Tuesday that's not due to open until Thursday.'

'Can you blame them?' I asked.

'No,' he said, 'that's life.'

The first night went extremely well, however, and when, at the week-end, the inhabitants of Swanage rolled in, in the footsteps of the opener, *The Secretary Bird* got a great reception.

There were still, of course, small imperfections to be ironed out – not so much in the play or in the cast as in the theatre. For instance, Tony and I noticed, at the premiere, that customers took some time coming back to their seats after the break.

'I can tell you why that was,' I said to Tony. 'There were no bells in the bar.'

'Good God!' he said.

Next morning, he informed the manager of this shortcoming.

'Bells?' the manager said. 'What bells?'

'Interval bells,' Tony explained, 'like they have in London theatres, to get the customers back in after the interval.'

'Oh, so that's what those bells are for,' the manager replied. 'I've often wondered.'

Back at home next day, I rang up every manager in London.

'Swanage?' they said. 'There's no theatre there.'

'All right, come to Plymouth, then.'

'To Plymouth? That's a long way.'

'All right, Street then,' I implored, in growing desperation, 'or, if not Street, Weston-super-Mare or Scunthorpe.'

'We'll see what we can do,' they told me. None of them did anything.

The play went well in Plymouth, too, and Harvey Crane, the local critic, gave it a first-class review. In spite of this, the London managers stayed put.

Then came a one-night stand in Street, and Tony, on his way to put the set up, saw a tape-recorder in the window of a shop. He hired it for the night and put it underneath the stage, and it recorded what turned out to be our most enthusiastic audience.

Meanwhile, a London manager, unknown to me, had somehow got hold of a copy of the play, and read it. He informed my agent, Aubrey Blackburn, a delightful and enthusiastic fellow, that he wished to have an option on it.

At the Derby dinner, in the week out before Swanage, I saw, sitting at a table nearby, Emile Littler and Peter Saunders, flanking an unknown (to me) young man. Emboldened by the grape, I wrote a note and sent it over to them. 'Which of you,' it said (to Littler and Saunders), 'is the lucky man who's going to get hold of *The Secretary Bird*?'

Back my torn-off piece of menu came. Written on it in a strange hand were just three words: 'Neither, I am.' Then the signature, 'John Gale'.

He came to Swanage next week. In the hotel after the performance, he suggested Kenny More for London.

'When?' I asked him.

'This time next year. He's booked up till then, but he's worth waiting for.'

He was. The youngest of our children, Dinah, was born while we waited for the services of Kenny More. Thus, 1964 provided us with an outstanding double. First, a fair-haired daughter (known thereafter as The Blonde) and secondly the most successful play that I had ever written – when assessed by number of performances at least.

We opened in the Opera House, Manchester. We came from Douglas, I, Rachel, two elder children and two dogs. We parked the two dogs in our bathroom in the Midland Hotel and went to the theatre. The house was full, the acting superb. By the time the manager, John Gale, director, Philip Dudley, leading players, Kenny More and Jane Downs, settled down to supper afterwards, we knew that we were on to a good thing.

We came to London some weeks later, into the Savoy. On the way back to bed, along the Edgware Road, near which we had a flat in nephew Charlie's house, I said to Rachel, *sotto voce*, with my daughter Sarah in the back, supposedly asleep: 'What will the critics say tomorrow morning?'

'I can tell you,' said a small voice from the back seat. 'Mr Home bores us again!'

She was wrong. One critic even, with a left-wing bias like a flat tyre on the near side of a car, wrote: 'Mr Home brings life back to the West End comedy' – or words to that effect. The clouds dispersed – so did the Inland Revenue officials. My bank manager, the next time that I met him, actually smiled. I felt like Charles the Second must have when he shook hands with Monk – the Restoration was a fact.

Thus did *The Secretary Bird* bring me back to London on a slow train, calling at all local stations – Swanage, Plymouth, Weston-super-Mare, Street, Scunthorpe – before puffing into the Savoy, where it remained for some years; Kenny More being succeeded by John Gregson, and John Gregson in his turn by Jeremy Hawk.

At a late stage in the run I lunched with Geoffrey Russell (now Lord Ampthill) who was one of the play's backers. During lunch the talk was of some suitable successor to one of those leading actors – I forget which.

'What about me, Geoffrey?' I said.

'Over my dead body,' he replied.

There, in one short, sharp phrase, my bid to make a come-back to the stage was trodden underfoot. My heart, however, was in no way bruised by the rebuff.

I knew my limitations as an actor, having heard them succinctly exposed by Matty when I played the juvenile lead in *The Chiltern Hundreds* for a fortnight, after letting Peter Coke go off on holiday. On my last night I followed Matty from the curtain-call towards the dressing-rooms and, as I went into my own, I thanked him for his tolerance.

'That's quite all right,' said Matty. 'You were very good, until you found your feet.'

My next post-war performance on the boards was also for a fort-night after Wilfrid, star of *The Reluctant Debutante*, had had a motor accident on the Bath Road. He rang me on his bedside telephone. 'Hired car, my boy – made of Ryvita,' he informed me. 'I'll be off for months. It won't do much good to your little play.'

In fact, the figures in his first week's absence topped the takings for all previous weeks.

I drove up to Hampstead to the house of Ballard Berkeley, Wilfrid's friend, in which my leading actor lay recuperating, with a bottle of champagne beside him on the bedside table.

'Thought you'd like to see last week's returns,' I told him.

'Good God,' said he, reaching for the bottle, 'I'd better come back quick!'

Of course, the takings at the box office could be attributed in no way to his absence, only to substantial advance bookings for the Motor Show – which opened in that very week. The same thing happened in the second week during which Wilfrid, still in ignorance of the true reason for the rise in popularity of the play in his absence, made a quite miraculous recovery – returning to it after two weeks' absence, at which, needless to say, due to his return exactly coinciding with the closing of the Motor Show, the takings dropped at once. However, since the penny had now dropped as well, he suffered no relapse.

I quite enjoyed my fortnight at the Cambridge, even though my father-in-law thought I was miscast, and told me so. I put it to him that perhaps the reason was that I was too young. 'Not at all,' he said. 'I must confess, however, that I missed the first act due to a late business appointment. I suppose that I was just beginning to get used to you when the play ended.'

'Come another night and see the first act,' I suggested.

'I'd like to,' he said, 'but I'm very much afraid that I'll be otherwise engaged.' He was.

My leading lady frightened me on my first night – not on the stage, but after curtain fall. While brooding on the past two hours as I removed my make-up, I heard someone knocking on my door. 'Come in,' I called, anticipating the news that many of the audience were queueing at the stage door, waiting to congratulate me on my acting.

'I'll take relations first,' I told the call-boy, as he entered, 'then friends – then, if it's not too late, strangers.'

'It's Miss Johnson wants to see you,' he said. Down the corridor I went, in trepidation, questions tapping at my brain like a neurotic woodpecker.

'Will she say she can't act with me?' I asked myself. 'And, if she does, would that mean we'd have to close the play till Wilfrid comes back?'

'Celia,' I called, through her half-open door. 'It's William.'

'Oh, come in,' she called back. In I went, to find her taking off her make-up. Studying her in the mirror, I decided that she looked quite friendly. 'Still,' I thought, 'one never knows with actresses!' I waited.

'Have a drink,' she said.

'Why not? What about you?'

'All right. Gin and tonic.'

'Ah,' I thought, as I poured out the drinks, 'she's softening me up. She's far too nice to give me the push without first anaesthetizing me.' I handed her her glass.

'Good luck,' I said.

'Good luck,' she answered. Then she struck.

'The breakfast scene in the last act . . .'

'Yes?' I said, thinking back in search of any major misadventure that had overtaken me in that scene.

'Where you pour my coffee,' she went on.

'Oh, yes?'

'In future, put more milk in it,' she said. 'I can't sleep otherwise.'

The long run of *The Secretary Bird* enabled me to push my foot a little further through the West End door, and get another play on at the same time, called *The Jockey Club Stakes*. Alastair Sim starred with Robert Coote and Geoffrey Sumner, playing three fictitious stewards of the Jockey Club. The last two I already knew. The first was still a stranger to me. Not for long, however.

I drove to Leeds from Southampton, having landed from South Africa that morning, to attend the first performance of the play. Murray Macdonald, the director (who had directed me in *Bonnet Over The Windmill* forty years before) came back to the hotel and introduced me to my leading actor. One of the first things he said to me, as I recall, in answer to some comment on a line of his was, 'Never mind the lines – it's what goes in between them that counts.'

I accepted this rebuke with equanimity, since, after watching him at work, I had sufficient proof that he had learned the lines with care and, having done so, given a superb performance in between them.

Some years later, after his death, his wife wrote to say that he had often talked of the play with nostalgia. Its author often does the same, recalling Alastair's inspired performance and the wonderful support he had from his companions in the Stewards' room and the rest of the cast.

Before we came to London, this play had had its problems. I had written it as fantasy but, in the following year, an event took place in real life which was very like my plot. This gave the Jockey Club some grounds for worry. Peter Saunders, who produced the play, and I were worried, too.

I took Sir Randle Feilden, a high-ranking steward of the Jockey Club, out to lunch at the Savoy Grill. He, legitimately, was concerned that if the play came on, it might give the Jockey Club an unwelcome image. Tactfully, I sought to calm his fears.

'It's just a fantasy,' I said.

'No longer,' he replied.

'Oh, yes indeed, it is. Don't tell me you think stewards of the Jockey Club are like those three old rogues in my play? If you do, you ought to be ashamed – sir!'

He smiled, enigmatically. 'Who's going to be the Senior Steward?' he asked.

'Alastair Sim.'

'Oh,' he said, and his face lit up. 'No one's going to take it seriously, then! No one could possibly believe that *he* could be a Steward!'

'Couldn't they?' I wondered.

So, the play began rehearsals with the Jockey Club on its side.

When we came to London it was well received, in spite of having two peers and one general as the leading characters. Perhaps, because they were portrayed as rascals, they got through.

When Alastair left after six months, Wilfrid came in, in his stead, and later played the part in Washington, and New York where he and his colleagues, Coote and Sumner still, secured a rave review from Clive Barnes.

I had had a West End double once before. On that occasion, Matty had said to me, 'When's your matinee at the Strand?'

'Thursday.'

'Right, I'll go,' he told me.

'I'll come with you.'

'No,' he answered, 'I prefer to be alone.'

'By God, I was,' he said, when he came back.

The fact that I had two plays running at the same time, did not mean that I was now *persona grata* in the West End theatre. I still had plays on the shelf that I could not get put on. Strangely enough, such plays sometimes turn out to be ultimately among the most successful.

There is no truth in the theory, held by some people, that a playwright who has had theatrical successes in the past has automatic entry into the production lists for his next play. The truth is each new play is treated as a stranger.

Impresarios are individuals with well-marked likes and dislikes, and they tend to put their money where their taste is. Consequently, any dramatist with a diversity of output should not let himself be hurt when impresarios, with whom he has been on the best of terms in the past, give him the cold shoulder. Let him smile instead, resignedly, then bandage up his wounded pride and cast his new play into hitherto uncharted waters. It's surprising what unlikely fish will take the bait. It's even more surprising when a fish swims uninvited into one's net and snaps up a bait from where it lies on the neglected shelf.

This happened to me with a play called *Lady Boothroyd of the Bypass* (later to be renamed *Lloyd George Knew My Father*). I first wrote it for Dame Sybil Thorndike and her husband, Lewis Casson. They rejected it for reasons not quite clear to me. Perhaps Dame Sybil thought Sir Lewis could not manage a long role at his great age. Perhaps they thought that the play was no good. Anyway, I put it on the shelf behind the chair in which I write and there it lay for some years.

One day, a young schoolmaster called Wheare, who had taught Jamie, called me up and asked if I had any spare plays for production.

'Who by?' I asked.

'Me,' he said. 'I've just been asked by Bobbie Bourne (an Eton House Master) to do a play with the boys in his house.'

'Sorry,' I told him, passed the time of day, discussed my son, by then at Bristol University, bade him farewell, put down the telephone.

Returning to my desk, I saw behind my chair, a script of *Lady*

*Boothroyd of the Bypass.* About-turning, I dialled Eton.

'Tom,' I said, when he came on the line. 'I've got a play. It's called *Lady Boothroyd of the Bypass.*'

'Splendid,' he said. 'Pop it in an envelope.'

I sent it off and heard no more about it for a long time. Then my telephone rang one day.

'Tom Wheare here,' his voice said. 'Just to tell you that we've got a winner on our hands.'

'Oh, yes?' I said. 'And what makes you think that?'

'Well,' said he, 'they've all learned their parts now, and we had a run through tonight. It looks good. There's not much doubt about it.'

'See you at the first night, Tom,' I said.

We took an impresario to Eton on the first night, and watched the play performed with a young boy called Charles Grant in the part of Lady Boothroyd (seventeen years old, and of the wrong sex, playing seventy). He acted with panache and an impressive technique. All the other parts, including that of Lady Boothroyd's husband, were played by boys who, on average, seemed even younger than Charles Grant. They, too, performed impressively. The impresario was gratified but declined to do the play. Anthony Roye later did it for a week in Boston (Lincs.) and Harold Hobson, out of kindness, came to see it. Still, the impresario would not take the play, and so I sent it to Ray Cooney, who at once agreed to a production.

At the Yvonne Arnaud Theatre in Guildford one night, after he had just performed in *Not Now Darling* (written by John Chapman and himself), we supped together in the restaurant.

'We'll start at the top,' Ray said, taking out a pencil with which he proceeded to write out a list of actors on the menu. 'In three weeks, I reckon we'll be getting near the bottom. Still, I think we ought to get a leading actor first, then see what kind of leading lady he wants.'

'Good luck,' I said, squinting at the list of names, headed by Richardson.

A few days later, Ray was on the telephone.

'I've got him,' he said.

'Who?' I asked, attempting to recall the name of the last actor on the list.

'Number one, of course,' he said. 'Sir Ralph.'

And so, indeed, he had.

I met Ray at the Ivy Restaurant one lunch-time, some weeks later. As I sipped my drink, I asked him just how firmly hooked Sir Ralph was.

'Very firmly, I think,' said Ray. 'He quite genuinely seems to like it. Still, we'll soon know.'

'What about the leading lady?'

'We'll find that out, too.'

In Sir Ralph came, with his agent Laurence Evans (now mine, too). We shook hands all round. Soon, our conversation turned towards the play. 'There's something underneath the surface,' said Sir Ralph to me. 'Don't ask me what it is, because I don't know. Nor will I ask you, because you won't know, either.'

Ray winked at me at that point, and I began to feel at ease. 'If he's prepared to volunteer a diagnosis of that nature, never mind how unsubstantiated it may be,' I told myself, 'he is indeed on the hook.'

We then began to talk about the leading lady.

'Who would you like, Sir Ralph?' asked Ray.

'Edith couldn't do it now,' he said, more to himself than to us. 'Old Edith couldn't do it, could she? I should doubt it. Poor old Edith!'

He stared into the middle distance, summoning replacements out of the four corners of the restaurant for 'poor old Edith'.

'Peggy,' he said, suddenly. 'I might give Peggy a ring.'

Then the conversation turned to other matters – clearance, for example, of Ray's choice of a director (Robin Midgeley), touring dates, potential London theatres and, much to my surprise, no talk of script revision, only of a change of title.

Whether at that lunch or not, I can't recall, but ultimately I came up with *Lloyd George Knew My Father*, which was well received by all concerned – and also by the public, as I like to think, although one impresario once told me that with any other name the play would have run even longer than it did. I wonder. Anyway, there is no proving that his calculation was correct, nor ever will be, although, marginally in my favour is the fact that, when they put it on in Paris with the name *Ne Coupez Pas Mes Arbres* it did less well than it had done in London. Possibly it should have been called

*Clemenceau Connaissait Mon Père!*

One night, Rachel and I went to Farnham for a poetry recital in which Peggy Ashcroft took part. Afterwards, we went to see her in her dressing-room. 'Ralph's talked me into doing your play,' she said.

'So they tell me,' I replied, and kissed her gratefully.

Thus, *Lady Boothroyd of the Bypass*, via Eton, Boston (Lincs.), the Yvonne Arnaud and the Ivy Restaurant, fell into the good hands of two great actors, and, not only that, two totally endearing characters.

Ralph won my heart at our first lunch, just as his predecessor, Matty, had, a quarter of a century before. He asked me, I recall, how my relations had reacted to the fact that I was in the theatre.

'They're used to it now,' I said.

'Ah,' said he, 'mine never will be. They're Puritans from the North Country. When I go to Newcastle in Lear or Cyrano de Bergerac – whatever – they come round to see me in my dressing-room after the play. They're all farmers. They all talk about their pigs. "I had swine fever last month, Ernest," one says to the other. "How's it going, George?" asks Ernest. "Better, Ernest, now," says George. And, never once, does any of them mention my performance in the play. They down their drinks and say goodnight until the next time, and go out into the street, still talking about swine fever among themselves. But as they drive home through the hills, I like to think they turn to one another in the car, and say "Young Ralph looked bad when we first saw him. Worried, weren't you, about him? But when he got all that stuff off his face after, he looked a lot better!" '

Robin Midgeley went through the script with me, patiently and gently, and then launched on the rehearsals in my absence.

One day, on my way through London towards Boston to see my faithful Anthony Roye launching yet another play, *At The End of The Day*, I called into the Savoy Theatre for half an hour. The cast were on the last scene, and a lot of talk was going on – and not much action – on the subject of the exiting of certain characters.

When the scene was finished, Robin Midgeley came down off the stage and joined me in the stalls.

'Well, what do you think?' he asked.

'I've got only one thought,' I said. 'Oxford, Monday evening.'

'Fair enough,' he said.

We lunched together in a restaurant some way from Ralph and Peggy, and, although I waved a greeting to them, I refrained from offering congratulations, being worried by the fact that I had witnessed too much talk and not enough rehearsal. Later, when I got to know her better, Peggy said to me: 'You looked into rehearsals and said nothing, except "Oxford, Monday evening". And you never came back!'

'That's because I had to go to Boston (Lincs.),' I told her.

But it wasn't. And she knew it.

In the Randolph Hotel, on the Monday evening, Rachel and I had a drink with Laurie Evans at the bar.

'I came down early,' Laurie said.

'Why?'

'Because Ralph's depressed about the play.'

'Oh, dear,' I said, downing my drink and calling for another. 'What's wrong?'

'Nothing. He just thinks it isn't any good. In fact, he wanted to get out of it this morning, but I told him it was too late. That's why I came down – to quieten him down.'

'And have you succeeded?'

'Hope so – touch wood.'

Rachel and I walked towards the theatre, a trifle worried, but not overmuch so, since we both knew from experience that actors tend to suffer from nerves just before a first night, and, not least, the stars. Indeed, I've heard it said that Sir John Gielgud suffers more than most, so much so that some drama critics write their notices on a first night on the assumption that the nerve-wracked piece of acting that they have just witnessed will never be repeated.

Ralph gave no such opportunity that night. From the first entrance to take breakfast with his piano-playing Peggy, he was in control, and, throughout the play, he never put a foot wrong. When we went to see him afterwards, we found him totally relaxed and smiling. Nor did we discuss swine fever. We congratulated him on a superb performance, and Peggy for precisely the same reason. Everyone, in fact, was happy, since there were no weak spots in the cast – no flaws in the production.

Only I, a few weeks later up in Leeds, found something that I thought was lacking in my script. A cut had been made in the last scene – three or four lines, only – and I thought that it should be replaced by something else.

At supper in the Queen's Hotel with Peggy, after Monday night's performance, I enlisted her in my support. 'I'll run up three or four lines in the morning, while I'm having breakfast,' I said, 'and read them to you at eleven, over coffee. Then we'll go to the rehearsal and sell them to Ralph and Robin.'

'All right,' she agreed. 'I'll see you at eleven.'

Studying the scene, before my breakfast came up in the morning, I decided that the missing lines should be replaced by something between Ralph and Peggy which, by being light and airy, would relieve the mood of the preceding scene and the scene after. My mind fixed itself with a tenacity which could not be denied on kestrel hawks. I seized my pencil and my notebook. Soon, the former flew across the page.

'Why is it, Sheila,' I wrote for Sir Ralph's approval, 'that one sees so many kestrel hawks on motorways?'

'Don't ask me, William,' was Sheila's reply.

'I'll tell you then, old girl. It's because of mice.'

'Oh, yes, dear?'

'Yes,' said William. 'And vibration. When the cars and lorries go by on a motorway, the mice get so excited by the consequent vibration that the little beggars dance around like dervishes and then the kestrel spots them. That's why there's so many of them hanging around motorways.'

I read it through and liked the whole scene. I liked the 'hanging around' phrase best, being something of an ornithologist, and therefore well aware of the unique method of flying practised by the kestrel hawk.

I took the half page down to Peggy, where she read it over coffee. 'Good luck with it,' she said, very sportingly I thought considering that Ralph was to have almost all the meat: 'Let's go.'

I drove her to the Grand. Ralph, seated on the stage, was studying his morning paper.

'Ralph,' I said, 'I've got a tiny scene here just to fill in that gap where I made the cut. You needn't say it all if you don't want to.

Just a line or two to break the mood of the preceding scene, and then restore it in the succeeding scene.'

I left him reading it. Robin's rehearsal with some of the other actors ended to his satisfaction, at which I told him about my new lines. We approached Sir Ralph together. 'Well?' I asked him. 'What about it?'

'Catastrophic,' he replied.

Director, cast and author all dissolved in laughter, as Ralph handed back my brain-child, smothered so succinctly in its infancy. From then on, the word 'catastrophic' was a standing joke between myself and Peggy. 'Catastrophic' we would say, if Ralph suggested, any minor changes. 'Which catastrophe is this?' Peggy would ask as she shook hands with one or other of our children, brought round for an introduction.

'It will take a bulldozer to get them out of the Savoy,' wrote Felix Barker of the *Evening News*, the morning after our first night in London. Peggy stayed until her six month contract had expired, to be replaced by Celia, who acted Sheila in a different way, but in an equally enchanting manner, until her six months expired, at which point Ralph too cried, 'Enough!'

'I've had two leading ladies shot beneath me,' he complained one day, then left to be replaced by Andrew Cruickshank, who played the part of Sir William with panache and, also, in a kilt.

Ralph played it later in Australia and Washington and Canada with great success with his wife, Mu. One day, as I still hope, he may be tempted to act in the film, the script of which I have already written.

When it left the Savoy, *At the End of the Day* (John Mills, Michael Denison and Dulcie Gray) moved in. By the time it came off in its turn, I had had plays in the Savoy for seven consecutive years.

## Chapter 12
# Sark and Great White Herons

My next theatrical adventure came about in quite an unexpected way. I had a play called *The Bank Manager*, at that time – (later, *In The Red*) which Tony Roye, with his usual devotion, had tried out in Boston but of which the London impresarios seemed strangely wary.

One of them, Ray Cooney, then embarking on an Oxford Festival of Plays, sent it to Celia to read. She said that she would do it on the understanding that she could secure a leading man. Ray sent it to John Clements who, on reading it, appeared to be, to say the least, a trifle lukewarm.

He invited me to lunch in Brighton, where he lives with his courageous crippled wife, Kay Hammond. It so happened that it was his birthday, so I took a bottle with me, pointing out, on my arrival at his door, that it was not intended as a bribe. He took the bottle in good part, but not the part in the play. Try as I would, I could not persuade him to share my considered view that *The Bank Manager* had merit. Indeed, he almost persuaded me that it was second rate, unfunny, not to speak of being in bad taste. He had this view confirmed to some tune by the critics when it came on in the West End some years later. That, however, is another story, which will be enlarged upon, in due course.

At his birthday lunch, John Clements' firm rejection of *The Bank Manager* caused Celia to throw her hand in. As she told me on the telephone, 'If John says he's too old, (one of his minor criticisms of the play at lunch) then I'm too old, too.'

'Right,' I said, 'forget it. But what will you do instead?'

'I've no idea,' she told me. 'Nothing, I hope.'

H.P.H.–L

I rang up Gyles Brandreth, who was managing the Festival for Ray.

'John Clements won't do it,' I said, 'and nor will Celia.'

'I know. Have you got anything else?'

'No,'

And then I had an idea.

'How long can you give me?'

'Tuesday week' (the day was Saturday).

'Keep Celia free, won't you, till then?' I besought him.

'Yes,' he promised.

Putting down the telephone, I searched my bookshelves and picked out a volume called *The Dame of Sark* by Sibyl Hathaway, a book which I had read with interest some years earlier, and made some notes on.

I re-read the chapters in the book devoted to the German occupation, and decided that a scene for each year of the occupation, making six in all, would be the best way in which to construct the play.

On Monday morning, I sat down and wrote the first scene. By late afternoon, that scene was done. The same on Tuesday – when Scene II was finished. So on, through the week, including Saturday – this last a departure from my normal routine which would have disturbed me greatly had the last scene not contained a sizeable slice of a speech by Winston Churchill. This lucky chance enabled me to write all my own dialogue before the racing started on the television.

Not that racing would have dragged me from my notebook had I been held up, so moved had I become by the whole project, and (I might as well confess it) by my dialogue. Specifically, I was moved by the newly-married German sentry, whom I had invented and whose death I knew, from the start, would provide a perfect ending for the play, conveying everything I wanted to convey.

Thus was *The Dame of Sark* completed in five days and one short morning, and I sat before my television screen that afternoon, not caring much which horse won which race, not even too sure which of them had been saddled with my money, such was the euphoria induced by having penned 'The Curtain Falls' six mornings after I had started with 'The drawing-room of the Seigneurie on Sark' –

the total satisfaction of a job well done.

My secretary, Anne Sergeant, typed out the play in record time, and got it to Gyles Brandreth by the deadline. He passed it to Celia and Celia accepted it.

The part of the aristocratic, anti-Nazi German Commandant was offered, at my instigation (since I felt I owed him something for his birthday lunch) to Sir John Clements, who rejected it, remarking that he did not want to play a German officer, and would prefer to play a gentleman (he could have done both!). Tony Britton, always Cooney's first choice, instantly accepted, and no better choice could have been made.

One hurdle lay ahead still, in the straight – the real-life Dame herself. I felt in duty bound to write and tell her that I had run up a play about her, and, as well, to ask her permission to call it *The Dame of Sark*. A letter came back in her strong handwriting, asking me to send the play to her to read. I did that.

Back a second letter came, with notes such as – 'Please change the name from Marie to Cecile as she has been with me for forty years' – 'I do not like your ending as it makes me sorry for the German soldier blown up at the harbour by a mine. There were two German soldiers blown up, in fact, and I wasn't sorry in the least!'

This final note, of course, struck at my ending which, for me, supplied the essence of the play.

I wrote back to that fierce old lady, telling her that had she known the little German soldier, Muller, as well as the Dame in my play knew him, she would have been sorry when he got killed – therefore, I had no intention of acceding to her wishes. My intention was to leave the scene exactly as it was, as I was very proud of having written it. In her reply, the Dame conceded that the last scene was indeed dramatic and that, probably, I was right to insist on it, although she did not like it. She enclosed the script with her written permission to name the play after her.

I then sat down and changed 'Marie' to 'Cecile', as she had requested and I wrote to Heinemann's who gave permission for *The Dame of Sark* to be the title of the play.

One last engagement still remained to be fulfilled – a week-end on Sark with the Dame, to which she had invited Rachel and myself, our younger children, Gian and Dinah, and my leading lady.

On the Sunday afternoon preceding this much-looked-forward-to week-end, I was playing a fierce game of croquet with some members of the family. Rachel came out and told me the radio had just informed her that the Dame had died that morning. The director of the play, Charles Hickman, had, however, been to see her the preceding week-end, had a long talk with her, had been greatly impressed by her courage and clear-mindedness, and had departed with the promise of a second meeting at the Oxford Playhouse in the autumn.

Looking through her photograph books, Charles had undergone a strange experience. In answer to his question, 'Have you got a photograph of Count von Schmettau in your book?' the Dame had replied, 'No, but I've got one of Private Muller,' (the young German sentry).

'But you can't have,' Charles had said, in some surprise, 'William invented him.'

'I know that,' said the Dame, 'because he wasn't in my book. But, none the less, I've got one of him.'

Sure enough, she opened up the book and there, before his eyes, Charles saw a photograph of Muller. I am quite aware, of course, that Muller is a German name as popular as Smith or Jones or Robinson in England. None the less, the young man in that photograph, both in appearance and in age, could well have been the prototype for my young German sentry. When, on his return, Charles told me this strange tale, I felt a surge of satisfaction, a conviction that the introduction of that minor, but important, character, had been inspired by something other than technique. I thanked God that I had stood firm against Dame Sibyl Hathaway's aversion to the final scene.

That summer, in the month before rehearsals started, we took a house on the Ile de Ré, and Celia came out to stay with us. One day, she read an article about the Dame of Sark, and noted that the Dame had limped from infancy as a result of a fall from her pram. 'I've got to limp, as well as learning all those dreadful lines!' she said.

I took this comment with a pinch of salt, because I knew, from long experience, that Celia was 'quite an adequate performer' (to employ a phrase her husband, Peter Fleming, had seen fit to use on the first night of *The Reluctant Debutante* in Brighton, many years before). In fact, their approach to life was very similar. They both used (only Celia, alas, now) understatement to disguise commitment, cheerful cynicism to conceal integrity, and caustic wit to decorate the obvious.

Once, at a dance in Eton, given by their great friend Harold Caccia, the then Provost, Rachel and I were proceeding up the stairs to meet our host and hostess, just in front of Celia and Peter.

'How is *The Queen's Highland Servant* going?' Celia asked (it was then at Windsor at the Theatre Royal).

'Splendidly,' I told her. 'Pamela Stanley is very good as the Queen, young in the first act, much older in the second, and a very great deal older in the third. It's quite astonishing,' I went on, my enthusiasm waxing, 'how incredibly she ages – through the use of cotton wool in her cheeks and not much else!'

'Ah,' said Peter's voice behind us, 'it's amazing how the theatrical profession always manages to catch up with the dental profession in the end!'

We sat on that enchanted island, studying the script for a few minutes every morning after breakfast, until Celia's modest requirements were fulfilled: a line cut here; a phrase changed there; her absence from the stage at curtain rise, for a few seconds, rather than discovery thereon – not, as a cynic might suggest, in order to secure herself a 'round' (no actress ever cared less about such irrelevances) but to give her line, conveying information to her patience-playing husband that the German troops were on the way, a greater sense of urgency.

With this re-write finished, Celia was happy, watching birds and playing bridge and only thinking intermittently of limping her way through the evening in the Oxford Playhouse for three weeks.

Among the trippers visiting the Ile de Ré – apart from my friend David Fraser and his family – are avocets, black-winged stilts, skuas, sooty terns, hoopoes, golden orioles and great white herons – these last fascinating in appearance and extremely shy.

Of course, the species named above are only a small part of the summer population of birds. Brother Henry, when he came to stay, compiled a more impressive list, although I'm bound to say that some thereon – the Spanish sparrow, for example – failed to thrill me as they did him.

'Stop the car, you bloody fool!' he would shout at his driver (all bird watching on the salt marshes, or most of it, because of Henry's physical affliction and the laziness of some of his relations, being car-borne). 'Stop the car, you idiot. You're not interested in anything that's smaller than a bloody eagle – that's a Spanish sparrow in that bush!'

'Well, what's it doing there?' I would enquire, endeavouring to stoke up my enthusiasm.

'It's on holiday, my dear boy,' Henry would reply, absorbing its apparent beauty.

'Not much different from an English sparrow, or a Scotch one, or a Welsh one.'

'No resemblance whatever, my dear fellow, but you're too much of a bloody fool to notice it.'

The minutes would slip by.

'Why don't you photograph it?' he would ask.

'Well,' I would say, in hesitation, 'my film's getting low. Besides, the car's at the wrong angle. And, if I get out, it'll push off!'

'Very likely,' Henry would reply, 'and I don't blame it. Being photographed by some damned fool who doesn't recognize one can't be much fun. All right, drive on. We'll go and look for your damned great white herons.'

We came on our first one together – Henry and I. It was sitting by a strip of water in the early morning. I thought that it was a stork, at first; and so, I think, did Henry, though he kept it to himself. It looked to me as though it had been roosting there all night. It seemed suspicious of the car, although we were a long way off and, finally, flew away, its long legs trailing out behind it, ending in black feet.

These feet proved to us that it was, indeed, a great white heron, rather than a lesser egret, whose feet, like its legs, are yellow. We read up the bird book, and discovered that such birds are marked as being residents of Turkey, here and there in Spain, and other areas remote from where we were. We saw no mention of them in our area, according to the maps, pin-pointing the location of each species.

Even French bird-watchers, when we broached the subject to them later, seemed to think we were discussing a mere egret. In the course of time, however, we discovered certain dedicated ornithologists who shared our view of their correct identity.

One evening, with my mother-in-law and my camera in tow, we watched a flock of knots for some time, in the shallow water of a pond, the sun being behind us, a sure method of getting near birds without disturbing them an hour or so before the sun goes down. Feeling I needed exercise, I left my mother-in-law where she was, and walked along the sea wall, over which I could see that the tide was high. I had not gone far, when I saw a great white heron, two salt marshes away.

Serpent-like, I crawled towards it down the path below the sea wall, flanked by little bushes and long grass that gave me cover. On arrival at the end of the first salt marsh, I paused to regain my breath and viewed my quarry flying over the dividing bank between the first and second salt marshes, towards me.

Crouching down, and getting my Pentax into a suitable position for a snapshot, through the long lens, as the bird flew over me, I watched its flight. To my amazement, it planed down and settled in the corner of the salt marsh in the shallow water, not ten yards from where I lay. I levered my equipment forward, took a reading through the grasses, found it good, and snapped the bird – and snapped and snapped again. It took no notice, and continued wading through the shallow water.

Suddenly, it raised its head, presenting me with what I thought would be a final photograph, before it flew away; then lowered it again, as yet another great white heron flew across the intervening bank and settled in the water by its side.

In anguish lest my mother-in-law, tiring of her contemplation of the knots, should walk in innocence along the sea wall and disturb my new-found friends, I snapped away until the film was finished. Then, triumphant, I disturbed my models, folded up my camera, retraced my steps and drove my tactful mother-in-law back to dinner.

Studying the casing of the film that I had used that evening, I discovered, to my chagrin, that the DIN or ASA or whatever (I am but an amateur photographer) had not been on the number that it should have been. My holiday was ruined, and, for three weeks, I spent sleepless nights, disturbing my wife's slumbers with the constant cry, 'The ASA should have been on eighty,' (or the DIN, whichever). Only when, a shadow of my former self, I drove to Petersfield one afternoon, picked up the film and saw the negatives and prints in the folder, did I smile again.

Parked off the main road (at the same spot, incidentally, on which I read the criticisms in the Sunday papers after my first nights), I came to the conclusion that, no matter what Lord Snowdon might think of my photographs (nor did he think much of them, when I showed them to him later, though he did his best to camouflage the fact), they were quite good enough for me. (I mean to show one here, if it will stand the transfer.)

'To Hell,' I said to myself, as I drove back home to wife and family, 'to Hell with ASA, DIN and all the rest of it. I have been closer to a great white heron (two great whites, to be precise) than most men have, and I have got a record of it.'

Next time we visited the Ile de Ré, I hardly saw my herons, except from a distance, on the edge of the receding tide, beyond the range of my lens even, which, by this time, was a Novoflex. Their absence from the marshes was, in fact – although I did not know it then – a blessing in disguise, because in spite of my expensive new lens, I was still an amateur photographer of quite astonishing incompetence. For instance, during all that year, I photographed birds (other, thankfully, than great white herons) which appeared, when I studied the prints, to come out rather smaller than they would have had I used an Instamatic.

Only when I got to Italy the next year, did I learn the reason why. Displaying, with some pride, my camera and lens to Oliver van Oss – a fellow guest of Caroline and Ian Gilmour's in a villa above Lucca, I was brought up short by a remark to the effect that, when I bought my Novoflex, it should have had a hood attached.

'I've always thought that,' I confided in him, 'but it wasn't attached.'

'Let me have a closer look at it,' he said, and, having done so, added with a smile, 'It was, you know.' He unscrewed the hood from

The author
with Dinah on
the lawn of
Drayton House,
East Meon.

*Previous page*
Great White
Herons

Goblin at Ascot. The Queen and Queen Mother are in the background.

the last section of the lens, reversed it, and then screwed it into its correct position.

'But I spent last summer on the Ile de Ré,' I told him, in deep anguish, 'photographing all the time, with that hood hanging useless round the end of the last section of the lens.'

'You're very lucky that you didn't lose it.'

Then, to comfort me, he told me how, once, he had bought a fog lamp for his car, and, thrilled by the performance of his purchase, driven through fog with a new-found feeling of security for some years.

'Evidently you don't like your fog lamp, Mr van Oss,' said the garage man, one day.

'Of course I do,' said Oliver. 'I find it quite invaluable.'

'Then why is it you've never had a bulb in it?'

A few days after I had picked up my white heron photographs, I walked into St James, Piccadilly, Church House, to watch a rehearsal of *The Dame of Sark*. I listened to a duologue performed by Celia Johnson and Tony Britton for ten minutes, shook hands with them and the cast and the director, and went out into the street a happy man. In those ten minutes, it had been conveyed to me with unmistakable conviction that the play was all that I had hoped it would be, and that the performances – all that I had seen, at any rate – were quite outstanding. When we came to Oxford, Rachel and I had no worries.

Sure enough, the first night went well. The drama critics wrote nice things and Donald Albery booked in the play to Wyndhams, if – and there was quite a big 'if' – Celia would go to London.

One assumes, of course, that every player, male or female, wants to go to London, except when a play is proved to be unwatchable on tour – and even, sometimes, then. Not so with Celia. The fact is that she only wants to go to Nettlebed, and, more specifically, to Merrimoles, the house enclosed by a romantic beech wood in which she lived for so many years with her husband and brought up her charming children.

Irritating to most playwrights as this preference is bound to be, this one, at least, though sharing in that irritation far too frequently, finds it refreshing. Analysed, it simply means that this enchanting actress puts life before acting, country before London, children before make-believe.

I learned this early on in our acquaintanceship, when Celia and the Clift/Minster/Home triumvirate sat round a desk on the top floor of the Strand Theatre in London, and we invited her to play the lead in *The Reluctant Debutante*.

'I'll ring you up tonight from home,' she promised Mr Clift, 'and tell you "yes" or "no" for certain.'

'Does that mean,' Clift asked her, 'that you have your reservations?'

'Oh, no,' Celia said placidly. 'It merely means I've got to get permission out of Nannie.'

Nannie gave her clearance and, at our next meeting, to discuss the casting of the other actors, Paul Clift said to Celia,

'The flash young man, Miss Johnson,' (we were formal in those days!). 'A most important part. What I might term the catalyst.'

'It is, indeed,' said Celia.

'Have you got any good ideas?'

'Jack Merrivale,' she answered, without hesitation.

'Is he good?'

'I don't know about that,' said Celia, 'but he can drop me off on Henley Bridge to pick up my car every evening on his way home.'

I laughed, Paul Clift looked non-plussed, and Minster smiled sardonically. Jack Merrivale was booked, and his performance was outstanding, which, of course, was no surprise to Celia. In other words, beneath this carefree attitude to her profession, lurks a dedicated actress of exceptional ability, who is a 'natural' and, too, a highly trained technician.

It occurs to me in passing, that one would be hard put to recall a single part that Celia has played, in a career that stretches over more than fifty years, that one would wish to criticize adversely, even in the smallest detail. Indeed, looking through her scrap book, if she has one (which I doubt) for hostile criticism of her acting, I would be prepared to bet a tidy sum that the most dedicated searcher would be hard pressed to find even one.

For how could anybody criticize her, on the stage or off it? On, her technique is outstanding, her integrity unquestioned, her vitality unrivalled, and her dedication total. Off, her charm is irresistible, her humour stimulating, and her modesty endearing.

'I come from a long line of bridge players,' she said to me once, 'beginning with my aunt who once remarked, as she finished playing a hand, "Had I known that hearts were trumps, I would have played it very differently." '

And yet, this paragon of all the virtues can induce an ulcerous condition in even the most complacent and well-balanced impresario by telling him at supper, after a successful first night on tour, that she has no possible desire to go to London.

'But I've got a theatre next month,' he tells her.

'Too bad,' says she, toying with her turbot.

At this point, a tactful manager like Ray, will turn the conversation towards trivia – asking her how long it takes her to get back to Nettlebed from Oxford, then comparing that with how long it takes his near-suicidal playwright to get back to Hampshire, or his leading man to London.

The meal over, he will then escort her, as indeed Ray did, to her car, and return, crestfallen, to the table.

'Don't discuss it now, she said,' he told us, calling for the bill.

'Then when will you discuss it?' asked his apoplectic playwright.

'Donald wants to know by Wednesday.'

'She'll do it,' Rachel told me in the car on the way home.

'How do you know that? She may hate the play.'

'She doesn't hate the actors, though. She likes them all, and the director and the manager and you.'

'And Merrimoles,' I said, with bitterness.

'She'll do it,' my wise wife repeated, composing herself for sleep.

On Wednesday, Ray Cooney rang me. 'First night, Wyndhams, 19 October,' he said.

'Well done, Ray. For how long?'

'Six months.'

'Oh, well,' I said, knowing, as I did, that that was her invariable contract, that however well a play is doing, at the end of six months Celia will wave goodbye and motor off to Nettlebed, another job concluded and well done, leaving behind a broken-hearted playwright.

So we came to Wyndhams and the play was a success, transferring to the Duke of York's when Celia left, with Dame Anna Neagle. Later, when performed on television, once again with Celia and Tony Britton, it was equally successful, being in the top spot for the week in which it was shown – an unusual place to find a straight play.

Reception of *The Dame of Sark* by London critics was enthusiastic on the whole, though one of them – by no means the least influential – irritated me by what he wrote and also caused me some disquiet. Between the lines of his review (and not only between them) I could sense again the blind antagonism that I had experienced during the New Wave revolution in the nineteen sixties – a determination on the part of the reviewer to dismiss the play as right-wing propaganda rather than a human story.

'The play's main thread,' wrote this critic, 'consists of the Dame's relationship with Count von Schmettau, the Channel Islands Commandant, portrayed as a gallant soldier of the old school loyally carrying out the orders of a government of which he was ashamed.'

Correct so far, but then he went on, 'This, of course, raises the question of German obedience. But Mr Home is not the one to open that can of beans.'

Well! Well!! – had not Mr Home opened that very can of beans in no less than three separate elections during the Second World War and finished up in Wormwood Scrubs for doing so! Was it likely, therefore, that in a play devoted to that theme, he would avoid the issue? Inconceivable – nor did he, as was noted by Harold Hobson in *The Sunday Times* – 'Slowly, delicately, at times very amusingly,' he wrote, 'Mr Douglas Home reveals to us the increasing peril of the Dame of Sark's position. But the striking dramatic merit of his play is that almost unconsciously the growing realization breaks upon us that the person who is really and most frighteningly threatened is not the Dame of Sark at all, but Colonel von Schmettau.'

There, to quote one favourable critic only, lies the proof that in *The Dame of Sark* the can of beans was well and truly opened by its author. There too lies the proof, alas, that the first quoted critic, fascinated by the trivialities outside the can of beans – such as 'the feudalism' of the Dame, the fact that Count von Schmettau was 'a perfect gentleman . . .' (I quote) – forgot to lift the open cover of the can and look inside it.

Calming down a little, I decided against taking any counter-action, as I had with *Aunt Edwina*. After all, the play was running well and my particular *bête noire* was only one of a minority. None the less, I kept a weather eye on the barometer, since instinct and experience both told me that the needle before long would point to 'stormy'. As it turned out, I was right.

## Chapter 13
# Drama Critics

I feel bound to write a chapter on dramatic critics, if only because I have a well-earned reputation for disliking some of them, namely, that section which devotes its time to damning plays for non-artistic reasons. Naturally, I've quarrelled with the others in my time as well – as in the case of *Aunt Edwina* when I thought their universal verdict was the wrong one – but such battles were not waged against their good faith, only with a view to questioning their judgement. Critics who review politically or socially, however, are the objects of my lasting enmity. Against such people, I wage public war and, although suffering from grievous wounds and, sometimes, near extinction, I feel bound to go on doing so in order to pin-point an ever-present danger to the theatre.

This danger is the possibility, remote admittedly, but none the less conceivable, that one day not just some but ALL dramatic critics might be guilty of political or social bias, thus ensuring that no plays by authors on their black list saw the light of day, except perhaps for a short time. Such censorship, in one form or another, has occurred and still occurs in other countries. It could happen here. The price of its avoidance is eternal vigilance.

Consider, for a moment, all it needs to institute such censorship. No Governmental edict is required, no police ban, no book-burning, no destruction of a canvas. The suppression of a play or rather, of its production, is a push-over. The sole requirement is for critics on the first night to unite in damning it since, in these hard financial times, few plays survive such treatment, impresarios being unwilling to spend money on a lame duck. Once a play is taken off and marked down as a failure, it is seldom revived.

Happily, two kinds of critics at present turn up at first nights. Also, happily, the dedicated critics still outweigh the propagandists.

Could the weight shift one dark night in favour of the latter? It is not impossible.

Imagine, for example, Miss Vanessa Redgrave being signed up by some London paper as their drama critic. Think of Messrs Wedgwood Benn, Clive Jenkins, Tariq Ali – any left-wing characters, in fact, you care to mention – manning the rest. 'What chance then,' one might ask, 'for any playwright tarred with the Establishment brush?'

'Quite impossible,' I hear the disbeliever say. 'Ridiculous! It couldn't happen that such people would be critics.' I agree.

But what if unknown people, with the same approach to politics, were critics – that each London editor signed up, unwittingly, a drama critic with an inbuilt leaning towards left-wing politics who found it very hard – if not impossible – to praise the work of those whom he assumed to be in opposition to his blue-print for a better world?

Some say I dream, like Walter Mitty in reverse, of persecution. None the less, my instinct tells me that I am not dreaming and the evidence at my disposal strengthens that conviction. Therefore I feel bound to spotlight the political or social bias in the writings of dramatic critics of whatever eminence.

Of course such folly earns me an unenviable reputation. 'Can't you realize you often write a bad play?' people say. Even my wife tells me sometimes that my theory that every play I write is first-class is untenable. My answer is that any playwright has to think that every play he writes is first-class, otherwise he loses confidence. As for the critics, let them criticize adversely if they will, but let me fight back, if they criticize unfairly.

Take a play of mine which flopped a year or two back – called *Rolls-Hyphen-Royce*. The theme was the collaboration between Henry Royce and Charles Rolls which resulted in their joint production, after many tribulations, of a splendid car. It then pursued the history of the firm – Charles Rolls's death at Bournemouth in an aircraft crash and Henry Royce's change of heart thereafter, in that he indulged in aeroplane production having been most violently opposed to doing so before his colleague's fatal accident. It ended with Royce's knighthood and his death.

A simple enough tale one would have thought, and a permissible theme, chosen for the drama generated by those two outstanding and divergent characters as well as by their joint achievement. Yet the critic of a well-known journal saw the situation from a different angle, baldly stating in his notice: 'Mr Home selects this theme in order to illustrate the operation of the gentlemen's club.'

There lies a prime example of the kind of criticism I deplore. Without one jot of evidence, this critic tells the public that I took the theme of Rolls and Royce for social reasons, rather than dramatic – that my purpose in writing the play was to make propaganda for what, in his world of fantasy, he called 'the gentlemen's club'.

Not content with this bizarre conclusion, he went on to say – I will not bore the reader with exact quotations, but the cutting is already pasted in my scrap-book by my faithful wife – that Henry Royce allowed himself to be seduced by Charles Rolls into joining the establishment (he even used that hackneyed phrase in his review) and, finally, betrayed his class by accepting a knighthood in his last years.

Small wonder, in such circumstances, that this most long-suffering and tolerant of playwrights sometimes finds himself wondering if the game is worth the candle. Of course, playwrights with financial independence might remain indifferent to such things and carry on regardless. I, alas, find myself in no such position. Unlike the picture of me, inscribed on the hearts of certain drama critics, I am no capitalist. In 1946 a letter came to me one morning from the family solicitor in Edinburgh. I recollect the thrill that I experienced on reading the first sentence –

'In view of the steep rise in taxation since the war, we have decided the £500 that each of you has been receiving annually as income, must be . . .'

Here I paused in my perusal and performed a jig around the breakfast table in anticipation of the goodies due to fall into my lap. Then I read on 'the £500, etc., must be reduced to £250.' That then is, or was, my private income, long since swallowed by the Inland Revenue.

In public life, the picture is a little different. In that sector, I have a large income – 83% of which is apt to go to the Exchequer leaving me with 17%, a weekly income (if I earn £1000 that week) of £170. Not a bad sum, one might think, until one recollects that if I wished to buy a new car to replace my Volvo (with 187,000 miles on the clock as I write) with its modern equivalent priced at £5000 plus, I would need to earn a sum of £30,000 or more. Though well aware that I am not unique in this predicament, I open this can up to show that flops are matters of great import to me, as to any other playwright, and that I am only mildly chuffed by my successes. That is why I bought a racehorse by the name of Goblin, since his winnings are not subject to taxation. I allow myself a wry smile at the thought that I, a geriatric dramatist with quite a few successes to his name, instead of shunting gently into honorary retirement, should be faced with the alternatives of either going into exile or buying a racehorse. By the time this book is published Goblin will have entered on his four-year-old career (or, even possibly, concluded it) with all that that implies for his proud owner.

To return to drama critics, certainly a playwright sometimes writes a bad play but, at the same time, I must confess to wondering how any playwright with a long list of successes to his credit can produce a drama quite so bad as some of his detractors say it is. He may be a shade off form on occasions. He may have selected a bad theme. His play may be directed badly. It may even be cast wrongly; but it seems unlikely that a playwright of experience should be so much off form as to earn the uncompromising 'thumbs down' treatment which is sometimes meted out to him. Indeed, one wonders whether any writer, painter, sculptor or musician ever falls so far below his normal level as to merit virulent abuse and ridicule, such as a playwright often suffers in the theatre. The years that he has spent maturing his style, polishing his dialogue, selecting his plots and perfecting his construction would seem to rule out the possibility that any play of his, spread over two hours, lacks all merit.

Yet experience – not only as regards myself but also certain of my colleagues – shows that, in the theatre, such total condemnation is not uncommon. Could this be, one wonders, because drama is the stuff on which dramatic critics feed – that some of them vie with those on stage in the production of dénouements, *coups de théâtre* and dramatic *tours de force*, and thus experience the thrill of giving a performance albeit in print? If this is so then it would seem that the important quality required in a dramatic critic should be strength of character, which would help him fight against the urge to slam on rouge and grease-paint and write his review on stage instead of from the semi-isolation of his stall.

Both Rattigan and Coward, to mention only two who in their later years confessed to having been destroyed, if only temporarily, by such criticisms, saw no future in producing plays in order to provide a row of sitting targets for those critics who had strayed, like killer sharks, into the waters in which they had swum, with buoyancy, for so long. Others like myself, with wives (and children still at school), sought vainly to persuade them that an artist has the right to choose his theme and that a critic who assails him for so doing is a Philistine.

When one looks back on it, of course, it has its funny side. Ken Tynan, for example, who assumed the role of self-appointed scourge of playwrights like myself, himself contributed to *Oh Calcutta*. Having been the Galahad and the St George of criticism, slaying the old-fashioned dragon known to students of the species as The Well Made Play, he shocked his friends and enemies alike by putting on a show (still running at the time of writing) which, whatever other merits it may have, is not the kind of favour that one would expect so dedicated a crusader to pin to his helm.

Apart from providing the title of this book, for which I am duly grateful, with his 'Mr Home (pronounced Hume), made me foam (pronounced fume)': he sometimes started his reviews of my plays with the phrase 'The Honourable William tells us'. Later, Clive Barnes, on the *New York Times*, took up the same theme, cracking jokes about my name and parentage. I sent a cable off in jest, reminding him that Tynan started the fashion, and concluding with the warning 'Look what happened to him'. When *The Jockey Club Stakes* came on in New York the next year, he gave it a rave review.

Once, in the first interval of a new play of mine, my wife and I went to a pub in order to avoid our friends and the dramatic critics. In the latter trooped in force. We hid behind our programmes. When the time came, they all left, excepting one who ordered eggs and bacon and a double whisky. We departed, trailing his more dedicated colleagues. On the pavement outside, I remarked to Rachel, 'I'll report that fellow to his editor. He isn't coming back.' 'Quite right,' she said, 'but wait for his review. It might be good.' It was – one of the best!

On another first night, we sat in the circle. As the lights went down, I left my seat to calm my nerves by pacing up and down. Just before the curtain rose, a figure tip-toed through the gloom and took my empty seat. My wife thought it was me, returning from the lavatory. At intervals throughout the act, each time some passage in the play or some forgotten line offended her, she seized my (as she thought) thigh in a vice-like grip, imbedding her nails in it. When the act concluded and the lights went up, beside her sat the critic of the *Morning Star* – behind her, with the other standing-onlys, stood her anguished husband. None the less, next morning, this brave, bruised and battered critic came up with an excellent review.

Once Tynan, noticing a modern musical he did not like, wrote, 'There is one tune in this piece of which Liszt would have been proud (and indeed was).' Well-informed and witty. Memories like these I cherish since they mellow me and make me long for an armistice followed by a peace treaty.

## Chapter 14
# The 'Bird' and the Kingfisher

Ten years ago or more I wrote a play called *Betzi*, on the subject of Napoleon and his last lady love on St Helena, a young English girl of sixteen. In the Salisbury production at the Playhouse, I enjoyed myself immensely in the company of Reggie Salberg, then the manager, and the director of the play, Oliver Gordon. The latter was a cricketer of some distinction, with an apt turn of phrase. The story went that once, directing *Romeo and Juliet*, he halted the rehearsals while he went to do what he was always pleased to call 'a weasel'. On returning, he called out to Romeo, 'OK cock – finish what you've got to say, and then piss off left!'

He did a superb production of my *Betzi*, with an actor called George Waring in the lead, and Patricia Brake playing the part of Betzi Balcombe, the young daughter of the representative of the East India Company in Jamestown. But, although the play was a success, the West End managers were lukewarm, so I put it on the shelf with *The Bank Manager*.

Some years later, interest revived, and Herbert Lom consented to play Bonaparte. We started our pre-London tour (and ended it) in Guildford. There, I had a salutary experience. On the first night, quite early in the play, I told myself (and Rachel, in a whisper) that one of the actresses was miscast, through no fault of her own.

Later in the week, profoundly worried still, I drove to Guildford for a matinee. I watched the first act, underwent the same reaction and, at interval time, left my seat, in order to parade my doubts before the manager and the director. On the way up the steep stairs, I found myself behind a couple.

'Geoffrey,' said the lady to her husband, 'what do you think of that girl?'

'I think that she deserves a better play,' said he.

I joined the manager for tea and biscuits with my criticisms routed, and reported 'Geoffrey's' verdict to him. 'That'll teach you,' he said, laughing loudly, and I had no option but to join him.

*Betzi* came to London to the Haymarket. The actress I had thought to be miscast came up trumps, but the play came off in the pre-Christmas period. Believing Herbert Lom would take this very much to heart, I went to say goodbye and thank you to him in his dressing-room.

'It's very sad,' I said, 'because you gave a great performance – the play should have run.'

'I'm sad, too. Not so sad as you are, though.'

'And why not?'

'Because,' said he, standing there before me in his riding boots and breeches and his green coat, every inch an Emperor, with his black hat in his hand, 'I've got a fortnight left in which to sell the Christmas trees I grow down at my farm in Kent, and if we had run on, I wouldn't have been able to get rid of them.'

*Betzi* came off at the end of 1975. During 1976, I had no play produced, so far as I remember, although plans for several productions in the following year were maturing: four plays, no less.

Jubilee year, it seemed, was all set to be a landmark in my life, with three plays running in the West End at the same time, all financial worries dissipated by the flow of royalties – distinction, acclamation and fame were to be my lot. In fact, my bottoms were all sunk, to quote Antonio in circumstances of comparable disaster or, where not sunk, prematurely towed to harbour and laid up, though still seaworthy.

*In The Red* and *Rolls-Hyphen-Royce* were the two plays which went down with all hands, holed below the water-line. *The Kingfisher* and *The Perch* were the two plays laid up, prematurely. *The Perch* at Pitlochry, directed by Joan Knight was well received by audience and critics but has not, to date, moved further southwards.

*In The Red* began in Windsor – Gerald Harper, Dinah Sheridan and a good cast. The first night there was not encouraging. I found myself depressed and nervous during supper in an adjacent restaurant after curtain fall. My family were there in force – wife, son and daughters, interested parties too, like David Barton my accountant, and, of course, the manager, John Gale. In spite of my doubts, however, the run at Windsor was a sell-out, breaking records for a straight play. My second visit and my third encouraged me to think that teething trouble was now past, that the cast was on top of its performance, and that *In The Red* was heading for a rosy future.

At this moment, when the clouds of doubt were lifting, John Gale informed me that he had decided not to take the play to London. This infuriated me, which fury turned to paranoia after we arrived in Richmond and broke records there as well. Then Allan Davis, the director, and I took a brave but foolhardy decision. 'John,' we told Gale, 'we are going to carry on with the play ourselves, take it into London and, together, make a fortune from it.'

'Good luck to you,' said he.

We informed the actors, some of whom were far from pleased to hear of our self-sacrifice. However, loyalty prevailed, and naturally, those members of the cast who had not yet appeared in London were delighted. Meanwhile, Allan and I tried to find a theatre. This task was made more difficult as a result of John Gale having dropped out. 'If a well known impresario,' the owners of the theatres that we approached would ask us, 'doesn't want to do the play, what makes you think that we will?'

'We don't think,' we would reply, 'we just hope.' That hope remained unfulfilled till the eleventh hour. By now we were in Brighton, where we played (as we learned later) to more money than *The Kingfisher* was to do some weeks later. None the less, in spite of lacking knowledge at the time of that encouraging comparison, we were elated. So much so that, when the Whitehall Theatre became available, we made advances to Paul Raymond and arranged for our arrival in the West End ten days later, with four nights of previews and a first night on the Friday.

Nothing could discourage us from this mad venture, not even the knowledge that for some years the Whitehall had been the home of Paul Raymond's revues and possibly, in consequence, had lost its straight play audience. Nor were we put off by the fact that every ticket agency and critic – even though the public may have been in blissful ignorance – knew that the manager had washed his hands of *In The Red*, in company with every other impresario in London – every owner of whatever theatre, except Paul Raymond, who at that

time was producing a review called *Penetration*, an advertisement
for which appeared on one page in our programme, to the consternation of those aunts of mine who came upon it on the first
night!

Allan and I had our blood up. We were going to prove that our
judgement of the play was sound – we would produce the damned
thing and be damned!

We *were* damned, and without equivocation, by the critics.
Although Brighton had been a triumphal march, although the
figures for the London previews rose excitingly each evening, the
first night was an unqualified disaster and the critics vitriolic –
witness random quotes from speeches for the prosecution the next
morning.

'You can imagine William Douglas Home scheming up this little
atrocity. How about a playwright, he thinks, a pleasant upper middle
class fellow like myself – though nothing aristocratic, what?'
*Guardian*.

'Once again WDH gallops forth in defence of an English elite
imperilled by the bureaucratic dragon.' *The Times*.

I wondered, wryly, why such critics always raised the spectre of
political and social privilege when noticing a modern play in which
the plot required the presence of some 'elite' individual – I use the
phrase 'a modern play' deliberately never having read a notice of
*The Merchant of Venice* couched in similar terms – for example,
'Shakespeare once again rides forth in defence of an elite city merchant beset by a proletarian Jewish money-lender'; or, of *Romeo and
Juliet* 'the offspring of the elite Capulet and Montagu families,
inhabitants of two large mansions in Verona, one of which employs
a Nannie, seek the help of an Establishment priest to resolve their
upper-class dilemma.'

I took the papers up to Rachel in the flat. It was unnecessary to
warn her of their content as we both knew *In The Red* was doomed,
in spite of Allan's brave attempt to subsidize it. So much for the
first leg of my West End treble.

The next play which came on was *The Kingfisher*. Some years
before, I had been asked, by a theatrical director who was a stranger
to me, to write a concluding act to three short one act plays respectively by Beerbohm, Wedekind and St John Hawkins. This I tried to

do for fun and as an exercise in playwriting, although there was no possible connection between any of the three and very little between any of them and my own.

Not unexpectedly there was no pay-off to this voluntary venture. He turned it down, in fact. Some years later, after reading through my little offering, I found it good and took it as the basis for the opening scene of a full length play called *The Hot Water Bottle*. This I offered to Sir Ralph, who first received it, as he told me later, on his birthday. Possibly in some way influenced by this coincidence, he also found it good.

At this stage, it is necessary to mention a long-standing contract that I have with Peter 'Mousetrap' Saunders which I entered into after borrowing the sum of £1500 from him (repaid a few months later) to help *Aunt Edwina* recuperate from her initial rape. This contract gave Peter three options on whatever new plays I might write – nor did he lose an option if he did not exercise it: it continued, intact and unscathed until he did.

At the time of *The Kingfisher*, he had one option still outstanding. In fact, had I let him do another play of mine which, as a great friend, he allowed me to withdraw from circulation, it being a skit on the Royal Family which I decided was a shade beyond the pale – our contract would, by then, have terminated. As it was, with one to go, he took up the option on *The Hot Water Bottle*, hereinafter called *The Kingfisher*.

Sir Ralph, however, felt that he would like to do it at the National, because he had been working there for some time and he wanted to continue the association. This both Peter and I understood. It also crossed my mind that to have a William Douglas Home play at the National would insert a much-needed feather in my cap. No longer would I be the West End 'boulevardier' alone; instead, I would join other playwrights of my vintage (ninety-two-year-old Ben Travers, for example) in a new, exciting world. I would no longer be described, disparagingly, as 'commercial' (a substantial subsidy, such as the National receives, excluding it, for some strange reason, from that company); I would be one of the immortals – Pinter, Ayckbourn, Shakespeare and the rest – who had received the accolade.

I therefore went to Peter Saunders and asked for *The Kingfisher* back. Peter let me have it on condition that I added yet another option to his contract, thus allowing him to stage two more new plays, instead of one. To this I instantly agreed, since I had set my heart on a production at the National.

I motored to the South Bank, and encountered Peter Hall for the first time. I liked him on the instant. He was sensible, unruffled, humorous and kindly, and these qualities, in such surprising contrast to the picture painted of him by some sections of the media, warmed my heart. Only one small cloud loomed on the far horizon, forecasting, perhaps, unsettled weather in the future. Peter did not like my happy ending, and required a sad one, which, in fact, he got – but not in the script!

During the ensuing month, I tried such endings – sad or semi-sad or tragic – of all shapes and sizes, tragi-comic endings even (as detailed by Hamlet) till the motive for performing all this overtime was overtaken by events. The log jam at the National, caused by delays in building, led to Peter handing over the production of *The Kingfisher* to Lindsay Anderson. At the same time, and due to the same causes, he told me that the play would be a National production at a West End theatre, where it would stay until it could be slotted into his revised National schedule.

I rang Ralph one morning, and I said, 'I'm meeting Lindsay at Marcelle's in Sloane Street for lunch. Tell me how I'll recognize him when he comes in.'

'You will see,' said Ralph, 'a little Caesar in a leather jacket.'

Sure enough, just such a figure came into the restaurant. I like to think we clicked at once. We talked of Ralph Richardson and Celia Johnson, who was to play the leading lady, of Allan Webb, who was to be Ralph's old retainer, and of Alan Tagg, the set designer at the National. This last (not Alan Tagg, the National itself), was not one of my new friend's favourites; indeed, he waxed eloquent against it. I was more concerned about the play, however.

'Will he,' I was saying to myself, as I sipped my Dubonnet, listening to his outspoken strictures on that great, much-longed-for, monument to British culture, 'will he tell me that he doesn't like my ending? Will he ask me for a tragic ending, just as Peter did, in which case I will have a lot more writing to do?'

In fact, Lindsay rode that problem with a light rein, indicating, more or less, that he was neutral, said that Celia was wrong in thinking she lacked glamour (which was also my conviction), and left me with the impression that the version of the ending I preferred would not offend him.

I left Marcelle's with the pleasant feeling that, although I came to meet a stranger, I was leaving having met a new and understanding friend. Events thereafter have not changed this first impression.

Peter Hall next fixed the dates for the tour and negotiated for a theatre in London. The barometer seemed set fair. William Douglas Home, the ageing playwright, was about to join his peers on the South Bank with a production at the National. I cannot say my children were excited by the prospect, living, as they do, a life detached from their ambitious father, but my wife and I allowed ourselves a measure of excitement.

I woke each morning with the sun already shining on my pillow. As I shaved, I saw the face of a successful playwright, just about to leave the field of 'commerce' and erect his tent, instead, on a subsidized site.

Then, suddenly, the storm broke. Laurence Evans, rang to tell me that the *Evening Standard*, if his information was correct, had just been briefed about the National's intended sally into the West End; that articles denouncing such a move had already been written; that they would appear in the next few days; and that his impression was that the Society of West End Theatre Managers had declared war on my vulnerable little *Kingfisher*.

A meeting was convened forthwith. It took place at Ralph Richardson's house in Regents Park. Among those present were myself, Peter Hall, Lindsay Anderson and Laurence Evans. Peter opened the proceedings with the firm assertion that he wished to carry on regardless – touring dates were fixed already, and a London theatre would shortly be forthcoming. He was more than ready to ride out the storm. Lindsay lay on the sofa, staring at the ceiling. Ralph, whisky in hand, sat watching us with a benign and fatherly affection. Laurence Evans summed up on behalf of all.

He readily conceded that the situation might be nasty if the *Evening Standard* articles were published, as he had good reason to believe they would be. He brought up the adverse effect that such opposition might have on the prospects of the play. Of course it might have none, the storm might blow itself out, Peter might well get away with it. 'It's really up to William,' he concluded.

Ralph's eyes turned to me, and so did Peter's. Lindsay still preferred to commune with the ceiling. I looked back at Peter, and a wave of sentiment engulfed me. 'This poor fellow,' I thought to myself, 'is going through a rough time. Almost every day an article appears in the Press, criticizing him adversely for the way in which he runs the National. Why should I be responsible for adding to his burdens? Why should *The Kingfisher* be used as a weapon with which to assault him further?'

My thoughts turned towards self-interest. 'Is it wise,' I asked myself, 'to let my fledgling hatch out in an atmosphere of conflict? Would it not be prudent to withdraw it from the battlefield?'

I made my mind up: 'Peter,' I said, 'can I have my play back, please?' He nodded. At this point, so far as I recall, Sir Ralph, benign and understanding fellow that he is, refilled my glass. There ended my association with the National – not yet renewed, my new-found friend having but recently turned down two plays that I submitted to him.

Back at home, I thought the situation over. Then, as is my custom in moments of stress, I wrote a letter to *The Times*, in which I gave my reason for withdrawing the play. Its publication clarified the situation, and explained the pressure to which I had been subjected. In the letter, I said I would make no plans for a production else-where – that is to say, by a West End manager – until I had an under-taking from that body that it was not their intention to dictate to playwrights as to where their plays should be performed.

'A playwright,' I asserted with profound conviction (and a measure of pomposity), 'must be allowed to place his play wherever he desires to place it.' (Many West End managers, no doubt, would have been happy to advise me of the right location for it!)

Naturally, I was aware that opposition to a National production had stemmed from the fact that the play had been given first to Peter Saunders, and it's possible that many West End managers may not have known the circumstances through which he had got it. None the less, I felt most strongly that an impermissible and, worse, successful attack had been launched against a playwright's freedom of choice. I therefore 'froze' the play.

A few days later, came a telephone call from John Gale.

'I'd like to do *The Kingfisher*,' he told me.

'Not until I have an undertaking from the West End managers,' I answered, 'that it's not their policy to influence a playwright in his choice of management.'

'Of course it isn't.'

'Well, it doesn't look that way to me. In fact, I have just been the victim of such an attempt. I want an undertaking, and in writing, that, in future, no such attempts will be made.'

'I can't speak for my colleagues.'

'Well, then, please arrange for me to get a letter from someone who can.'

The necessary letter came from Michael Codron, an important figure among West End managers. In it, to my relief, I found the undertaking I was seeking. Consequently, I unfroze the play, imposing the condition that John should attempt a joint production with the National. For reasons still obscure to me, this effort fell through. Not entirely happily, I settled for a straight West End production.

The play opened in Nottingham to instant acclaim. Some weeks later, we came into London, to the Lyric. On the night in question, at about five thirty, just as we were changing for the first night, Rachel's Uncle Dick rang through from Boodles Club to say that many theatres were blacked out in the West End. On arrival at the Lyric, we discovered that the power cut was confined to those in and around Shaftesbury Avenue, of which, of course, we were one.

In the foyer, we found friends and relatives, including all the usual aunts and uncles ('rent-a-crowd', as Jakie Astor calls them). After half an hour, the bar was opened, thus providing the frustrated customers with a welcome diversion. Lindsay made a speech to the effect that curtain rise would be postponed till nine o'clock (instead of seven) adding: 'And thanks for being so British!'

Cheerfully, the audience debunked into the damp street. Rachel and I went backstage to call on Ralph and Celia. We found the former sitting, hunched in his unheated dressing-room, awaiting the incursion of the sore throat which assailed him later in the week; the latter looking for a game of bridge. Indeed, she told us off for not selecting some bridge-playing member of the audience in order to make up a four.

The curtain rose at nine o'clock. Next day, the critics on the whole were friendly, a few even eulogistic. We looked set for a long run. Meanwhile, the third play, *Rolls-Hyphen-Royce*, was in rehearsal at the Shaftesbury while, at the Whitehall, *In The Red* was dying on its feet.

The Shaftesbury play opened without a tour, because the scenery consisted of a replica of a steel balcony which would have cost a fortune to transfer from town to town. Wilfrid Hyde White, Alfred Marks and Peter Egan played the leads: Wilfrid as commentator, doubling that part with that of Rolls' manager, Claude Johnson. Alfred Marks played Henry Royce, and Peter Egan, Charlie Rolls.

So far as I could ascertain, there were no weak spots in a large cast, with the possible exception of one, whose addiction to ad-libbing as a substitute for learning his lines properly, bid fair to throw the whole play out of gear. However, previews came and went, producing a replacement for the missing tour, and the reaction from the audiences was encouraging.

Then came the first night. The reception was as good as *In The Red*'s had been (which should, perhaps, have acted as a salutary warning). Even Wilfrid, nature's leading pessimist, retired to bed convinced that we had hit the jackpot. In the morning came the cold douche, for the second time in three weeks.

'Mr Douglas Home,' wrote our old friend whom I have previously quoted, 'has apparently been drawn to this subject as a surviving relic of the old British Class structure, and his treatment of the two partners is designed to show the democratic operation of the gentlemen's club.'

Many of his colleagues followed suit, though not (I'm happy to record) basing their notices on such a questionable premise. The play folded three weeks later, as had *In The Red*, a fortnight earlier.

My only representative in London now was *The Kingfisher*, living on its own unsullied reputation, unmoved by the fate of my other offspring, guaranteed, as I thought then, to keep me solvent through that year, the next and, hopefully, into the nineteen eighties.

I was perfectly aware, of course, that Celia would only stay six months, but I was not unduly concerned. Ralph, although not a stayer of the calibre of Matty, had already given evidence of stamina in *Lloyd George Knew My Father*, playing in it first with Peggy Ashcroft and then with Celia. I felt that, when six months was up, another leading lady would come in instead of Celia – perhaps Dame Peggy, in a vice-versa version of the previous play.

In the autumn, though, I felt the tremor of a warning shell exploding suddenly across my unsuspecting bows. John Gale informed me that he was 'concerned' about the Lyric Theatre.

'Concerned about it – why?'

'The owner got a little worried in high summer when the takings went down.'

'So did I, but they're coming up again.'

'That's right. I've told him that that trend is certain to continue, and that, in a month or so, we'll be playing to capacity. I hope he'll see sense . . .'

'He can't throw us out,' I interrupted, 'as we've never dropped below the get-out figure,' (this being the figure at which impresario or owner are entitled to give one another notice).

'That's right, but the fact is that I've a contract with him which contains a clause, which I confess to having overlooked when I signed it, which gives me the Lyric Theatre for only twenty-six weeks.'

Sure enough, the owner of the Lyric took advantage of that most unusual clause. No doubt considering that Celia's replacement might cause problems, he decided to be prudent and back a new play to replace *The Kingfisher*.

In the last weeks, I fought like a tigress for her cub in an attempt to force my impresario to find another theatre, to replace Celia, and to persuade Ralph to continue with another leading lady. It was all to no avail. We came off, playing at the box office to over £14,000 a week.

Apart from the financial loss I suffered (10% of the gross takings, for the information of those interested in worldly matters), I was shattered by this ending to a venture which had been bedevilled by misfortune from the start. I thought back to the arguments that had been put up by the West End managers, in order to secure the play for themselves – one set, cast of three, the kind of play exactly suited to theis budgets and their audiences – so on and so forth. Yet, while it was still in its prime, they took it off.

'Oh, what a fall was there, my countrymen,' I murmured to myself, 'then you and I and all of us fell down.'

Then, turning from the Bard, I wrote my own effusion and dispatched it to my leading actor, who acknowledged it with thanks:

One morning in the month of May
(The ornithologists all say)
A kingfisher to London flew
A brilliant flash of azure blue
And settled in the Avenue.

And there this lovely little bird
(So ornithologists have heard)
Would preen his plumage every night
In London's fading evening light
Until he suddenly took flight.

Some impresario, it's thought
(So ornithologists report)
Considering the crowds he drew
In summertime were far too few
Then clapped his hands and shouted 'Boo!'

But still the little creature stayed
(As ornithologists had prayed
He would) and when the autumn light
More quickly faded into night
The little kingfisher sat tight.

And sure enough his presence drew
(As ornithologists well knew
It would) the watching crowds again
To see him there, though under strain,
Defying darkness, wind and rain.

But, came the winter and he knew
(As ornithologists knew, too)
He could no longer face the clown
Who 'shooed' at him when he was down
So sadly he flew out of town.

But there will come another day
(The ornithologists all say)
When London's citizens will view
Another flash of azure blue
Along the sunlit Avenue.

And people passing in the street
(The ornithologists repeat)
Will stop and look and smile and say
'This time – on this red letter day –
The kingfisher has come to stay!'

That day has yet to dawn, but I still live in hope.

# Chapter 15
# Goblin

Though disaster struck during the year of which I have just written, causing me to stagger through the spring and summer like a punch-drunk boxer, autumn brought me compensation in another sphere – the Sport of Kings gave me my first success.

For seventeen years I had been a racehorse owner, ever since I went to stay with Aidie Darby – Alec's son-in-law – an Oxford Don who, as an undergraduate, had got a First in Economics and been master of the Drag at the same time. I saw a little creature standing in a field while we were waiting for a pheasant drive and Aidie told me that its mother was a racehorse – or its father, I forget which.

Long before the routine crows and blackbirds swooped by, heralding the advent of the beaters, we decided that it should become a racehorse in its turn. We sent it to Bill Wightman, no cash having passed between my nephew and myself since this was a joint venture: and we shared the training fees between us. Sad to relate, we shared nothing else, speaking financially. Aunt Bridget (as we named her) never reached a place once. None the less, each time she ran, I felt the thrill of ownership, the ecstasy of seeing my own colours (lent to me by Rachel's family) worn by a jockey riding a horse running under my name on the race-card (my co-owner being incognito, believing that Keble College might look on a racehorse-owning Economics Don with some disfavour).

At the same time sister Bridget, after whom the animal was named (since she is Aidie's aunt by marriage), underwent acute embarrassment each time her namesake appeared on the television screen. Deep in her armchair up in Scotland, with her knitting at the ready, she would hear the commentator saying such things as: 'There goes Aunt Bridget, spanking down to the start.' She felt better when the horse was seldom mentioned once the race had started.

Other horses followed this pathfinder (a pathfinder who had failed with such consistency to blaze the trail) because I was now bitten by the bug of ownership. One of them, Springer, cost £800. He never earned his purchase price.

Bill Wightman, at a time when I had one or two long running plays, bought a horse for me for £4000 which I called Hafiz. On his first appearance, in a race at Newbury, he threw his jockey, Willie Carson, at the start, and bit his finger. A month later, Willie rode him in a sprint at Epsom, his finger still hurting (as he told me in the paddock with some feeling) and he finished second to a good horse. Later on, at Salisbury, Hafiz was runner-up to Pitcairn. The prize money that he won on each occasion, being untaxed, was the most rewarding income I had ever earned.

Thereafter, Hafiz went sour. I retained him for another season, during which John Oaksey rode him, telling me, as he dismounted, that, in his opinion, Hafiz should take up some other sport, like golf. Certainly, he made no impact on the race course, though he carried Jamie, my son, on the gallops in the days when he was learning about racing from Bill during his vacations from the University of Bristol.

Then I lost my head and bought two horses – having sold the film rights of *The Secretary Bird* to Italy before the Houghton Sales at Newmarket. My first acquisition, Songful, was a filly by Song, and the second, Sparkenbroke, a colt by Busted. This latter was chosen by myself and Rachel, a choice deplored by Bill who, in loyalty, agreed to train him. Songful went to Jakie Astor, who had chosen her. In her first race at Windsor, ridden by Joe Mercer, she came second to a two-year-old who had already won. 'A sharp one, Mr Astor,' said Joe to the trainer on dismounting. 'You'll need to win with her quick.' But she never did win. Sparkenbroke was never placed.

More horses came and went – one called My Learned Friend, which I shared with John Oaksey. It, too, finished second, at Wincanton with his lordship on board. Second, second, always second, never first.

In spite of this frustration, I was by now hooked on racing, being unable to envisage an existence in which some racehorse or other was not carrying my colours. These were now the property of David Hampden, Rachel's uncle, who once said to me, 'I'm naturally delighted that you use the Hampden colours, but I'm wondering if they aren't a shade conspicuous for your racehorses.' Alas, Uncle David did not live to see them triumph in the end.

Towards the end of 1976 I decided on the purchase of another racehorse, in anticipation of the flood of income which was likely to be pouring into my account in the New Year. I wrote to Bill, my patient trainer, asking him to go to Ireland to buy me a horse for not more than £3000. A few days later, I received a postcard on which he wrote, 'Come and see your yearling that I bought at Ascot yesterday for £3600, Bill.'

Excitedly, we drove to Upham to be introduced to our new colt, out of Rocelle by Sun Prince. Rachel liked the look of him, forgot about his purchase price being above the limit, then returned home satisfied and looking for a suitable name. 'Sun of York' and 'Goblin' were our nap selections – 'Sun of York' because 'Now is the winter of our discontent made glorious summer by this Son of York', established some connection with Sun Prince, however tenuous; 'Goblin' because 'I'll make a Goblin of the sun', was penned by Dante Gabriel Rossetti, as I learned from my much-thumbed quotation book. We pondered for a while on the respective merits of these two names, finally deciding that to call an unknown yearling Sun of York might seem pretentious, whereas Goblin was a modest, unassuming name, the definition of the word in my *Concise Oxford Dictionary* being 'mischievous, ugly demon'.

We rang up Weatherby's to learn to our delight and surprise, that the name was free. After consultation with Bill, who approved the name because of its conciseness (I was just about to write concision, looked it up to find it equalled circumcision, and abandoned it), our colt was registered as Goblin, and went into winter quarters. Through the long dark months, we waited. 'Will this be *the* horse?' I asked myself and Rachel. 'Will the taxmen be confounded by the income he will earn, which they can't get their hands on?'

Rachel counselled caution. 'Anything can happen to a horse,' she said, 'especially a racehorse. Anyway, he's one of Sun Prince's first crop, and no one knows how good they're going to be.'

As I sat watching *The Perch* at Pitlochry, *In The Red* at Windsor, *The Kingfisher* down at Brighton, or *Rolls-Hyphen-Royce* in the Shaftesbury Theatre, my mind would wander from the business in hand. Nightly, I would dream about myself at Ascot, leading Goblin in to the ecstatic plaudits of the crowd.

'Congratulations, William,' I would hear the Queen say, 'even though you beat mine.'

'Thank you, Ma'am, that's very sporting of you,' I would answer, bowing low, grey top hat in hand.

Came the spring, and Goblin ran at Newbury – Rachel and I with Brian Rouse and Bill together in the paddock, Jamie watching us from the rail.

When I first became an owner, I assumed that detailed orders were routine between the trainer and his jockey in the paddock. Not at all. They talk – assuming that they talk at all – of shoes and ships and sealing-wax, indeed of anything except the job in hand.

'How's Mary? Has she got over the measles?' asks the trainer.

'Better, thank you,' says the jockey. 'Back at school, now.'

Then the bell rings. 'Jockeys, please mount,' calls the speaker. 'Good luck,' says the owner. 'Thank you, sir,' the jockey says, and rides down to the start. The owner, this owner at least, then hurries to the rails to place his standard wager.

'There goes Goblin,' the loudspeaker tells us. 'Royal blue and white stripes, red cap.'

In his first race, he came back some way behind the leader. Bill, however, was quite satisfied. 'His first race,' he explained, stroking the sweating animal, 'in heavy going.' 'Good old Goblin. Well done,' I said, patting his extended nostrils.

In his second race, he finished third, again at Newbury, on harder going. In the Champagne Stakes at Salisbury, he finished third again. Once more at Newbury, he finished fourth, having, according to the pundits, suffered much bad luck in running. At Goodwood he finished second, in a record-breaking run, to Tumbledownwind, who went on to win the Gimcrack.

His next race, at Newbury, was run while we were spending a week-end in Brussels on our way to Italy. He finished second to the Queen's horse, English Harbour, bringing me just that much nearer the fulfilment of the dream I mentioned earlier.

'Congratulations, Ma'am,' I would have said on that occasion, 'even though you beat mine.'

'Thank you, William,' she would have replied, 'that's very sporting of you!'

'He must get his head in front,' said Bill, when we returned to England.

'How will he do that?' I asked.

'I'll have to find a maiden race before the season ends.' He found one, God be praised, at Newmarket. We went to stay with Jakie, Rachel and I. In the morning, I played golf with Jakie on the nine hole course at Worlington. He beat me handsomely, remarking later that his game had been impaired by the stream of imaginary orders pouring from my lips throughout the round.

'Now look here, Wightman,' he insisted he had heard me muttering on every fairway, sometimes in mid-stroke, 'either you tell Lester what to do, or I do – which is it to be?'

The services of Lester Piggott had been sought and gained as a result of Jamie having told us, some days earlier, that he was likely to be short of a ride in our race. I rang Bill Wightman's stable to be told that he had left for Newmarket. His secretary, Diana Ross, however, promised she would tell him when she rang him in the evening. Sitting, worrying about the possibility of losing Piggott in the interval, I heard the telephone ring, hurried to it, to hear Diana report that Bill had engaged Piggott.

'But I thought you said he'd gone to Newmarket.'

'He had,' she said, 'but he forgot the drinks, and came back for them.'

With our round of golf completed, Jakie and I ate our sandwiches, then drove to Newmarket to watch the Cambridgeshire, which race was run in record time, a gale-force tail-wind blowing. As the time drew on towards the four o'clock race, Rachel and I stood beside the preliminary ring, watching our opponents pacing round it. Out came Goblin from the stable into the main ring. We followed. From the jockeys' changing-room came Lester, (royal blue and white stripes, red cap), I shook his hand (they say one shouldn't even do that!).

I had met him previously at the dentist, some years before. In the waiting-room, we had chatted until he went in to have a filling. When he came out, I replaced him.

'Lester's given me a winner,' said my dentist, 'for this afternoon in the first race at Epsom.'

'Thank you,' I said, trying to talk over the saliva sucker, 'I'll back it.' Which I did. When the results came through, I found the horse in question had been beaten into second place by an outsider with L. Piggott up.

I did not reminisce, however, in the ring, that afternoon. Instead I listened to Bill, talking, not, for a change, about measles, but about my Goblin.

'He can go,' said Bill, 'but you may find he's not too keen on passing other horses, tending to duck in behind them.'

'Don't you worry about that,' said Lester.

'Good luck,' I said, hurrying towards the stand to watch him go down.

'There goes Goblin,' said the commentator. 'Royal blue, white stripes, red cap.' Down he went, with Lester holding him. I followed with my glasses to the start.

'He went down marvellously,' Rachel said. 'If he comes back like that, he won't be beaten.'

I looked at the board, and saw that he was favourite, Rhineland second favourite and Welsh Jester third.

'They're under starter's orders,' said the commentator. 'They're off!'

I raised my shaking glasses to my eyes, and steadied them.

'Where is he?' Rachel asked me.

'I can't see him.'

'He's not left,' she said, with panic in her voice.

'Nobody's left,' I told her. 'I can't see him, that's all.'

Then I saw him, Lester's red cap. Suddenly, the commentator called him. He had struck the front rank on the outside, moving forward steadily. The field came closer. He was in the centre now, having come over, level with some other horses between him and the near rail.

The commentator called their names, but I forget them now. Indeed it's doubtful if I even heard them, watching Goblin as I was, and Lester coming up the centre.

'Goblin's gone to the front,' said the commentator. 'Two or three lengths clear. It's Goblin leading. Rhineland with Welsh Jester in third place. It's Goblin . . .'

I put down my glasses when the field was still a furlong out, embraced my wife, and warded off a strong congratulatory blow from Oaksey. Goblin passed the post three lengths ahead of Rhineland, with Welsh Jester three lengths back in third place. Rachel and I were already running for the paddock, absorbing the fact that, after seventeen years, we had won at last.

We stood by the unsaddling enclosure, waiting for the royal blue and white stripes and the red cap to appear. Lester rode in, beside our trainer, travelling head lad and stable boy. The great man wore a grin as he dismounted.

'Kiss the horse and not the jockey!' shouted Oaksey, thus providing himself with the motivation for his article next Sunday, in which he was to inform his readers that I tried to kiss the rider. Even had that kiss been placed on Piggott's cheek, it could have been excused in the euphoria of winning. Mikey Seely, Rachel's cousin, asked me what my future plans were. 'Fluid,' I said, and repaired to the bar. There we learned that we had broken the course record for all ages over seven furlongs on the Dewhurst Course, in spite of Lester having told Bill, 'I won very easy.'

'Never mind the wind,' said Bill, champagne in hand, 'it was a very fast time.'

'Thank you, Bill,' I said, and raised my glass to him.

Jamie came in and joined us. He reported that, while standing by the entrance to the weighing-room, Pat Eddery and Lester had walked past him.

'The next time that those two horses meet,' he heard Pat say, 'the placings will be reversed.'

'Balls!' said Piggott.

Through that winter, that word was inscribed on my heart like Calais on Bloody Mary's.

As we drove back towards Jakie's house that evening, talking over Goblin's future prospects, Rachel turned to me and said, 'We've only won a maiden race. From the way we're talking, anyone would think we'd won the Derby!'

'We'll do just that,' I said. 'But we'll have to wait till next year.'

Next year, Goblin ran last on soft going in the Guineas Trial. He ran next in the Free Handicap. Again, we stayed with Jakie.

During breakfast on the morning of the race, he turned to me
and said:

'You and your horse are very similar you know.'

'In what way, Jakie?'

'You're both rather second-rate. You ought to learn to act
accordingly.'

'There speaks your dear old mother,' I replied, recalling with
nostalgia how stimulating she had been in her outspokenness – a
quality that she had handed down with compound interest to her
youngest son.

That afternoon, we finished some way back in the Free Handicap,
behind Remainder Man – and Jakie was the first to offer sympathy.

Thereafter Bill's enthusiasm for the Derby – never very strong –
was on the wane. It took some effort to persuade him that the horse
was up to the task. He agreed to leave him in, however, and I paid
the necessary forfeit.

Then came a diversion. Tony Roye, playing the lead on tour in a
new play of mine, *The Editor Regrets*, rang me from Bath to say he
was about to undergo an urgent prostate operation.

'When?' I asked him, panic in my voice.

'As soon as possible.'

'Who's taking over from you?' I enquired, already knowing.

'You are,' he replied.

I drove to Bath that evening, Wednesday, with two suits and some
clean shirts in my suitcase and sat through the play. On Thursday
I rehearsed all day – the same on Friday. In the hotel, during supper,
Tony said, 'I wonder if you ought to play the matinee tomorrow.'

'Not on your life,' I said. 'I don't know the part yet. I'll start next
week in Bournemouth and do Brighton the week after where the
tour ends.'

'Right,' he said. 'Agreed.'

I woke next morning with a change of heart. I took my script in
one hand and my early-morning tea-cup in the other and went
through the part. Then I went down to breakfast and confronted
Tony.

'You were right,' I said, 'I'll do the matinee today.'

'I thought you said you didn't know it yet.'

'I don't, but that's not the point. The point is that if I don't do the matinee today, I'll have the whole week-end ahead of me in which to worry about Bournemouth. I'll either have a nervous breakdown or shoot myself – or both.'

I drove into Bath, feeling like some French aristocrat aboard a tumbril, heading for the guillotine. The day was hot, though not so hot as I was. I ran through my part; those members of the cast who shared the scenes in which I was involved co-operating like the troupers that they were. I took a light lunch in a restaurant next to the theatre with Tony Roye and then went to his dressing-room to rest before my first performance, a rest made less restful than it might have been because of a dedicated piano-tuner, working just outside my door.

I rose and dressed – Bill Berkeley lent me make-up and reminded me how to apply it. Came the call 'Beginners, please' and I went on stage and stood in the wings (a cigarette in each hand), listening to Marcia Fitzalan and Robin Marchal opening the play. Their dialogue continued, the stage manager came round from the prompt corner to assure himself that I was in position. I trod out my cigarettes and moved towards the outside of the set door, shaking like a jelly. When I heard my cue, I took a deep breath, thought of Rachel, turned the handle of the door, and went on.

'Getting everything you want,' I said to Robin, who was slapping his fiancée's bottom. I heard a laugh from the thin audience (remember that there was a heat wave). Maybe the laugh came from Tony. Anyway, it gave me confidence. The afternoon progressed – the prompter gave a great performance – and I drove home, feeling like some Roman Emperor coming back from a successful campaign.

One night, during the next week in Bournemouth, Rachel and I and Bill Wightman and his daughter Dulcie, dined together in the Royal Bath Hotel after the play. Bill congratulated me on my performance.

'Do we run?' I asked him.

'Who? The play or Goblin?'

'Never mind the play. That's my concern – the horse is yours.'

'He runs,' said Bill, 'provided that the weather stays like this.' I raised my glass to him.

Next Wednesday in Brighton I rose early, picked some members of the cast up at the Theatre Royal, drove to Epsom and met Rachel on the course.

Bill Wightman won the race before the Derby with Bell Tent, which I regarded as a favourable omen, since we had been galloping with him.

'Good luck,' we said to Taffy Thomas, in the paddock, and then hurried back to watch the parade. Goblin looked a picture.

Down at the start, being drawn two, he was one of the first to be loaded. Fifteen minutes later all the horses were in. While he was awaiting the completion of the loading, Goblin fell asleep. As a result, he came out very slowly – one but last in fact. He held that place until the field had reached the straight.

'He's going to be last,' Rachel said. 'Not him,' I answered, false bravado in my tone. As if in answer to my words, he started running at that moment, passing fifteen horses in the straight, and finished tenth to Shirley Heights.

'I would have been fourth or fifth,' Taffy said as he dismounted, 'if he hadn't gone to sleep.'

'Could Taffy not have noticed that?' I asked Bill later.

'Well,' said Bill, 'horses sleep standing up you know, and jockeys can't keep looking over their ears to see if their eyes are shut or not.'

Thus ended my sole tilt to date at winning the Blue Riband of the Turf – I could not have enjoyed it more.

And Goblin? Time alone will prove his true worth. Will he, in his fourth year, having eschewed sleeping while on duty and been pardoned for it, as Napoleon pardoned his sleeping sentry, beat the nine who were in front of him on that exciting afternoon, less Shirley Heights, now at stud? With two wins, by six and five lengths respectively, to finish up the season, hope still springs eternal in his owner's heart. And hope, of course, is what the owners of racehorses live on. Nobody can take away from us our dreams of future glory. That is why I felt no jealousy when my old schoolmate (Wood then, Halifax now) won that Derby – not because I had once shared a lodging-house with him at Oxford, but because I had already won the race two or three times a week in my dreams during the preceding winter and, to win it in fact, might have been an anticlimax.

This may help to explain why the race course is – and always has been – popular with the theatrical profession, sharing, as it does, the ups and downs, the unpredictable results, the dreams and the excitement common to both callings – with the added bonus that most horses, unlike most plays, at least, run.

Goblin's two victories at the end of the season took place while his owner was aboard the QE2 *en route* for and returning from America.

On the way over, one day out from England, we were sunning ourselves in our deck-chairs on a clement afternoon. The loud-speaker asked me to take a telephone call. Hurrying down in the lift and then along the furlong or so of corridor, I wondered whether the call could be about Goblin, Wightman having warned me that he might be running, that day, at Newmarket or Brighton. After studying my wrist-watch I rejected the idea since neither race could yet have taken place.

I reached my cabin, got through to the operator waited a few minutes and heard the voice of my good friend Commander Phillips, sire of Michael Phillips, *The Times* Racing Correspondent, telling me that Goblin had just won at Brighton.

'But he can't have, Jo. The race hasn't been run yet.'

'Yes, it has, you bloody fool, and Goblin won.'

Then, I remembered that, according to the Captain's dictate, I had put my watch back one hour on the previous night.

'Thank you, Jo,' I said and hurried back to Rachel with the glad news.

We arrived in Philadelphia to attend the opening of *The King-fisher*, starring Rex Harrison, Claudette Colbert and George Rose under the eye of Lindsay Anderson. The audience liked both the play and the cast. So did Rachel and myself and the dramatic critics. By the end of the week after minor changes here, a few cuts there and one word 'faucets' being substituted for 'taps' to give Rex a missing laugh, the play was set for Baltimore, Boston and New York. On our passage home, one day out from Southampton, we were sitting in our deck-chairs once again.

'Do you remember,' I remarked to Rachel, as she poured the tea, 'that we were sitting just here at this very hour on the way out, when Jo rang up to tell us about Goblin's win?'

The words had scarcely passed my lips when the loudspeaker called me to the telephone. I took the well-worn path to my cabin and repeated the routine of two weeks earlier. Again, I heard Jo's voice informing me that Goblin had just won – this time, at Lingfield.

What a double! What a treble, if we put in *The Kingfisher*.

I returned to Rachel and my deck-chair, seriously contemplating living on a lightship at that spot in the Atlantic during Goblin's four-year-old career.

# Chapter 16

# Conclusion

The year of which I wrote in the last chapter is now drawing to its close, with Goblin in his winter quarters and *The Kingfisher* in Melbourne (John MacCallum, Googie Withers) and in New York. Thus the first two legs of my suggested treble are already past the post and all that is required for its completion is hard-going in the coming year for Goblin – and good luck.

Not that much lasting benefit, in the financial sense, is likely to accrue to me from *The Kingfisher*'s journeys overseas although the income gained from such productions should, in theory, result in its proud author dancing his way to the bank. Instead my bank manager comes out, at intervals, as did his predecessors and, no doubt, will his successors, for a cup of coffee and a chat with Rachel and myself. We sit him on a jack-knife sofa, plying him with chocolate biscuits, as he talks of mortgages and warns us against cashing cheques until the overdraft has been reduced to such a level as to make Head Office happy. Indeed, last month, on just such a visit, warnings came not only from him, but from our accountants as well – 'Watch it,' all three of them cried in unison, 'expenditure must be cut down to the bare minimum, no Christmas "splash" indulged in, every penny must be watched, a mortgage on the property must be secured against the overdraft and then – but only then – can any cheque be drawn without the prospect of it bouncing.'

'So I've had it, unless Goblin wins a big race next year?' I say, bitterly. 'No more than you have always had it,' they reply. 'You should have emigrated years ago.'

I see them off, *en route* for their respective offices and, as they drive out through the gate in convoy, I look back towards the house where we have lived for nearly thirty years – and, in my heart, I know that we could never emigrate, for here we have found happiness and here we hope to go on finding it.

After all and at the risk of seeming sentimental, it is here that Rachel has brought up four children through a quarter of a century, from the days when her first-born, aged six, used to dress as a French policeman to the day this autumn when my telephone rang and a voice from a house down the hill said, 'Dinah's pony's feeding in the field here with no rider in the saddle.' I drove down to the valley in a panic, to find search-parties already out and, ultimately, Dinah being tended by a friendly farmer's wife, nursing a broken arm.

All kinds of things have happened to me in this house along the years – the telephone has rung conveying sad news sometimes, but more often good news, telling us, perhaps, of some new child born to a niece or nephew.

A mile along the valley, in East Meon church, by permission of the Vicar and at Rachel's instigation, my play *The Lord's Lieutenant* has been acted by a group of local amateurs. So well did they perform it that I think it likely they have launched it on a long and popular career.

My eldest daughter, Sarah's wedding to Nick Dent took place here, with a marquee on the lawn in mid-December, Dinah as her bridesmaid and one of her godfathers, Jakie Astor, asking the assembled company to drink the bride and bridegroom's health in just those words, no more – the shortest and most relevant speech ever given, perhaps, at a wedding.

What of these four children? Do they get on with their ageing father? Possibly they lack respect for him as a prolific (not to say distinguished) playwright. Once, while driving through Chalon-sur-Saône, I saw a poster advertising *Le Canard à l'Orange* (*The Secretary Bird*) and applied the brake in prospect of a happy evening attending the production. As I did so the children cried in unison: 'No. Drive on, Daddy.' Should they, perhaps, all be drama-critics?'

In so far as any father can assess his children, I would mark down Jamie as an independent fellow – the assistant trainer, as I write, to Peter Walwyn, doggedly determined to become a trainer himself. Will he train a Derby winner one day, possibly for his old father, should that hard-pressed forebear ever have the wherewithal to buy himself another racehorse? Ah, well – dreams cost nothing.

What of Sarah and her husband? Both are gentle, kindly, creatures who dream too; not of racehorses but of fish-farms and a fishing-boat equipped to carry paying passengers, and of a house, perhaps in Southern Ireland, and, no doubt, of children. Should the fish-farm and the fishing-boat both fail to surface, maybe they can fall back on their other talents – his, a marked ability for writing on the subject of the sea and hers, outstanding skill at china-mending.

And, Gian, twenty-one next year, who likes to live in France and is a notable eccentric, even in this family – what will become of her? She is imaginative, absent-minded, a cross between a Lambton and a Seely and she writes well and may end up with a literary career.

Dinah, fifteen next month, is a friendly child, indulgent to her parents. We like to think we do not spoil her, but she certainly spoils us – she also pulls our legs. While driving to school last term, she told me from the back seat, without batting an eyelid, that her mother and myself were clearly unaware how psychologically disturbing it was to young children to be separated from their parents for long periods. I squinted in the mirror and observed a twinkle in her eye which twinkle, I am glad to report, seldom leaves it.

On the whole, I find these children satisfactory. Nowadays, we seldom see them all together, save at Christmas and then only for a short time. Last night – since I write these lines on Christmas morning – the whole family attended Midnight Mass, less Jamie, standing in for Peter Walwyn at his racing-stable. As the congregation sang a seasonable hymn, I looked along the pew that held my son-in-law, my three daughters and their mother and gave thanks to God for all things bright and beautiful.

Returning home, we called Rex Harrison in New York to learn that he had just re-married and was about to read the lesson at his local Midnight Mass. Imbued with good will, I drank one last nightcap and went to bed, to find a stocking hanging from the bed-rail, Father Christmas evidently having called – according to a note in Dinah's handwriting stuck on the bedroom door – while we had been in Church. This morning, I woke to yet another Christmas morning to find Dinah, opening her stocking, tucked beneath the eiderdown, leaning against the bed-rail, which had once supported Jamie and her elder sisters and, beside me, Rachel, opening hers.

What a woman! Married at the age of twenty-one – to a cashiered ex-Army officer, aged thirty-nine, an old lag and a dicey dramatist already wedded to an overdraft for life – what can I say of her; in view of my inherent reticence and intense dislike of wearing my heart on my sleeve?

No other woman could have run the course with such consistent loyalty and humour, with such stern and yet constructive criticism of her husband's work, with such tolerance of his shortcomings. Once, admittedly, she threw a poker at me, as she stirred the damp logs in a Scottish fireplace and I mildly criticized her mother over some forgotten episode in our first years of marriage – a back-handed throw that struck me on the kneecap. My reaction was deep-seated admiration both for her aim and her spirit. Otherwise, she has been tolerant beyond the call of duty, for which tolerance my gratitude can never adequately be expressed in words except, perhaps, by saying that, whenever I drive past the Albert Hall, I think of the first time I met her – a blonde beautiful girl with a bandaged forearm and a gaiety which struck me to the heart on that enchanted evening when I fell in love with her.

'Who can explain it? Who can tell you why? Fools give you reasons, wise men never try.'

Maybe, maybe not. None the less, I hazard the suggestion that God smiled on Rachel that night in the Albert Hall just as, with inter-mittent lapses, He has always smiled on me – and, by so doing, fixed her beauty for eternity.

I offer no apology for mentioning the Deity because, although I'm well aware that, in ever increasing circles, He is looked upon as being out of date, if not extinct, I find it difficult, to put it at its mildest, to envisage life without Him.

For this reason, every night and morning, I repeat The Lord's Prayer to Him, lying on my back in bed with closed eyes – Tommy, Rachel's pug snoring beside me – not, as did my father, audibly, nor, as was also his invariable custom, with a number of additional requirements, aimed at influencing events, such as the presence of a roebuck at a certain cross rides at a certain time. My custom is to play the Lord's Prayer straight with only one short postscript, added in my own words, in which I require God to ensure that Rachel and I go on loving one another and that we continue happy. To date, He has complied with this request.

Thus, twenty-seven years on, as I sit on this December morning in my study, looking through the window at the snow-flakes on the branches of the yew-tree on the lower lawn, spring is still in my heart and deep contentment. I ask nothing more – I have my wife, my family, a host of friends and relatives, my house, my garden, my swimming-pool (known as The Secretary Bird Pool) and my croquet lawn. I have my week-end shooting (sometimes mid-week, in an arid period devoid of inspiration), bird photography, racing on television, golf and bridge. I also have my writing, half-past nine to half-past twelve, two thirty until four or later, should a new play be in the process of creation.

I can see no prospect of retirement from this routine, even though I am an old-age pensioner – nor should I wish to. Never mind the fact that I keep very little of my income; I am content to go on writing plays until my dying day for the good reason that I do so for the love of it – and in the hope of immortality.

And what of death, seeing that death will come when it will come? I do not much look forward to it, even though I like to think I am a Christian. None the less, in spite of being nervous of the prospect to the point of carrying, on all my travels, as a mascot, a small brown cloth duck that Rachel gave me when we got engaged, attired in red and white check trousers and a tam-o'-shanter, I anticipate a future life – and for this reason.

Thinking back on all those relatives of mine, now dead and buried, mostly in the Border land, both north and south of Tweed, the strange thing is that were my study door to open now and one or other of them – or, indeed, all – walk in, I would experience no nervousness. I would look up and say, 'Hullo there, Dadda (or Mamma or Claud or George or Vi or Johnny). You've just come in time to read this. If there's anything you don't like, let me know and I'll cut it out.' Then I would pass them each a carbon copy and continue with my writing.

Death, in fact, means little to me, after the first impact, for the reason that, in my book, people never die. They live on as I saw them last or in the situation that I gain most pleasure from recalling – Uncle Hugh, his gun raised at the fox; my Uncle Johnny in the Members Stand at Goodwood, taking in the message that his horse was running and might win; Aunt Joan, dressing a wooden mouse at her work-table; Uncle Brackley and Aunt Violet (bandaged)

H.P.H.–O

coming down to dinner; Hairy Mary pouring out the tea in Draycott
Place, while talking sixteen or more to the dozen; Mouldy Margaret,
smiling warmly at her white knight; Rumbling Reggie, demon-
strating how he caught his big brown trout under the oak tree;
Uncle Claud, interrogating me when I came out of Wakefield;
my father-in-law laughing in the Fortune Theatre at *Aunt Edwina*.

And the same with both my parents. Though I have them round
me in my study as I write, I do not need their photographs. I see them
still as I remember them, as vividly as ever: Charlie, standing on the
steps of Coldstream Church – a little Lord Lieutenant in a bowler
hat – impatient with the 'little devil' of a parson's lengthy sermon
on a snowy day; Lil, following him round the Hirsel drawing-room
with the shovel from the fireplace, saving the tobacco scattered on
the carpet from his unlit pipe and handing it to Mr Collingwood for
future use –

'The world is peopled well with men
And men are flesh and blood and apprehensive.'

Would not people feel less apprehension – not about death, perhaps,
but about the prospect of eternal life – were they to spend more time
recalling other men and women who, although no longer flesh and
blood, live on as happy memories, therefore unmourned and, for
that reason, I would guess, immortal?

# *Index*

# Index